SUPPLIER EVALUATION
AND
PERFORMANCE EXCELLENCE

A Guide to Meaningful Metrics
and Successful Results

Sherry R. Gordon

ISBN-10: 1-932159-80-6
ISBN-13: 978-1-932159-80-6

Printed and bound in the U.S.A. Printed on acid-free paper
10 9 8 7 6 5 4 3 2

Library of Congress Cataloging-in-Publication Data

Gordon, Sherry R.
 Supplier evaluation and performance excellence : a guide to meaningful
metrics and successful results / by Sherry R. Gordon.
        p. cm.
Includes index.
ISBN-13: 978-1-932159-80-6 (hardcover : alk. paper)
1. Purchasing. 2. Vendors and purchasers--Evaluation. I. Title.

HF5437.G65 2008
658.7'2—dc22   2007052783

Phone: (954) 727-9333
Fax: (561) 892-0700
Web: www.jrosspub.com

CONTENTS

FOREWORD

Back in the mid-1990s I spent three months working with the Toyota Motor Company in Japan. Why? Well, our early work at the Lean Enterprise Research Centre at Cardiff University, Wales had demonstrated that Toyota had managed to outperform every other manufacturing company on the planet in performance and ability to improve. I was interested to find out what the secret to their success really was. In this work I identified four key areas: Policy Deployment, People-Enabled Process Management, the Toyota Production System, and their ability to spread these three areas to the wider supply chain.

Bearing in mind that Toyota buys in about 80 percent of what it produces, it soon became apparent in my mind that the most critical element to Toyota's success was not its internal excellence but its ability to spread this into its wider direct and indirect supplier network. What was also apparent, in contrast to what I typically saw in Europe or North America, was that the focus of the buyer-supplier relationship was on analysis, measurement, and development, not traditional negotiation, fire-fighting and recrimination.

So what can we learn from this Toyota experience? Well, there are a number of key messages:

1. Understand the power and profitability that can be created by unlocking the hidden potential of your supplier community.
2. Understand strategically what you need from your suppliers in order to become world class yourself.
3. Find a way to convert your relationship with suppliers from an arm's-length one to one of common destiny.
4. Measure the current performance of suppliers in the areas that really matter (not in areas that are just easy to measure).
5. Develop an approach to improve suppliers.
6. Find a way to recognize and reward success and turn around setbacks.

7. Develop a sustainability approach to make sure that the first round of improvements is not just a one-off but the start of a continual-improvement process.

This is definitely not an easy job. As a result, it is necessary to get some guidance and help along the way. This book I believe is an excellent starting place, as its simple step-by-step approach will help guide you in your journey toward having a world-class supplier base.

I wish you luck.

— **Professor Peter Hines**
Professor of Supply Chain Management,
Chairman of Lean Enterprise Research Centre,
Cardiff University, Wales

PREFACE

Supplier performance management (SPM) has become an area of increasing interest as supply chains have become global and supply risks have increased. Companies are aware that the more insights they have into their suppliers' performance, the better decisions they can make regarding which suppliers are meeting their requirements, which suppliers need to improve and have the potential to do so, and which suppliers should be disengaged. Awareness is the first step. But an evaluation and performance measurement process without action is ineffective and does not last.

WHY THIS BOOK WAS WRITTEN

When companies describe their efforts to evaluate suppliers and improve their performance, I find that the majority are measuring supplier performance in some fashion, but few are satisfied with how they are doing this and the results they are getting. Many firms are unclear about what and whom to measure and how to effectively use the measures they do collect. Procurement, quality, and supply management professionals understand how critical supplier performance is to their firms, but many find that making a compelling business case to senior management and gaining support and resources are challenging. They know it's a good thing, but they have trouble selling goodness to senior management in a way that senior management can support. The problem is that many companies do not know how to develop a good SPM process, especially one that gets measurable results and shows return on investment.

There has been a dearth of information in the literature that explains how to put a good supplier performance management process in place—one that can be tailored to work effectively in a particular company's environment. Some articles and research describe programs or approaches at specific companies, while others offer generic and theoretical models that are difficult to apply. Many books and articles are focused on the quality function and offer detailed information on auditing and conformance to quality standards. The technical nature of this information and level of detail are not easily accessible to management or to functions outside of quality. While the quality literature adds valuable insights, techniques, and ideas, this information can be difficult to utilize outside the quality function and doesn't take into account procurement and supplier management issues.

Another impetus for writing this book was my work with companies who wanted to implement a software solution to support SPM and were challenged by the business issues and processes that they needed to address in order to ensure a successful software implementation. The need for a practical book on this subject has become clearer with the increasing attention to some of the more spectacular and visible supply chain risks and failures, such as the pet food poisoning scandal and the lead paint found on children's toys, both attributable to supplier performance management issues. Warnings about supply chain risks and disasters abound, but approaches to reduce those risks are scarce. Corporations have begun to put supply chain management higher on their lists of important areas to pay attention to and are eager for real tools and techniques to avoid and mitigate these risks.

And last, I recognized the need for a book on supplier evaluation and performance management to help senior management and practitioners understand and develop an effective process that really works in their firms. This became clear from the many questions that companies have been asking me about the supply management challenges that they are facing and the increasing interest in the topic of supplier evaluation and performance management at my various speaking engagements.

HOW THE BOOK IS ORGANIZED

The book is organized according to the flow of the supplier evaluation and performance management process from development to implementation. It starts with creating the business case and getting management support, including how to link organizational goals and strategies to the supplier evaluation and performance management process. It describes how to create the team and develop the plan for defining, developing, and implementing the evaluation process. The book then outlines an approach for developing a supplier evaluation strategy, including how to segment the supply base for evaluation and choose which suppliers to evaluate.

Next, the book addresses how to determine what to measure by developing supplier performance expectations and evaluation criteria aligned with overall company goals and specific supply management and quality objectives. In determining what to measure, the book covers how to get from evaluation to specific outcomes and actions. The book outlines advantages and disadvantages of different evaluation approaches, including ways to understand supplier capabilities and capacity for future performance and how to choose approaches that are most suitable in your environment. The role of technology in supporting the evaluation process is discussed.

The book then describes how to design an effective supplier evaluation and performance management process and how to build evaluation tools, such as surveys and scorecards. How to develop a process to communicate with suppliers about performance, including how to give feedback, is described. Next in the process is how to recognize and reward good performers, including how to plan and run a successful supplier conference. The book also covers supplier certification, including the benefits of it and how to create a supplier certification process or program. Finally, the chapter on supplier development describes approaches for working effectively with suppliers to get from measurement to improvement and to achieve a return on investment.

FEATURES

Some of the practical features in the book include the following:

- How to structure a supplier performance management project, including roles and responsibilities and senior management support and guidance
- A complete project plan for an SPM implementation, including tasks, key decisions, and challenges
- A supplier segmentation model specifically for supplier evaluation, including types of performance information to use by supply base segment
- Sources and types of supplier performance information for evaluating both direct and indirect suppliers
- A process for developing supplier performance expectations
- A hierarchy for developing a business measurement model
- How to choose metrics that are meaningful to your organization
- Pros and cons of different evaluation approaches
- Suggested supplier evaluation processes
- How to create a good supplier survey
- How to conduct a supplier site visit
- Specific tips on the dos and don'ts of giving supplier performance feedback
- How to create a process for supply risk planning

- How to develop a good supplier certification process
- How to plan and run a successful supplier conference
- How to conduct a successful supplier development process

WHY FIRMS FIND SUPPLIER EVALUATION AND PERFORMANCE MANAGEMENT SO CHALLENGING AND HOW THIS BOOK CAN HELP

This book addresses the challenges and pitfalls of evaluating suppliers and enabling performance improvement. Putting a supplier evaluation process in place and getting outside supplier firms to improve their performance is not an easy task. However, it is too risky not to develop a robust SPM process. For those companies involved in process improvement and continuous improvement, lean, Six Sigma, or another high-performance or business initiative, developing a good SPM process will be a familiar and similar exercise. You already know much of the drill. This book will add subject-matter-specific knowledge, tools, and techniques. Knowing what to do is the first step in the journey. This book was designed to help guide firms in this journey. Like all continuous-improvement projects, implementing SPM is a process, not an event. If you follow a good process to develop, implement, and maintain it, SPM is very approachable and is not mission impossible.

Where do companies run into trouble? Many firms neglect to address the multifunctional participation required. Businesses typically look at supplier evaluation and think that it belongs to one function: Procurement or quality can take care of it. SPM cannot be developed and deployed within just one department, such as just purchasing or just quality, as it can touch many stakeholders within the firm and the supply chain. Or, some firms believe that implementing a software application with scorecards will provide the silver bullet to solve performance problems.

Executives feel proactive and in control with dashboards. I call it "managing from the control panel." Using executive dashboards can be effective, but it is not a substitute for building the relationships with suppliers that provide insight and understanding and help avoid risks. Sitting at arm's length and reviewing too few, too many, or not the right metrics doesn't work. Some companies look at evaluating suppliers and managing their performance simplistically—just find the right metrics to put on the scorecards. And the way that they try to determine the right metrics is to find out what metrics other companies are using. Bolting other companies' metrics onto your scorecard may not produce sufficiently meaningful or actionable results. Your firm may not have even a means to collect the same metrics as another firm. Neglecting to use metrics aligned with your company's goals and strategies can cause a failed initiative and may not produce successful results. Trying to evaluate suppliers without having a good SPM process in place is another pitfall.

Another important reason that firms find SPM challenging is that it involves organizational change. Business processes will change. Employees from the senior executive to associate level will need to be involved. Good communications is needed. Time is needed. Internal and external stakeholders are involved. Not addressing the important change management aspects of supplier evaluation and performance management as well as supplier development can result in a less successful process and provide less return on investment than anticipated.

All of these factors make supplier performance management more challenging than viewing it as simply the quest for the perfect scorecard. This book covers all of these issues and gives practical suggestions on how to overcome the roadblocks and develop a successful process that gets real results and engenders continuing management support.

ACKNOWLEDGMENTS

The impetus to write a book can come unexpectedly. I became an author when Drew Gierman, the publisher at J. Ross Publishing, asked me to write this book after hearing me speak at the 2006 ISM Conference in Minneapolis, Minnesota. I was hesitant at first, as I had never written a book before, but then decided that I was up for the challenge because supplier evaluation and supplier performance management is an area where there is much hunger for practical information. Writing this book gave me new respect and admiration for the job of author and an appreciation of the huge amount of work required.

There were many sources of inspiration and knowledge in the book-writing process. I would especially like to acknowledge Charles Ballard and Terrence Majerski, supplier development managers at The Boeing Company. Some of the thought process that went into this book came from the ideas and synergies borne out of many years of working with Charles and Terry. Their deep knowledge of supplier management, best practices, and supplier development greatly enhanced my own.

I would like to acknowledge Emptoris, Inc., which acquired my software company, Valuedge, and provided the opportunity to work with many companies facing the challenges of managing supplier performance and to increase my knowledge of how software can scale the supplier management process.

There are numerous people and companies who helped found and support the former New England Suppliers Institute (NESI) and from whom I increased my understanding of and insights into the needs and challenges of the customer-supplier relationship. Some of them include Bob Fulford, Ron Pariseau, John Rabbitt, Dave Miller, and Peter Novello, all founding board members from customer and supplier firms, as well as Wallace Patterson, from the Air Force Research Laboratory at Wright-Patterson Air Force Base, the original funder for New England Suppliers Institute. Their steadfast support of NESI helped spread lean practices in the New England supply chain and gave me some of my initial inspiration to develop ideas that ended up in this book.

Other acknowledgments include Terence Burton, who demonstrated to me that it is possible to write practical and useful business books; Robert Rudzki, author, consultant, and former CPO, who contributed some of his ideas; and Jean Scoon, a dear friend and a professional writer, who helped me understand that all that I was experiencing during the writing process was perfectly normal.

I acknowledge AME, Association for Manufacturing Excellence, whose enthusiastic volunteer membership helped expand my knowledge of lean and supplier development and who gave me opportunities to give back to others in manufacturing. I acknowledge the many companies who shared with me their struggles in supplier evaluation and from whom I synergized information that went into this book.

I acknowledge the Lean Advancement Initiative (LAI) at MIT, whose synergies with New England Suppliers Institute enabled NESI to develop relationships with member companies and gain additional knowledge about spreading lean principles and practices in the supply base.

And finally, I would like to acknowledge Stephen A. Smith, my dear friend and husband, who provided unconditional emotional support throughout this book project.

ABOUT THE AUTHOR

Sherry Gordon is President of the Value Chain Group, a supply management and performance excellence consultancy. She was previously Vice President, Supplier Performance at Emptoris, a leading provider of enterprise supply management software solutions. Emptoris had acquired her previous company, Valuedge, where she was founder, President, and CEO. Valuedge offered a software solution for supplier evaluation, certification, and performance management and improvement. This solution became part of Emptoris's software suite. She is a pioneer in enterprise measurement and process improvement techniques and considered a thought leader in supplier performance management.

Before founding Valuedge, she ran the New England Suppliers Institute (NESI), a nonprofit organization funded by the Air Force that she led and developed from idea to execution. NESI focused on improving the business relationships between customers and their suppliers. It also developed innovative programs for improving supplier performance via lean enterprise practices adoption in the supply base, supplier development, and education. NESI offered some of the first public workshops in the country for suppliers on the topic of lean manufacturing practices.

Sherry also worked for manufacturing and distribution companies as well as the consulting firms of Arthur D. Little, Inc. and the former Arthur Young. In addition to supply chain management, Sherry has a functional background and expertise in quality, materials management and lean enterprise and spent two years as an examiner for the Baldrige-based Mass Excellence Award.

In 1999, she wrote an e-book, *Improving Company Performance Through Supply Chain Management Practices*, published by Lionheart Publishing. Sherry produced a video in 2000 entitled *Creating the Lean Supply Chain: Implementation*

XX Supplier Evaluation and Performance Excellence

Stories, based upon supplier development projects done by suppliers of aerospace defense prime contractors. She appeared in the February 2002 ISM Satellite Seminar on "Complexity Management: Webs, Chains and Other Business Relationship Models." In 2002 and 2005, Sherry was chosen by *Supply and Demand Chain Executive* magazine as a "Pro to Know." Her article "Seven Steps to Measure Supplier Performance" appeared in the August 2005 issue of *Quality Progress.*

Sherry is a frequent speaker on enterprise performance improvement and supply chain topics and has spoken at events for ISM (Institute for Supply Management), The Conference Board, ASQ (American Society for Quality), the Supply Chain Council, ASMI, PMAC (Purchasing Management Association of Canada), and others. Sherry has been active in AME (Association for Manufacturing Excellence) as Chairperson of the 2004, 2005, and 2006 AME/IndustryWeek Best Plants Conferences. Ms. Gordon has a BA from University of Michigan, an MA from Columbia University, and an MBA from Simmons Graduate School of Management.

Web
Added
Value™

Free value-added materials available from
the Download Resource Center at www.jrosspub.com

At J. Ross Publishing we are committed to providing today's professional with practical, hands-on tools that enhance the learning experience and give readers an opportunity to apply what they have learned. That is why we offer free ancillary materials available for download on this book and all participating Web Added Value™ publications. These online resources may include interactive versions of material that appears in the book or supplemental templates, worksheets, models, plans, case studies, proposals, spreadsheets, and assessment tools, among other things. Whenever you see the WAV™ symbol in any of our publications, it means bonus materials accompany the book and are available from the Web Added Value™ Download Resource Center at www.jrosspub.com.

Downloads available for *Supplier Evaluation and Performance Excellence: A Guide to Meaningful Metrics and Successful Results* consist of value-added supplier evaluation tools and templates including: a supplier evaluation implementation plan template, a supplier assessment topics hierarchy, a sample scorecard, a list of common supplier performance metrics and their definitions, and a presentation on the business case for implementing a supplier performance management program including the cost of poor supplier quality, the value proposition and return on investment.

INTRODUCTION

SUPPLY MANAGEMENT TODAY

The field of supply management has been undergoing a transformation from a tactical, transaction-oriented function to a strategic capability at many companies. Senior executives are discovering that a good, integrated supply management capability is not only a necessity but also a competitive advantage. Management is realizing the potential for procurement to add cash to the bottom line instead of viewing procurement as just a cost center. And where supply management often worked as an arm of materials management or finance, it now operates at executive levels. A function that reported low in the organization now has assumed titles like CPO (Chief Procurement Officer) and Corporate Vice President of Supplier Quality and Performance Management, positions that didn't exist until several years ago and now report directly to the CEO in many large organizations. No longer the purview of administrators and clerks, procurement and supply management have come of age. Now master's-level degree programs in supply management and procurement at universities attract bright and capable candidates who can look forward to a profession with a career track and a future in the executive ranks.

What are the forces transforming supply management?

- Increased dependence on outsourcing goods and services
- Globalization
- Supply management technology
- Time and market responsiveness
- Performance improvement methodologies

Companies have been steadily increasing the percent of goods that they outsource over the past 10 years. Increased outsourcing has in turn increased the level of dependence on suppliers for the elements of cost, quality, time/responsiveness, and technology.

Information technology has become a key enabler in supply management. Information technology has facilitated order-of-magnitude improvements and scaling of supply management processes such as sourcing, negotiation, spend analysis, contract management, and supplier performance management. These and other software tools are radically changing the way business is conducted between customers and suppliers. Initially, and in some cases even today, sourcing software was perceived negatively, as a way for customers to get the lowest price in a reverse auction at the expense of suppliers and as a detriment to the customer-supplier relationship. Technology cannot overcome longstanding poor purchasing practices such as choosing suppliers on price alone; it will only speed up that process. When well deployed and within a set of good business processes and practices, procurement software is an indispensable supply management enabler. It has been a driver in the transformation of supply management. Typically, business processes take longer to catch up with technology. However, technology tools and their rapid adoption are revolutionizing the supply management profession and have become a competitive necessity.

VALUE OF EFFECTIVE SPM

The immediate return on investment in a sourcing event is simple and visible: The price was $X; after the event the price is $Y, so what you saved ($S) = $X − $Y. Most procurement people are measured by price savings for products and services. And these savings will directly impact the bottom line. As the cost of goods sold goes down, profit margins go up. Sourcing and negotiations technologies have improved and scaled the process and are now widely accepted and adopted. However, focusing only on price savings in sourcing means potentially missing some big opportunities. A huge opportunity exists with your suppliers who are on board: capitalizing on the relationship. What is the value of a high-performing supply base? Sourcing focuses on cost reduction of goods and services. Optimizing the customer-supplier relationship and achieving performance excellence also reduces cost and risk, two of the biggest concerns of companies today. The better you know your suppliers, good points and bad points, the less likelihood of unpleasant surprises. But it is distinctly different from the sourcing process in that it is more than a cost reduction function—it can also *create value* for both the customer's enterprise and the supplier. In fact, excellence in supplier performance management can help enhance the sourcing process so that you choose those suppliers more likely to add value to the company.

Do any of these questions pertain to your company?

- Have you negotiated with suppliers and squeezed out most of the cost?
- When prices of certain commodities such as oil, steel, and transportation rise, do they impact your suppliers' cost structure to the point where their margins cannot tolerate any further price reductions? Could demanding lower prices weaken or put some of your suppliers out of business?
- How do you derive value from the relationship beyond lower prices?
- Do you know whether your suppliers are fully compliant with contract terms and that you are actually getting what you negotiated?[1]
- Do you know how well your supply base is performing?
- Do you know who all your suppliers are and which are most critical to your company?
- Does your company have quality problems, customer complaints, and warranty returns? Do you know what portion of them is caused by suppliers?
- Are you aware of what types of risks lie in your supply base? Do you know where they are and how to begin to uncover them? Mitigate them?

When suppliers are viewed as an extension of the customer's enterprise, ideally their importance to the business can be viewed less as cost centers and more as partners with the potential to add value to the business. Some of the ways that suppliers can add value include the following:

- Using suppliers as a source of new technology in areas that complement customer competencies but where customers do not wish to invest.
- Working collaboratively with suppliers to develop new technology.
- Gathering best practices and great ideas from suppliers and adopting them within one's own organization.
- Capitalizing on the synergies of collaborative problem solving and idea sharing.

---

1. An Aberdeen Group study for the *CPO Agenda*, Winter 2006, reported that the typical company implements about 70 percent of the savings it negotiates (Aberdeen Group, *The CPO's Strategic Agenda*, p. 9). Areas where savings did not materialize include "lack of internal customer awareness and compliance" (p. 2).

- Working jointly on improvement projects that benefit both parties. Initially, the project may benefit the supplier, and ultimately, improved performance benefits the customer.
- Being able to get innovative new products to market due to supplier contributions in new product development.
- Developing faster cycle times in the order to delivery process due to the agility of one's supply base can give companies a competitive advantage in speed of order fulfillment.
- Choosing a diverse supply base. Doing business with diverse suppliers can help strengthen a company's ability to conduct business across all cultures and geographies in its area and expand its market potential.

However, when relationships are purely arm's-length, adversarial or price-driven and performance is unpredictable, suppliers are in the position to indeed drive more cost than value. And even though unpredictable performance is not acceptable, a customer may be unable to do anything about the situation, at least immediately. Or, more likely, the customer may be unaware of the dimensions and root causes of the problems with supplier performance. Some of these root causes may even originate with the customer, whose own business practices exacerbate performance problems and reward the wrong supplier behaviors and business practices.

WHAT IS SUPPLIER PERFORMANCE MANAGEMENT?

We define supplier performance management as:

The process of evaluating, measuring, and monitoring supplier performance and suppliers' business processes and practices for the purposes of reducing costs, mitigating risk, and driving continuous improvement.

Managing supplier performance helps companies focus resources on value-added activities instead of reacting to supplier-performance-induced problems (i.e., defects, expediting, excess inventory, late deliveries to customers, work stoppages, reduction of market competitiveness, etc.). By better understanding supplier performance via increasing performance visibility, companies can better monitor and manage key relationships by taking steps to prevent or remedy problems. And, on the positive side, they can identify and leverage suppliers capable of innovation and continuous improvement who will add value to the relationship.

Supplier performance excellence gives companies competitive advantage. To the extent that suppliers perform well, companies enjoy a competitive boost, since this performance is reflected in lower costs, improved responsiveness to customers, better-quality goods and services, and technological advantage. Thus, there has been a recent increase in interest in measuring supplier performance.

Suppliers, however, do not view their companies as needing to be "managed". In fact, many may have business practices and processes that are better and more robust than those of their customers and may have a thing or two to teach their customers about performance excellence. Thus, supplier performance management (SPM) might be more appropriately viewed as business relationship management, which we define as:

> *In what ways, and how effectively, the firm ensures a two-way flow of understanding between the company and its suppliers, specifically as it pertains to communicating and negotiating requirements and performance expectations with the supply chain.*

In order to get from the concept of managing supplier performance to managing business relationships for mutual benefit, a lot of insight is needed into not only supplier performance, typically defined as quantifiable performance metrics, but also the means to achieve performance excellence through best business processes and practices as well as through enabling behaviors and culture. Business relationship management entails involving the appropriate functions and using effective methods to communicate with suppliers. In the case of key suppliers, the communications will likely include exchanges of information about company history, capabilities, financial and market performance, and future business plans. These communications will involve multiple levels of staff starting from senior management on down from both sides.

Currently there are several terms being applied to this area. One is supplier relationship management (SRM), which includes elements of performance tracking and management, relationship development and management, and even supplier performance improvement activities through supplier development. Others include SPM, which implies a focus on performance only. In this book, we address what business practices, processes, tools, techniques, structures, approaches, culture, behaviors, and even technology can enable supplier performance excellence as well as excellence in business relationships.

Some companies approach supplier performance as an area where measurement means only those metrics that can be objectively quantified. Any metrics that do not come from an objective source, usually defined as the company's internal enterprise management system or financial systems, are considered qualitative and therefore unacceptable. In the realm of relationships, not all is objectively quantifiable. In fact, the saying is that perception is typically reality, whether or not there are any measurements to back up the perception. For that reason,

SPM cannot give supply managers a complete picture without including qualitative metrics. Relationships are messy, subjective, and open to perception. And both perceived objective and nonobjective measurements can ultimately be disputed. Therefore, both objective measurements and perceptual measurements are needed to assess suppliers because, ultimately, even quantitative measurements in an enterprise are open to subjective actions. While the saying is that you manage what you measure or you get what you measure, the corollary is that "whatever you can measure most easily and accurately is what you end up measuring."[2]

As an example of how even one of the most hard-core quantitative metrics is still open to subjectivity, let's take a look at on-time delivery. When a supplier's product arrives at the customer, it can be considered to be on time because a date is entered into a system at the time it is received. However, on-time delivery can still be open to dispute. Perhaps the item sat on the customer's dock for three days before it was officially received into the system. Or, it was several days early, and the customer changed its policy and rejected early shipments. Or part of the shipment was rejected by the customer for a quality problem that the customer caused by not giving the supplier the most up-to-date work instructions. Or the customer gave the supplier the order in significantly less than the supplier's agreed-upon lead time. Or the customer bricked in the dock, the supplier's driver could not find the dock, which was now moved to a different building, and the driver returned with the item undelivered (a true incident that happened to a small electro-mechanical supplier). Or the customer even closed off the dock at the end of a quarter and turned away deliveries in order to reduce its inventory position (an incident that occurred in a semiconductor industry business downturn). The possibilities for the subjectivity of quantitative supplier performance measures under the guise of being strictly quantitative are endless. And the possibilities for disagreement on the parameters for these metrics within the customer's organization itself are also endless. How many organizations have arguments about whether on time means plus-or-minus three days? Or whether on-time delivery to a customer is measured by the date the shipment left the dock plus a few days and not what time it actually arrives at the customer?

Therefore, the purpose of measuring supplier performance is not to come up with foolproof, fail-safe, neat, and perfectly quantifiable measurements and metrics and to judge each supplier thumbs up or thumbs down. It is an ongoing and iterative process of communicating expectations about performance and the relationship and continuously working to improve both performance and the relationship in that process. This ongoing iterative process is taking place both within the customer's organization among the various stakeholders and among customers and their suppliers. The perfect scorecard, much like the concept of the

---

2. Hughes, Jonathan, "Supplier Metrics that Matter," *CPO Agenda*, Autumn 2005.

perfect order, is a moving target and a nirvana at which a customer is never going to arrive. But, nonetheless, it is a discussion and negotiation point that helps customers and suppliers come to terms with and improve (or dissolve or rethink) their relationships.

CURRENT STATE OF SUPPLIER PERFORMANCE MANAGEMENT

With the global economy and increase in global sourcing, interest in improving ways of managing supplier performance has been increasing. When I speak to groups of supply managers and supplier quality managers, I typically ask the group how many of them are measuring supplier performance. Usually about 50 to 75 percent of the room will raise their hands. But when I ask how many are satisfied with their systems or approaches for doing this, very few—and often no—people will raise their hands. Managing supplier performance is full of challenges and difficulties for a number of reasons. The biggest challenge is that just coming up with metrics, even what appear to be the "right" metrics, does not typically produce any results. The questions that I am asked most often are

- What metrics should I use?
- What metrics do others (in my industry) use?
- My boss says that I need to get a scorecard in place in the next six months. Where do I begin?

Standalone metrics or metrics borrowed from other companies have a low chance of success because

- They are not part of an overall supply management program.
- They do not relate to any overall company or procurement goals and objectives.
- They are often data collection exercises with no teeth enforcing compliance and no actions resulting from them.

The purpose of this book is to provide a guide to developing a successful SPM and improvement process and to demystify the process and make it accessible to most types of companies and organizations.

For manufacturing companies, the traditional approach to measuring performance has been through scorecards derived from enterprise resource planning (ERP) system data. Based upon an AMR Research survey of 100 manufacturing companies in 2006, Figure 1.1 shows the most common metrics that the surveyed manufacturing companies track.

Several things are striking about these metrics: how few of them are tracked in common by more than 60 percent of the respondents, how internally focused

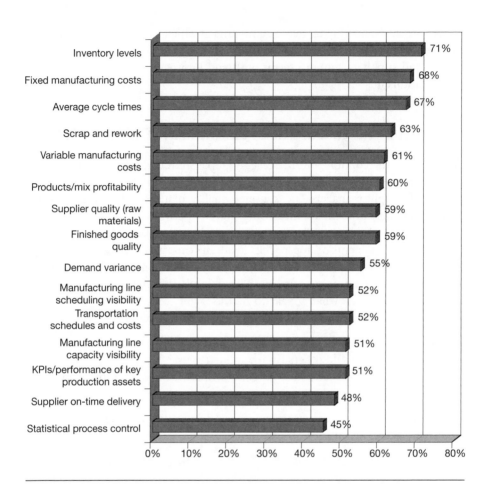

Figure 1.1 Commonly tracked metrics.

many of the metrics are, and how few of the metrics provide data useful for driving continuous improvement. One is left to wonder what these companies actually do with the data. In the case of supplier-oriented metrics (supplier raw material quality and on-time delivery), one may question whether the information is shared with suppliers in any meaningful way or at all.

As the argument has just been made for the need to develop metrics that are unique to the requirements of each organization, ERP systems lend themselves to specific types of information that can be readily captured, such as on-time delivery, incoming supplier quality, and in-process supplier quality. While these are important metrics, there are limitations on what can be learned from ERP types of data, which are usually limited to product quality and not business process and practice quality.

In the case of service organizations, internal data available to be harvested into scorecards is even more limited. The important measures of customer satisfaction and quality for indirect purchases are not captured routinely in the enterprise systems of service-oriented companies. The key metrics captured are typically limited to financial measures based largely on price variances. Even the emerging metric of contract compliance—that is, making sure that purchase terms, prices, and service level agreements meet the terms of the signed contract—is almost impossible for most firms to capture in any meaningful or routine way, as they lack the computer systems and internal disciplines to do so. How do you measure supplier performance and supplier contract compliance readily so that you can manage these areas? And if you are not sure what to measure and don't have a system and processes in place to do so, how are you going to prove to your management that measuring supplier performance is worth doing and has a compelling return on investment? Those are some of the challenges of the current state to be addressed in this book.

COST DRIVERS IN THE SUPPLY BASE

Unlike the highly visible and clearly understood metrics of price and purchased price variance, the cost drivers attributable to suppliers are less visible and transparent. However, when identified and reduced, they have much higher potential return on investment than price reductions. And, for those companies depending on their suppliers, the cost drivers in the supply base pose higher risks and create more waste and competitive disadvantage. The challenge is how to find and remove these cost drivers to improve supplier *and* customer performance. Executives tend to be focused on quick hits and need to understand the business case for investing in SPM and improvement, as it requires an integrated, breakdown-the-stovepipes management system to obtain the return on investment (ROI) and an investment in technology to scale the process.

One approach to understanding cost drivers is to identify the components of the cost of poor supplier quality. To the extent that these components are measurable, you will be able to uncover

- Potential financial savings from reducing or eliminating some of these cost drivers
- Which metrics will help you understand the root causes of these problems
- Which suppliers are driving the most cost
- Where improvements need to be made

Table 1.1 Cost of Poor Quality—Elements

• Call center expenses	• Warranty costs	• Quotation errors
• Excess inventory	• Warranty costs in	• Rejects
• Service calls	excess of reserve	• Warranty returns
• Shipping errors	• Customer complaints	• Rework
• Incoming inspection	• Excess inventory	• Reinspection
• Counting	• Shortages	• Moving
• Schedule changes	• Expediting	• Invoicing problems
• Order changes	• Poor process control	• Lost time
• Scrap	• Poor communications	• Additional overhead
• Concessions	• Stocktaking	• Shipping and packing
• Claims adjustments	• Replacement	for returned items
• Goodwill	• Long lead times	
• Excess freight	• IT system issues	

These cost drivers can impact both the supplier's operations as well as the customer's. That is, inefficiencies at the supplier can cause waste and inefficiencies at their customers. Issues such as customer complaints, warranty returns, quality problems, excess inventory, service failures, long cycle times, and so on drive cost and are part of the supplier cost of poor quality.

The classical view of cost of poor quality (COPQ) categorizes the costs into four categories:

- *Preventive costs.* What do you need to do to prevent poor service or product quality, such as policies and procedures, planning, and training?
- *Appraisal costs.* Money spent inspecting, reviewing, or testing the quality of goods or services.
- *Internal failure costs.* Cost of fixing quality problems, such as rework.
- *External failures.* Cost of dealing with customer support, customer complaints, lost business, and so forth.

Table 1.1 gives a partial list of some components of the cost of poor quality that fall within the internal and external failures category.

There are various rules of thumb for quantifying the cost of poor quality as well as its subset, the cost of poor supplier quality. The cost of poor quality has been estimated to be 10 percent to 25 percent of sales. And the cost of poor supplier quality ranges from 25 percent to 70 percent of COPQ.

One large manufacturer of home appliances estimated its supply base's contribution to the cost of poor quality to be in the 70 percent range and is working to understand the causes of this level of waste and reduce it. Some of the metrics that they regularly track and that have led them to conclude that suppliers are responsible for such a big portion of poor quality include the following:

Table 1.2 Total Resources Calculation

Activity Resulting from Poor Quality	Cost Location	Cost Location	Cost Location	Total Cost of Resources	X	Percentage of Resources to Counter Poor Quality	Total Cost for Activity
Final inspection	Wages and benefits	Training		$127,000		80%	$101,600
Rework	Wages and benefits			$87,500		12%	$10,500
Customer complaint resolution	Wages and benefits	Training	System maintenance (telephone and computer)	$63,750		100%	$63,750
Total Cost of Poor Quality							**$175,850**

Source: Adapted from http://web2.concordia.ca/Quality/tools/8costofpoorquality.pdf.

- Parts and labor
- Inside warranty
- Call center
- Liability expense
- Product exchange
- Product adjustments
- Recalls
- Repair and rework
- Parts per million (PPM) defects

While some may feel that these estimates are grossly inflated, it is my experience that in most companies, there is more than sufficient waste to attack without the need for exaggerating it. However, the symptoms are more visible than the causes. The easiest approach to quantifying some of the cost is to identify wasteful processes or resources, calculate the cost of that resource, and then estimate the percent of the resource devoted to countering poor quality. Tables 1.2 and 1.3 illustrate this approach in a manufacturing environment.

COPQ is not limited to manufacturing. Jay Hughes writes in an article in *Physician Executive* that COPQ is: "20 to 35 percent of gross revenues or budget in manufacturing and service industries. ... [however] quality engineers who consulted with clinics and hospitals during the National Demonstration Project for Quality Improvement in Health Care agreed that the cost of nonproductive work (COW) in medicine might well *exceed 40 to 50 percent of the total health care*

Table 1.3 Unit Costs Calculation

Activity Resulting from Poor Quality	Cost Location	Cost Location	Cost Location	Frequency of Activity (#/yr)	X	Average Cost	Total Cost for Activity
Final inspection	Wages and benefits	Training		12		$8,125	$97,500
Rework	Wages and benefits			7		$2,600	$18,200
Customer complaint resolution	Wages and benefits	Training	System maintenance (telephone and computer)	37		$2,050	$75,850
Total Cost of Poor Quality							**$191,550**

Source: Adapted from http://web2.concordia.ca/Quality/tools/8costofpoorquality.pdf.

Table 1.4 Cost of Nonproductive Work (Example)

Technician time	0.5 hr at $ 8/hr	$4
Nursing time	0.5 hr at $18/hr	$9
Film cost		$7
Developer		$2
Machine maintenance		$1
Patient care delay (affecting other services)		$10
Calculated COW of one unreadable film		$33
Calculated annual COW*		**$60,225**

Source: Adapted from *Physician Executive*, Sept–Oct, 1998 by Jay M. Hughes, pp. 1–10.

*$33 per film x 5 per day x 365 days per year.

dollar [italics added]."[3] An example of a cost of poor quality analysis (here called cost of waste, or COW) in a service environment is shown in Table 1.4. The table shows the yearly cost of Caring Memorial Hospital creating an average of five unreadable portable chest X-rays daily.

These are only a few examples of the cost of poor quality or waste. If the first manufacturing example came from a supplier, consider not only COPQ for the supplier but also the impact on a customer. Would you as a customer wish to be

---

3. Hughes, Jay M., *Physician Executive*, September–October, 1998, pp. 1–10.

footing the bill for hundreds of thousands of dollars of waste at the supplier? What if these defects were not caught at the supplier and escaped into your system? The impact multiplies. Not only would the supplier's cost structure be higher due to the inefficient use of resources and suboptimal processes, but the customer could end up using its own resources to rework a product, send it back to the supplier, carry excess inventory to protect shipments, and so on.

In the hospital example, radiology is often an outsourced function. The same costs and impacts will apply and depend upon which aspects are outsourced. Any wasteful costs from the supplier will be passed along to the hospital and ultimately the patient.

In looking at the total picture, a company with sales of $1B is could be harboring anywhere from $200M to $350M of cost in poor quality or waste. The cost of poor supplier quality could range from $50M up to $245M.

Quantifying the cost of poor supplier quality serves these purposes:

- Quantifying the cost also quantifies the problem.
- A quantified problem is easier to prioritize.
- A quantified cost problem is more visible to management.
- Both quantification and management visibility increase the chances that resources will be applied to the problem.
- It will be easier to estimate ROI for applying resources to reducing COPSQ and to understand what resources will be needed.

It is important to try to measure and to understand the cost drivers, risks in the supply chain, and root causes of supplier performance issues if they are to be uncovered and eliminated. Focusing on reducing purchasing prices misses one of the biggest opportunities for cost reduction: identifying waste in the supplier's business. How well do suppliers run their businesses and have business processes and practices in place to perform well and add value, not cost, to the customer? Measuring cost drivers and waste in the supply chain is not an exact science, and some supplier performance problems are complex and not quickly solvable. Companies should not focus on quantifying supplier performance problems precisely. Accounting systems can make this a difficult task, so you will need to make estimates and educated guesses about some of the elements. By developing a process to consistently measure performance and costs, companies can focus on the trends and information rather than on data gathering or impractical precision.

The Supplier Performance Benchmark Report by Aberdeen Group, first published in 2002 and then updated in 2005, supports the business case for measuring supplier performance. In its survey of 197 companies of varying sizes, it found that the performance of suppliers of companies with an SPM in place improved— particularly in the areas of price, on-time delivery, and quality—more than that

Table 1.5 Average Supplier Performance Improvement

	Price	On-Time Delivery	Quality	Service
SPM Program	23%	23%	21%	21%
No Program	13%	11%	5%	17%

Source: Aberdeen Group, Supplier Performance Benchmarking Report, September 2005.

of the suppliers of companies with no program. Table 1.5 compares companies with SPM to those who do not have such programs in place.

The Aberdeen Group also found that suppliers perform better when measured, which has long been the thought process behind "you manage what you measure." In other words, supplier performance improves somewhat simply because people are paying attention to it—that is, "they [the suppliers] know you're watching". So simple metrics can have some impact. But even more interesting is that more formal, system-based, and enterprise-wide measurement systems brought about even greater improvements in supplier performance.

This study looked at only measurement-induced performance improvement, without examining the additional variable of supplier development. Supplier development ensures that maximum ROI from an SPM program is more likely to occur. Once the metrics reveal performance problems, then the causes of those problems must be identified in order to fix the problems. Supplier development helps close the loop from problem identification to problem resolution. Data collection must be transformed into action.

Another study by two professors at Georgia Tech demonstrates the impact of supply chain glitches on stock prices and shareholder return.[4] Researchers expected investors to be more punitive if the malfunction was caused by internal problems within a company. But stock plunged 8.29 percent when internal problems caused the glitch, compared with an 11.97 percent decrease when a supplier caused the problem and an 8.48 percent drop when customers caused the problem. So there was no mercy for incidents out of the control of the company. The researchers found that the stock began to dip 90 days before a problem was announced, possibly due to information leaks, and then continued to dip for another 90 days, with an average of a 20 percent loss during that period. This was an average loss of $120M per company. Can a better understanding of supplier performance prevent these types of problems?

---

4. "Quantifying the Impact of Supply Chain Glitches on Shareholder Value," by Prof. Vinod Singhal of Georgia Tech, 2003.

Table 1.6 Supplier Managers' Top Five Risks

Type of Disruption	Percent of Those Surveyed
Supplier disruptions (critical supplier failure)	49%
Logistics failure (port strike)	17%
Natural disaster (Hurricane Katrina)	14%
Strategic failure (selling the wrong product in the wrong market)	13%
Geopolitical event (regional instability causes supply disruption)	8%

Source: "Three Techniques for Managing Supply Risk" by Mark Hillman, March 9, 2006, AMR Research, based on a poll of 150 people attending a webinar.

RISK FACTORS

With suppliers now spread around the globe, risk avoidance is a hot topic. What happens when an Asian supplier has a quality or delivery glitch? Or an Indian call center has employee turnover that impacts service quality? Or a supplier unexpectedly goes out of business? According to an AMR Research Alert,[5] the top risks that keep supply managers up at night include the five types of disruptions shown in Table 1.6.

While one can't control acts of nature or political events, preparing for uncertainty by gaining a better understanding of who one's suppliers are, how they are performing, what their strengths and weaknesses are, and even how they are running their business are some important steps toward preventing and mitigating risk. Developing closer relationships with important suppliers also helps companies mitigate risk. You are more likely to work with valued supplier partners in times of adversity and they with you. You may even decide that risks and total cost of pursuing cheaper but far-flung suppliers may be greater than the rewards. What you don't know can hurt you. So, finding ways to increase visibility into the supply base is critical to risk avoidance.

SELLING THE BUSINESS CASE FOR SPM

SPM requires resources. Getting those resources requires an understanding and commitment from senior management, who need to understand the ROI for these resources. So far, we have discussed several ROI approaches:

---

5. Hillman, Mark, "Three Techniques for Managing Supply Risk," March 9, 2006, AMR Research, based on a poll of 150 people attending a webinar.

- Describe and quantify elements of the cost of poor supplier quality to your organization.
- Quote results from studies about the impact of measuring suppliers.
- Look at some of your biggest internal issues, such as customer complaints, call center costs, or quality rejects, and analyze the extent to which your suppliers contribute to these costs. (For those companies involved in Six Sigma, this would make an excellent Six Sigma project.)
- When SPM is well deployed, companies can more readily identify supplier problems and their root causes. Take one or two supplier problems and calculate the savings to both the supplier and to your company if the problem were fixed.

The business case is solid and the benefits clear. First, SPM provides quantifiable bottom-line impact. SPM provides executives with uninterrupted supply and enables them to establish productive and sustainable relationships with suppliers. Both the research by Denali Consulting and work with customers showed that SPM can drive 3 percent to 6 percent total supply chain cost reductions through continuous improvements.[6]

---

6. Minahan, Tim, "The Business Case for Supplier Performance," *Supply Excellence*, http://supplyexcellence.com/blog/2007/04/18/the-business-case-for-supplier-performance-management.

2

GETTING STARTED

ORGANIZATIONAL READINESS FOR SUPPLY MANAGEMENT

This book, like many companies, focuses on what *suppliers* need to do to improve their performance. We are looking at how customer companies can work with their suppliers to help improve their performance. Conventional wisdom says that performance problems lie predominantly with suppliers, particularly smaller suppliers. When I was running the New England Suppliers Institute (NESI), a regional organization that focused on improving business relationships between customers and their suppliers, we worked with some prominent larger manufacturing companies who wanted their suppliers to improve their performance and adopt lean manufacturing practices. Since NESI offered lean workshops and supplier development to smaller suppliers, we had the chance to get the supplier view of their customers. In addition, our board was made up of representatives from both customer and supplier companies, and we were given a lot of input on the topic of customer-supplier relationships. A key insight came from examining what these smaller suppliers were saying about their customers' performance "as customers"—and it wasn't a pretty picture. Customer companies were regularly unable to provide suppliers with critical information such as supplying timely and accurate product demand forecasts, reliable order releases, current engineering documentation, and other information required before suppliers could even begin to react. Strategic issues like sharing of business plans and product strategies that could provide a foundation for longer-term, productive customer-supplier relations were not addressed often enough. We heard many stories about customers making it difficult for suppliers to perform well for them. There was the customer who bricked in its receiving dock and never told the supplier where to deliver the parts. Another typical scenario was the customer who left supplier shipments on its dock for days or even weeks, and then, when it finally received the shipment into its system, dinged the supplier for being late. Other customers gave suppliers the wrong drawing revision and then were upset at the supplier for building to the wrong revision. And, instead of communicating with suppliers about requirements, one company suddenly closed its dock near the end of a month in order to improve its financials by not receiving any shipments, forcing suppliers who had built to order to eat the inventory and forego planned revenue. Another company would stop paying suppliers at the end of the year in order to make its financials look good for Wall Street analysts, often for over 90 to 120 days, and still expect continued, regular shipments and good service. At the end of every year, some of the suppliers to this Fortune 500 company would go out of business due to the late payments, and the purchasing director would get calls begging him to save their businesses by sending a payment. (It was a corporate policy that this manager was unable to alter.) Yet, at the same time, this company had a preferred supplier partner process that was recognized for its excellence. Some of our supplier members recounted supplier conferences where the customer would talk about developing customer-supplier partnerships, then tell the suppliers that they would no longer be doing business with half of them by next year. These suppliers began to refer to partnerships as "the P word," as they saw little in it for them. In a buyer's market and in the short term, these tactics may work, but they lose impact and can fail in a seller's market or as a long-term strategy, particularly with key or strategic suppliers. One of our supplier board members called this the "helmet and sledgehammer" approach to supplier management (with the supplier wearing the helmet).

While many important concepts—and to some extent buzzwords—such as early supplier involvement, long-term partnerships, and sharing of information are finally becoming reality for some companies, these are still at the talking stages for many. While many companies' goals are to improve the customer-supplier relationship and derive maximum value from it, the reality is that many companies do not have the business processes, practices, and enabling behaviors in place to pull this off. And when it comes down to it, many procurement people are looking for price, price, and price as the top criteria, not total cost or added value.

Many customer firms have internal processes that create cost and waste both for themselves and for their indirect, service, or nonmanufacturing suppliers. We define waste in the lean enterprise sense as any process or activity that does not add value to the customer. Poor communication of requirements can cause suppliers to deliver services that are incorrect or poor quality. For example, unclear or insufficiently detailed specifications to offshore information technology vendors can produce disappointing, if not completely incorrect, results and end up costing more than if higher-priced internal or local resources had been used. The money saved by lower prices may be lost in additional administrative attention needed to manage offshore programmers. Many companies have learned about this communications gap when they have pursued low-cost-country software development resources. Similarly, the trend toward sourcing with suppliers in Asia-Pacific requires good processes and precise communication of requirements to avoid poor results. Customer competency is needed to manage a global supply chain.

Our work at New England Suppliers Institute in the 1990s led us to the insight that, as one of our customer company members said, "It's the customer, stupid." Companies tend to focus on supplier performance—where suppliers need to improve. They often are not focused on what they do as an organization that either degrades or diminishes their suppliers' ability to perform and meet their requirements. Customers need to have supply management competencies in place if they wish to enable good performance from their suppliers. We learned that supplier performance depends not only on the supplier's own capabilities as a business but also on the capabilities of its customers. As in many relationships, both parties contribute to problems. This is one of the reasons why different customers can have different perceptions of the capabilities of the same supplier— and why the measurement of a supplier's performance by one customer may produce significantly different results than the performance experienced by another customer of the same supplier. And why some of the responsibility for poor supplier performance lies with the customer company.

As a result of our work at NESI, we developed the Supply Base Management Improvement Process. This was a tool designed to identify supply management competencies and areas of opportunity for improvement at the customer.

SUPPLY MANAGEMENT SYSTEM COMPONENTS

The Supply Management System Framework (see Figure 2.1) is a development tool and a best-practices model based on a functional model of the supply management system. This functional model is a prototype for achieving excellence in supply management practice. In addition, it played a key role as the foundation for NESI's Supply Base Management Improvement Process. This process outlined the skills, competencies, and enabling behaviors that a customer needs to have to enable excellence in supplier relationships, enable good supplier performance, and help improve that performance.[1] It is a business improvement model for the buying organization, but it is also applicable down the supply chain.

---

1. Gordon, Sherry, *Improving Company Performance through Supply Chain Management Practices*, Lionheart Publishing, 1998.

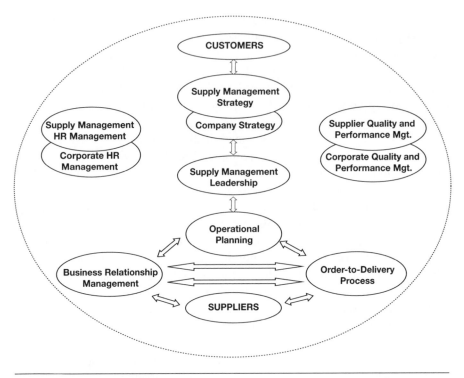

Figure 2.1 Supply management system framework.

1. Supply Management Leadership

Supply management leadership addresses in what way and how effectively company leadership sets the direction, designs, deploys, and improves the supply management system. To be most effective, supply management should report to the CEO and be part of the senior leadership of the company. Supply management has evolved in the twenty-first century to more of a leadership role, as it continues to prove its value to the bottom line of the company. The position of CPO or chief procurement officer is a fairly recent development.

2. Supply Management Strategy

The supply management strategy component considers how effectively a firm's requirements for purchased materials and services are expressed and communicated to suppliers, how well aligned the supply management strategy is with overall corporate goals and strategy, how the company allocates resources to support supply chain management operations, and how well these resources are aligned with the company's customer and market strategies and other resources within the company. Supply management strategy is part of the overall company strategy and requires the input of various functions in its development. Having supply management strategy as part of the overall company strategy helps set the direction of initiatives in procurement and ensures alignment with overall corporate goals.

3. Operational Planning

Operational planning is the process by which the company specifies the objectives, tasks, resources, and measurements needed to guide supply management operations. It clearly defines what an organization is looking to accomplish, typically within a one- to three-year time frame, as well as how it will be accomplished, in what time frame (when) and who will be responsible The focus includes areas such as commodity planning, production and inventory planning, and sourcing. Operational planning takes into account sales projections, new technology, and marketing strategy. It includes the processes that are necessary to manage suppliers, measure their performance, and ensure that supplier performance is supporting overall business objectives and internal business requirements.

4. Business Relationship Management

The business relationship management component addresses how effectively the company ensures a *two-way flow of understanding* between the company and its suppliers as it pertains to communicating and negotiating requirements with the supply chain and the mutual exchange of information, plans, and ideas. A good, effective relationship can enable a company and its key suppliers to create maximum mutual value. For example, good business relationships are the cornerstone of collaborative new product development with suppliers. Business relationship management with key and critical suppliers can take procurement beyond the purchase of goods and services and even beyond cost savings to enable the creation of real value for the corporation. Companies must develop criteria for and then select those suppliers with whom to focus their business relationship efforts in order to create this value.

5. Order-to-Delivery Processes

Order-to-delivery processes comprise the methods and effectiveness of how the firm directs the process of getting products and services from suppliers to the company. The order-to-delivery process is often measured in terms of the perfect order or the extent to which every step of this process is free of error. Included are processes such as order release, receiving, incoming inspection, accounts payable, customer service, and internal material or order handling. This component touches many functions, most of which are outside the purview of a single functional group like procurement but heavily impact suppliers' ability to perform. An operations manager I once knew characterized the order-to-delivery process as how efficiently you can get from "ring to ring"; that is, from the time the phone rings when the customer places the order until the cash register rings after the customer pays for the order. The extent to which this key process operates smoothly and effectively impacts the overall company's cash flow and customer satisfaction. Therefore, the supplier role in this process is critical to overall company success.

6. Quality and Performance Management

Quality and performance management for supply management addresses activities undertaken by the company and its suppliers to ensure that purchased materials and services meet agreed-upon requirements and service levels. A subset of the overall company quality and performance management system, it includes providing specific and timely feedback to key suppliers on nonconforming parts and on service failures, and tracking and providing feedback on supplier quality, responsiveness, on-time delivery performance, and any other performance areas that are important to the business. Quality and performance management includes supplier performance improvement activities such as working with key suppliers on product or service quality, cost, responsiveness, and cycle time improvements.

7. Human Resource Management

Human resource management for supply management is a subset of the company's overall human resources management system and encompasses activities to develop people with the skills, knowledge, and attitudes that support the performance of the supply management system. The assumption is that employees need *specific* training and education to work with suppliers in areas such as sourcing, supplier quality, supplier site visits, business relationship management, contracts, supplier management and procurement systems, and so on.

SUPPLY MANAGEMENT ENABLERS

Having the seven components of this framework in place is a start, but more is needed: enabling behaviors at the customer level. Even if the functions and skills exist, supplier performance excellence is still dependent on cultural and environmental factors and core values. These enablers are sometimes referred to as the "soft stuff," or the people side of things, as opposed to the "hard stuff," or the actual output or work product. The extent to which these enablers exist and are in sync or aligned at both customer and supplier supports improved performance. Enablers are critical for driving overall performance of the supply management system over time. The supply management enablers allow and sustain a firm's achievement of high-performance supply management practices. The processes and practices of supply chain management are difficult, if not impossible, to implement without the following underlying enabling behaviors. Supply chain management rests upon a cultural and behavioral system and mind-set, which is the primary difficulty that American companies face in its implementation. American companies are typically focused on the hard stuff, particularly tools and techniques, because it is easier to understand and control, while the soft stuff can thwart success. Below are some key business enablers that facilitate the deployment of good business practices in supply management. Identification of these enablers was influenced by the Baldrige National Quality Program.

1. Customer-Supplier Focus

Customers and suppliers are both internal and external to the organization. Efforts are dedicated to ensuring the complete satisfaction of not only the end user or customer for a product or service but also the satisfaction of the suppliers whose products or services are incorporated into the end customer's order and whose performance impacts end customer satisfaction.

In firms with large supplier dependencies, the business health and well-being of suppliers are critical to the overall ability to provide value to the end customer. Supplier satisfaction includes stable business relationships in which the rules of the relationship are clear and mutually understood and acknowledged. The long-term profitability and success of the supplier is an important consideration. The increasing struggles of American auto manufacturers support this notion. As automakers demanded price concessions every year from their suppliers, the suppliers either improved their operations to do this or went out of business. At a certain point, some suppliers had restructured themselves heavily and refused to reduce their prices for fear of going out of business. Their customers had relied on the price cuts and had few alternatives.[2] In part, relationships had been strained and trust no longer existed. Operationally this can also be seen in supplier involvement in new product or service development and in improvement in the design of existing products and services. Supplier expertise in contributing to the success of its customer should be recognized. The regular sharing of business goals and objectives and market conditions also demonstrates supplier focus.

Most companies would say that they are customer focused, meaning that they are trying to add value to their customers and provide them with the goods and services in a way that meets their needs and satisfies them. Not all companies view

---

2. "New Detroit Woe: Parts Makers Won't Cut Prices," *Wall Street Journal*, March 20, 2007, p. 1.

supplier satisfaction as a goal. Supplier focus means that the relationship is viewed as two-way and suppliers are treated as valued business partners.

2. Fact-Based Management

Fact-based management means that effective decisions are based on the analysis of data and information, rather than on guesses and feelings. The measurement and analysis of performance should be derived from business needs and strategy. Per the Baldrige National Quality Program, "The measures or indicators you select should best represent the factors that lead to improved customer, operational, financial and ethical performance."[3]

Fact-based management is based upon measurement. Measurement is the starting point for knowing where you are now, finding out about opportunities for improvement, and understanding where to focus sustainment and improvement activities. Measurements should be clearly connected to the processes that use and act on them. Measurement is a means to an end and not an end in itself. For example, if a company generates report cards to measure supplier performance, these are useful to the extent that they are used as a dialogue and improvement tool with suppliers.

Measurements can and should drive behavior. Thus, it is important to be measuring the right things and to align the measurements with overall business strategies and objectives. Otherwise, measurement can drive wrong or even unintended behaviors.

3. Alignment

Alignment refers to a unification of goals throughout the company and consistency of processes, actions, information, and decisions among company units in support of these goals. Within the supply chain management system, alignment is a key organizational enabler. Since most of the highest-value processes and outcomes require cross-functional as well as intercompany activities, the stakeholders must work together toward mutually recognized goals and objectives. Good alignment requires that supply management leadership sets goals, objectives, and strategies that are in sync with overall company goals and that support successful supplier relationships. For example, if management rewards purchasing primarily for obtaining low prices from suppliers, then it will be difficult to develop partnerships or close relationships with those suppliers, as the buyer will need to view the supplier primarily in terms of price and thus disregard potential value that the supplier could bring to the table. If there is an overall culture

---

3. 2007 Criteria for Performance Excellence, Baldrige National Quality Program, p. 4.

of distrust within a company, then it will be reflected in the supply management system and relationships with suppliers.

The other side of alignment is between customer and supplier—how well a supplier fits with its customer's culture, business processes, and practices; general ways of doing business; goals and objectives; and so on. For example, if a customer is deploying a high-performance system such as lean, it may want the supplier to do the same. When performance issues with the supplier arise, the supplier needs to fit with the customer's ideas of continuous improvement to resolve problems. In lean, the supplier may need to reorganize its workplace in order to satisfy customer requirements. Lack of alignment means that this type of request will appear absurd to some suppliers. Some suppliers will not and/or simply cannot comply with such business directives. Some are family-owned "lifestyle" businesses that are focused on supporting the lifestyle of the owners rather than developing a business that will be sustainable in the future. Or, the supplier may be at a beginner level in understanding lean and has other urgent business needs and few resources. In other cases of poor alignment, a supplier may have more advanced business practices than its customer, such as EDI (electronic data interchange) capability or a lean one-piece flow that works best with small, frequent shipments to the customer, who still wants large and infrequent shipment. In this case, the supplier may find working with its customer frustrating and even costly. These are examples of lack of alignment.

4. Agility

Agility is the capacity to rapidly, flexibly, and effectively respond to changing customer, supplier, stakeholder, and market requirements or expectations. With global competition, compression of business cycles, and pressure to improve products and services, agility, or at least the willingness to work toward an agile enterprise, is critical. As companies focus on time-based issues such as order velocity and compression of product development cycles, improvements in areas such as quality, cost, productivity, customer responsiveness, and so on can result. The customer cannot successfully address time-based issues alone, without the cooperation of its suppliers.

5. Continuous Improvement

Continuous improvement refers to a never-ending effort to expose and eliminate root causes of problems. Continuous improvement requires periodic review of processes, programs, or systems. Periodic review is a cornerstone of a continuous-improvement culture, whose premise is that there is always room for improvement. All supply management processes should be reviewed periodically for improvement. Since most processes evolve over time rather than by intentional design, this is particularly important. Companies should focus on periodic review of self-contained processes (such as the purchase order process) as well as on the core business processes that impact successful supply management, such as the order-to-delivery process. It is impossible, however, to segregate periodic review as only a supply management process, as it is a behavior that pervades the entire culture of most companies.

In the realm of customer-supplier relationship development, a culture of continuous improvement is particularly important. The improvement of supplier performance depends upon the supplier wanting to improve. If the supplier's culture is resistant to change or sees improvement opportunities as flaws that need to be justified or denied rather than exposed, then improvement will be less likely to occur. Some suppliers have the will but not the way to improve. Having at least the desire to improve puts the supplier in alignment with a customer who wants to improve supplier performance. A supplier can learn specific continuous-improvement tools and techniques, but only if the supplier regards continuous improvement as a genuine value, rather than simply an empty slogan or lip service to the customer. The customer firm must, of course, have a corresponding commitment to continuous improvement if it expects its suppliers to improve. Otherwise, its improvement expectations may be met with resistance and resentment.

6. Participation/Involvement/Teamwork

Inclusion of all stakeholders in decision-making processes helps ensure the continued and future success of a product, process, system, or service and is an important cultural characteristic of high-performing companies. A culture of involvement means that leadership, business processes, hierarchy, decision making, and information systems create and sustain participation. Participation and involvement in supply management can include asking key suppliers to help design customer business processes that affect them, listening to feedback not only from suppliers but also from other departments within the customer company, allowing problems to be raised by suppliers and taking action to correct those problems, and encouraging cross-functional involvement by key internal departments in evaluating suppliers.

Participation and involvement supports the notion of customer-supplier partnerships: that strategic and key suppliers can bring additional value and complementary competencies to customers.

7. Process/Systems Approach

A process/systems approach views activities and resources as connected steps in producing value and identifying, understanding, and managing interrelated processes as a whole to drive the company's effectiveness and efficiency in achieving its objectives. The performance management and improvement systems, both within the company and with suppliers, work as one system to succeed. Per the Baldrige National Quality Program, "A systems perspective also includes using your measures, indicators, and organizational knowledge to build your key strategies. It means linking these strategies with your key processes and aligning your resources to improve overall performance and satisfy customers and stakeholders."[4]

A high-performing supply management system should encompass the elements at the customer as described. Many firms ask suppliers to improve performance without having an adequate supply management system in place in their own workplace. The system just described is not a prerequisite for managing suppliers, but a framework to help companies recognize the elements of and develop a good supply management system in order to be more effective at managing their suppliers and enabling performance improvement and to avoid exacerbating supplier problems. If customers can get their own houses in order first, or at least be cognizant of how a good system works and be working toward it, they can be in a much better position to enable supplier performance excellence.

IDENTIFYING STRATEGIES AND GOALS

The first step in developing a supplier performance management system is to understand your company's overall business goals, objectives, and business strategy. The types of suppliers you choose, your performance expectations of those suppliers, how you work with them—just about every aspect of supplier management—can be influenced by corporate goals and strategies. And in turn, procurement should be actively supporting those strategies. If procurement is out of sync with corporate goals and strategies or operates without knowledge of or alignment with them, it could be working at cross-purposes with the rest of the company or not adding its full value. Senior management may be less likely to support procurement initiatives if it cannot see the link to overall goals. For example, if the company is trying to reduce cycle times, procurement must do more than just look at price without regard to suppliers' abilities to reduce cycle time. Perhaps the longer cycle times are a part of the root cause for higher prices. Or procurement could find that its request for sourcing software might be better justified if it can show how using the software will support corporate objectives beyond just procurement internal objectives. Without alignment, support for procurement initiatives will be difficult to obtain and appreciation of its contribution to the company will be lacking or limited, if not invisible. Yet many procurement people are unaware of corporate goals and strategies, not always due to their own fault.

---

4. 2007 Criteria for Performance Excellence, Baldrige National Quality Program, p. 10.

Senior management may never communicate its goals and strategies beyond themselves. I have had to ask purchasing management to look in their own annual reports to see if they can glean their company's strategy and objectives.

This process of flowing corporate objectives down to the operational level is not a new concept. It is typically called policy deployment or strategy deployment, a derivative of the Japanese method Hoshin Planning. Many companies use some sort of a corporate strategic planning process; however, with some exceptions, the smaller the company, the less likely it is to be codified in written form. Executive management develops a yearly strategic plan covering the next year or sometimes a three- to five-year period of time. During this process, various market and financial data and projections are considered and incorporated into a plan. The result is a document with goals, objectives, and strategies for the next year or some future time period.

The challenge with strategic planning is the execution of the plan. Policy deployment is a method for gathering the voice of the customer[5]—that is, the customer's true needs and requirements—inputting them into the plan, and then flowing the objectives through the organization to the points where they will be made operational—that is, the points of impact. Policy or strategy deployment takes the critical strategic imperatives and makes them operational at every level of the organization with the goal of achieving measurable business results. Each department and even individuals develops their own goals and objectives that relate to overall corporate goals, specifying owners and due dates. Then metrics are identified to help measure progress toward these goals. This management process helps align an organization in order to achieve its strategies and goals. In order to do so, the goals of all departments and/or units must be in sync with overall goals. Successful policy or strategic deployment starts with senior management and requires strong organizational discipline and follow-through. Strategy deployment works best when the workforce is trained to work as teams, find root causes of problems, and is familiar with continuous-improvement tools and techniques. It is a good way to ensure alignment and constancy of purpose and increases the chances for success. Yet, according to one study, only 60 percent of U.S. companies have a written strategic plan.[6] So it is likely that even fewer companies are flowing their strategic plans throughout the organization in a systematic fashion.

An example of a company successfully using strategy deployment is Medrad, Inc., a medical device manufacturing company and a 2003 recipient of the Malcolm Baldrige National Quality Award. Per the National Institute of Standards

---

5. The voice of the customer is a process used to capture requirements from internal or external customers and to create and provide the best possible service/product quality to customers.

6. Minnesota Council for Quality Stakeholder Update, July 2005. Available at http://www.councilforquality.org/Documents/2005Newsletter07.pdf.

and Technology (NIST), "Medrad's Executive Committee uses a systematic strategic planning process to review the company's five corporate scorecard goals, to set one- and five-year targets, and to identify the Top 12 Objectives to achieve those targets. Medrad's 'Waterfalling Process' is used to deploy the scorecard goals and Top 12 Objectives throughout the organization. Managers create departmental objectives and plans to support the corporate scorecard and Top 12 and then work with employees to develop individual goals to support departmental goals. This process results in the alignment of the corporate scorecard goals down to the individual employee."[7]

So let's go back to supply management and alignment with corporate strategy. With strategic plans

- Unwritten
- If written, not fully communicated in many organizations

and with strategy deployment an ideal but unlikely to be a reality in most businesses, where does that leave supplier managers on the challenge of aligning their supply chains with overall corporate objectives? Alignment of procurement is important not only for obtaining and keeping senior management support but for determining supplier performance requirements. For example, if your company's corporate goal is to develop new products and supply management understands that there are suppliers currently playing an important role in the development of many new products, your company's future depends, in part, on those suppliers having the requisite capabilities and being able to meet your performance expectations.

If your company has a full-fledged strategic planning and strategy deployment process, then you are probably already familiar with developing a procurement and/or supply management strategy in alignment with the corporate strategy. However, many individuals will need to derive or infer corporate goals and strategies, rather than having something formal or written to work with. Even in cases where there is a written plan, it is not always easily accessible, for some reason, as if it were a top secret not available to employees, who, after all, are the ones who execute the plan. When procurement reports to the C-level in an organization, communication and understanding of corporate goals should be simpler. But where no formal corporate plan exists or is readily accessible, I am recommending that you create a supply management strategy, making it support corporate goals and strategies as much as possible, *as you understand them.*

---

7. National Institute of Standards and Technology, Malcolm Baldrige National Quality Award 2003 Award Recipient, Manufacturing Category: Medrad, Inc. Available online at http://www.nist.gov/public_affairs/releases/medrad.htm.

Table 2.1 Example of How Procurement Strategy Can Support Corporate Strategy

Area	How Supply Management Can Support
Technology	Partner with technology suppliers on product development and value engineering
Globalization	Develop a global supplier network

Some publicly traded companies publish some of this information in their annual reports. For example, from the GE 2006 annual report, the CEO describes goals and strategies and the results. Here are two as an example:

* Focus on technology
* Focus on globalization

How can this relate to supplier management and be incorporated into a procurement plan? Table 2.1 gives an example of how procurement strategy can support and align with corporate strategy.

How ever you go about it, you will next need to define or understand your existing procurement and supply management strategy.

In the chapter "Linking Suppliers through Policy Deployment," in his book *Total Quality in Purchasing and Supply Management*, Ricardo Fernandez addresses the issue of aligning suppliers and supplier performance with strategic plans in order to bring about mutually beneficial changes. Figure 2.2 illustrates how the vision of the future state of the entire organization can be cascaded down to the

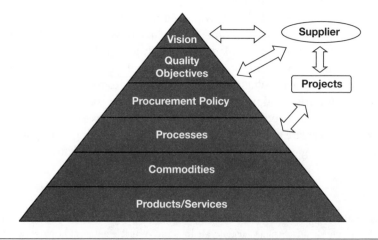

Figure 2.2 The supplier within strategy deployment.

products or services, which contain supplier inputs. The organization develops overall objectives related to the quality of its products and services. Next, procurement policy that supports the quality goals and targets must be developed and signed off not only by procurement executives, but by the executive management of the organization. Processes include major business processes such as manufacturing, service delivery and administrative processes. Commodities are similar items used by a process or group of processes, which in turn lend themselves to categories of suppliers who supply these commodities. Once the organization has identified key suppliers to work with, supplier projects are launched to improve their products and services. The policy/strategy deployment process helps align and prioritize organizational and procurement goals. The organization then needs to figure out how to evaluate these suppliers to promote alignment and to identify supplier development areas that will improve performance as it relates to the supplier and its support of customer objectives.

DEVELOPING A PROCUREMENT STRATEGY

To develop a meaningful procurement strategy, there are many considerations: products, services, technologies, financial plans, global presence, geopolitical and economic risks, growth plans, competition, customer satisfaction, corporate social responsibility, regulatory and political environment, and employee growth and satisfaction. Procurement should gather information on these areas, using company strategic plans, operational plans, the annual report, executive management input, and awareness of overall business and procurement/supply management trends outside the company. The information should be reviewed in terms of its impact on and potential support by procurement and supply management.

Here is a sample outline for a procurement strategy:

1. Introduction
2. Strategy
3. Objectives—Vision and values of procurement, goals, key issues to address
4. Policy—Principles for decision making, procurement policies
5. Overview of procurement process
6. Internal and external issues to be addressed in context of the process
7. Action plan (can be separate)—With milestones, tasks, timetable, and metrics

Table 2.2 illustrates a structure for developing a procurement strategy. Table 2.3 gives some examples of how corporate objectives might align with supplier performance management objectives. The extent to which corporate objectives are visibly supported by supply management and supplier performance strategies

Table 2.2 Procurement Strategy Structure

Milestone	Timetable
Key strategies supporting each milestone	
Major goals	
Tasks (the programs or implementation plans for the key strategies)	Responsibility, completion date, actions required, evidence of achievement Resources, objectives, time scales, deadlines, budgets, and performance targets
Supporting business practices, processes (performance targets) that help determine if tasks are accomplished	

Table 2.3 Aligning Supplier Management Strategies with Corporate Objectives

Corporate Objectives	Supplier Strategies
Reduce cycle time	Suppliers implement cycle time reduction techniques
Reduce product cost	Value engineering with suppliers Implement lean enterprise methodologies
Reduce service costs	Low-cost-country outsourcing
Improve service to customers	Put service level agreements (SLAs) in place with suppliers
Improve customer satisfaction	Suppliers implement quality at the source

not only helps a firm achieve its overall goals but also increases support (and resources) for the purchasing/supply management function.

The journey from corporate strategy to supplier performance excellence has been described in terms of a policy or strategy deployment process. Once you know your company's strategic direction and operational priorities, you can then set procurement and supply management priorities and subsequently develop supplier performance expectations. These performance expectations will be the backbone of your supplier performance management process and the basis for decision making about suppliers.

This book has free material available for download from the
Web Added Value™ resource center at *www.jrosspub.com*

3

CHOOSING THE TEAM AND DEVELOPING THE PLAN

DEVELOPING A SUPPLIER PERFORMANCE MANAGEMENT PROJECT TEAM

An SPM project is a change management undertaking, which means that you will need a clear plan, senior management support, stakeholder representation, and ongoing communication with internal and external stakeholders. You will need to create a team and team structure for the entire project. Depending upon the size of your company and how you are organized, there are a variety of approaches that can be successful. Figure 3.1 shows a sample proposed SPM project structure for a transportation services company.

This organization created a procurement steering committee with participation at the executive level in order to better leverage procurement as a way to improve enterprise performance. Some companies may have an executive-level council. Others will have a procurement or supplier management council at the senior management level. One example of this is Boeing, which has used its SMPC, or Supplier Management Process Council, chaired by a senior vice president-level supplier management leader, as a senior executive decision-making group regarding new processes, policies, practices, and technology within its supplier management organization. The fact that Boeing has a senior vice president of supplier management indicates the importance procurement and supplier

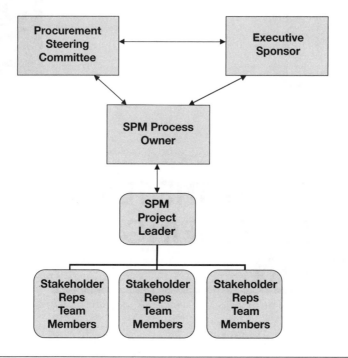

Figure 3.1 SPM project structure.

management has in the company. There should be some reporting relationship and oversight of the SPM project to the overall procurement council to ensure that SPM project activities are aligned with overall procurement strategies and objectives and have senior management buy-in.

However a company goes about organizing major initiatives, it is important to ensure the visibility, communications, and support for SPM, as it requires support, resources, and management commitment to ensure maximum impact on the company and a full return on investment. Inevitably, other priorities will arise in the organization, and supplier performance can easily get lost in the shuffle if its contributions and results are not kept in front of senior management. Because supplier performance initiatives have less specifically predictable ROI than do other initiatives, such as price reductions obtained through sourcing initiatives, many senior managers feel as if they are taking a leap of faith that supplier performance will pay off. If supplier managers neglect to keep a supplier performance initiative on the executive radar screen, then senior management can more easily have "senior moments" about why they authorized it in the first place.

To ensure a successful SPM project, there should be an executive sponsor. This person can sit on the procurement council or steering committee. The responsibilities of the executive sponsor can include the following:

- Championing the SPM process with senior management
- Helping obtain and then maintaining the commitment and financial support of senior management
- Ensuring the link and alignment between the SPM project and corporate strategies, goals, and objectives
- Providing communications about and maintaining support for SPM with the procurement council or steering committee
- Providing input and guidance about corporate internal matters (i.e., politics) in relation to SPM

Ideally, SPM should be more than just a project. It should be a process, and there should be a process owner for supplier performance management. This is because it is a key enterprise process that touches multiple functions beyond just the procurement or quality organization. In a cross-functional process, it is important that one individual has ownership for the health and success of that process and responsibility for coordinating the various functions and work activities at all levels of a process. Otherwise, the process can fall between the corporate cracks and be left to languish and wither unattended because it does not belong to anyone. This person should have the "authority or ability to make changes in the process as required and manage the entire process cycle to ensure performance effectiveness."[1] This person may be the same as the executive sponsor in some companies. The process owner's responsibilities would also include the following:

- Providing input and guidance on the project
- Providing organizational knowledge and insights to make SPM successful
- Developing an understanding of and advising on best practices in SPM

For example, this person may have a better understanding of the organization so that he or she can ensure such things as the proper composition of the project team and identifying key stakeholders. If the process owner is other than the executive sponsor, the process owner ensures good communications throughout the project regarding its progress and any issues or obstacles that arise that may need executive assistance to overcome.

---

1. The Six Sigma and Lean Glossary, http://www.onesixsigma.com/onesixsigma/glossary.

The project manager leads the SPM project. This person is responsible for:

- Working to select and manage the SPM project team
- Guiding procurement and other impacted functions through the SPM process
- Planning and development of all project deliverables
- Defining components and tools of the SPM process as well as the process itself
- Developing and deploying the project plan
- Managing the day-to-day activities of the project
- Working with stakeholders for participation and buy-in in the process
- Internal and external project communications with the process owner, senior management, suppliers, internal stakeholders, and so on

The SPM project team performs the detailed work of developing the SPM system. It consists of representatives in the organization who are impacted by supplier performance or who actively work with suppliers. Some of them serve in an advisory role, representing the stakeholders in the process throughout the organization. Others actually perform the detailed work: develop and implement all aspects of the supplier performance management process, from supplier performance expectations, process design and development, and implementation to ongoing process monitoring and improvement. Since suppliers are important stakeholders in the development and deployment of SPM, they should be represented on this team through participation of selected supplier representatives. The suppliers do not necessarily need to be involved as closely as the other team members. Their input is valuable and needs to be part of the process in order to make SPM successful. Some companies have a supplier council, which is a formal organization that is used to get supplier input on all matters affecting suppliers. The input on SPM can be obtained from a supplier council, if applicable, and/or directly from supplier representatives that advise the SPM team.

STRUCTURING THE EVALUATION PROCESS

To have a successful supplier performance management program, there are two critical success factors: management support and a defined, robust evaluation process. One reason for supplier performance programs not having much impact is that they are developed and deployed in a vacuum. Even if the measurements are well aligned with overall supply management and organizational goals, supplier evaluation cannot operate standalone. In a truly robust program, you may need input and thus cooperation from a variety of stakeholders in your organization and in the supplier organization. Even when a company is using scorecards where the data is derived from an internal business system, such as ERP or a financial system, a defined process is still needed. Collecting information is just one step in the process. A company also needs to take action on the information. While procurement can be the focal point for the supplier relationship, other interested and involved stakeholders need to be involved in supplier performance management, as supplier performance can impact a variety of stakeholders. These may include quality, accounts payable, legal, warehouse personnel, materials management, customer service, manufacturing, engineering, and field service. Other functions may be impacted by supplier performance issues on a daily basis (or they themselves have an impact on supplier performance) and may need to give performance input, work with suppliers on performance improvement issues, and conduct supplier development activities. Various stakeholders in the company will look at supplier performance from their own unique perspectives and will have different views of performance expectations from procurement. If and when actions such as supplier development or even supplier disengagement need to be taken, stakeholder involvement and support can be important.

Because of the recommended and critical cross-functional participation of others, the evaluation process should be clearly defined and documented. After gaining executive support for supplier evaluation, there should ideally be an executive sponsor for a supplier evaluation initiative who can make sure the appropriate resources are committed and serve as a communication link with senior management. One function or person needs to be designated as the process owner. Depending upon the organization, an SPM initiative can be overseen by different types of management councils or groups within the organization such as a supplier quality management council or a procurement council. For example, Con-way, a transportation and logistics services company, created a procurement council consisting of the executive management team of the company to oversee procurement initiatives, such as sourcing, spend analysis, and supplier performance. In companies deploying Six Sigma or lean enterprise, a senior steering committee that oversees prioritization of improvement initiatives may already exist and it may be appropriate to have the initiative report to it.

Table 3.1 summarizes how a supplier performance initiative can be organized. This relates to the diagram in Figure 3.1. Three key elements are suggested. First is the establishment of a procurement or supplier management council or steering committee at a senior level that meets regularly to set priorities, oversee initiatives, review progress, and make policy decisions about procurement and supply management strategy and operations. Supplier performance management is typically just one of the areas where this council or steering committee provides leadership and decision making. Another role is that of the executive sponsor for the SPM project. This person may be part of the procurement council or may even be a higher-level executive. If not a regular member of the procurement council,

Table 3.1 SPM Project Roles and Responsibilities

Key Player	Roles and Responsibilities
Procurement or supplier management council or steering committee	Consists of the senior executive team or of senior procurement management
	Oversees procurement initiatives
	Meets regularly (at least quarterly)
	Reviews procurement's progress
	Discusses current issues
	Sets priorities
	Makes decisions that impact how procurement works within the organization
Executive sponsor	Makes key decisions using advice and information supplied by supplier performance team
	Champions the supplier performance management (SPM) process
	Provides communications about and maintains support for SPM with the procurement council or steering committee, as appropriate
	Provides input and guidance about management matters (and political matters) in relation to SPM
Process owner	Provides input and guidance on all aspects of the project
	Provides organizational knowledge and insights to make SPM successful

the executive sponsor should attend its meetings. Whatever the actual job title, the executive sponsor has position and clout in the organization to champion the SPM process and ensure support and resources. The executive sponsor runs political interference for SPM as needed and provides guidance and support to the SPM project team. The process owner has the operational ownership of the SPM process. This person coordinates the various functions and work activities at all levels of a process. In other words, the SPM process owner has a vested interested in the success of the SPM process and any projects designed to develop or improve that process.

In situations where a company is implementing SRM or SPM software and an SPM process at the same time, it is particularly important to make sure that there is a good project structure in place. You will need to deal with both the business issues and the software issues. Therefore, it is important to have the users of the software running the project, but with the software specialists playing a key support role in implementation and training. However, the software or IT people should not be running the project (other than the technical aspects of the project), since SPM is about developing and enabling a business process, not just implementing software. However, IT people should play a key role on the project team as major stakeholders, as described next.

The next step is choosing the SPM project team. While every important stakeholder in the organization will not be able to be on the project and you may not want or need them to be, their input (or that of their representative) into the project must be solicited. This will help ensure their buy-in, make implementation later on easier, and also make certain that you are not missing any important components. Who are potential stakeholders in the SPM process? Internal stakeholders might include quality, finance (such as accounts payable), information technology, contracts, legal, materials, product development, engineering, production, customer service, sourcing personnel, and employees who deal with suppliers and/or suppliers' goods and services. You want an understanding of process and business issues in supplier performance. Table 3.2 shows different functions in the organization that are stakeholders in the supplier performance management process, the specific types of input they may be able to provide, and the kinds of input that can be expected from all stakeholders.

The composition of the SPM team will vary depending on the type and size of the business. Obviously, smaller organizations can use a simpler structure and smaller team, as their scope will not be as big. Whatever project structure is developed, some of its components must be left in place to monitor and improve the resulting supplier performance management process that is developed. The main takeaways here about setting up an SPM project and team are that the project must be structured to be transparent in order to

- Obtain and maintain senior management support.
- Get input from all stakeholders, including suppliers.
- Communicate progress and results to stakeholders and senior management during *and after* the project phase and then on an ongoing basis.
- Ensure that the supplier performance management process is part of daily work, is institutionalized, and is not the "project du jour."

DEVELOPING A PROJECT PLAN

As the project structure and the roles and responsibilities are being identified, the SPM plan needs to be created. This plan describes the central process for developing a supplier performance management system. A project plan is applicable whether your company is starting from scratch or almost from scratch, is rethinking its current approach, or is adding to its current toolset. The tasks and strategies in the plan make up the foundation for this book and are described in more detail in subsequent chapters. Many companies come up with a few key performance

Table 3.2 Supplier Performance Management Initiative Process Inputs

Stakeholder	Specific Input	Common Input
Quality	Supplier quality problems Quality requirements Quality performance of suppliers Quality goals Noncompliance issues Evaluation strategies Corrective action and continuous improvement strategies Choosing SPM pilot suppliers Supplier development	Performance expectations Performance metrics Desired outcomes Business process development Creating new process workflow Getting stakeholder participation Setting goals Supplier development Communications
Finance	Supplier financial issues Payment processing issues Procure to pay process E-commerce	
Materials	Inventory issues Supplier knowledge Performance insights Supplier delivery issues	
Information technology	Current information systems and their capabilities Sources of metrics data Implementation of new systems Evaluation or development of IT alternatives Technology aspects of evaluation techniques IT interfaces with suppliers, such as e-commerce and supplier portals	
Legal/contracts	Understanding of or input into SLAs Types of contracts with suppliers Contractual issues with suppliers Contract change insights, implementation Legal issues in performance management Supplier disengagement contractual issues	
Engineering	Supplier capabilities Supplier problems and issues related to engineering Value engineering with suppliers	

Table 3.2 Supplier Performance Management Initiative Process Inputs (Continued)

Stakeholder	Specific Input	Common Input
Product development	Identifying development suppliers Development supplier capabilities and performance expectations SPM process development SPM metrics	
Customer service	Issues and impacts caused by supplier performance Customer complaints	
Production	Supplier problems, such as rejects, scrap, rework	
Procurement (sourcing and supplier management)	Category knowledge Knowledge of specific suppliers Supplier segmentation Evaluation strategies Choosing SPM pilot suppliers Recognition and rewards Supplier development strategies	
Miscellaneous stakeholders with knowledge of or contact with suppliers	Supplier strengths Supplier problems	
Suppliers	Customer issues that cause supplier problems Ease of doing business Evaluation techniques SPM process inputs Communications Recognition and rewards Customer evaluation	

indicators (KPIs) to track and consider that adequate—or at least hope it will be. There is nothing wrong with starting small, so long as your company does not keep SPM as a small, standalone process, disconnected from other supplier processes. It is important to have a plan and know where you are going with it. Implementing SPM is a challenge that supply managers are struggling with, and they are realizing that there are no silver bullets. The steps described in this book are far more comprehensive than approaches many companies have been using. They are not technically difficult but are perhaps more organizationally demanding. The process is easy to understand, makes a lot of sense, but is harder to actually do. The perform-ance management and improvement system that can be created using this process will be closed-loop and robust and has the potential to provide a real and visible return on the investment of resources. This book is organized around the flow of the process.

The major milestones in a supplier performance management plan include the following:

1. Initiate project plan and kickoff.
2. Segment the supply base.
3. Develop evaluation strategy.
4. Define performance expectations.
5. Define KPIs and scorecards.
6. Develop data collection instruments.
7. Plan transition from metrics to action.
8. Develop SPM business process.
9. Conduct SPM pilot.
10. Fully deploy SPM.

Table 3.3 shows a supplier performance management project timeline. The actual elapsed time will vary, depending upon the scope of the project. This proj-ect timeline is intended as a suggestion or guideline and an illustration of the key milestones involved in an SPM implementation. The development of the plan and completion of the suggested milestones and their components are dependent upon a good understanding of the organization's strategies and goals. If those are not clear, an understanding of procurement strategies and goals may suffice. Without this knowledge, however, it will be difficult to do an adequate job of completing tasks such as segmenting the supply base, defining performance expectations, and developing plans to transition from metrics to action. In reality, these tasks can be done, but in an organizational vacuum, making development, support, and sustainment of SPM more challenging.

1. Initiate Project Plan and Kickoff

The project team and project structure need to be determined, as described ear-lier. With the team and structure in place, the plan can be developed with inputs from the team and then approved. Team members represent major stakeholders, so they are expected to communicate with these stakeholders to ensure buy-in. Of course, as with all planning, the plan represents an iterative and continual process and not an end state—as in the classic continuous-improvement Plan-Do-Check-Act (PDCA) cycle. There will be many unknowns at the start and some risks. For example, you may not know at the start the kinds of data that are available for use

Table 3.3 Supplier Performance Management Project Timeline

Milestone	Months									
	1	2	3	4	5	6	7	8	9	10
Project Plan and Kickoff	▪									
Supply Base Segmentation		▪								
Define Performance Expectations			▪							
Develop Evaluation Strategy			▪							
SPM Pilot Plan, Run, Modify		▬▬▬▬▬▬▬▬▬▬▬								
Define KPIs and Scorecards				▪						
Develop Data Collection Instruments				▪						
Metrics to Action Planning				▪						
Develop SPM Business Process					▪					
Full SPM Deployment							▬▬▬▬▬▶			

in developing KPIs. You may need to change your ideas about what will be on the scorecards if certain data are not available, or you may need to look into alternatives. Or perhaps some information will require IT department efforts to obtain. Such issues will be uncovered as the process progresses. The details of the plan will become clearer as it is deployed and reworked.

2. Segment the Supply Base

In order to determine which suppliers to measure, you will need to segment the supply base. This is the process of putting suppliers into groups or categories based on common attributes such as dependence, strategic importance, switching costs, and risk. Supplier segmentation is done in order to apply the appropriate resources toward managing, developing relationships, and working with key suppliers to improve their capabilities and performance.

Table 3.4 shows some of the major tasks, decisions, and challenges of segmentation. Supply base segmentation is important not only for SPM but in general for deciding about applying limited company resources to work with types of suppliers and specific suppliers. Segmentation can be a continual process. It is not rocket science. The segmentation process can be ambiguous, and you do not want to get

Table 3.4 Supply Base Segmentation

Tasks	Key Decisions	Challenges
Define segmentation parameters	Developing parameters useful and appropriate to the organization	Defining segments that require measurement data that may not be available or ultimately prove less meaningful
Perform segmentation	Deciding how detailed segmentation needs to be for business decisions	Sufficient information about suppliers available for good segmentation decisions
Choose suppliers to measure	Identifying the most important suppliers to measure Prioritizing suppliers for supplier performance monitoring	Finding a representative supplier cross section willing to participate in pilot

stuck on this step. You want to make overall decisions rather quickly, then fine-tune them as you get into the details of developing the evaluation system. Segmenting the supply base will help you decide which suppliers you want to measure and how you want to measure them. Your segmentation efforts will be tested by the selection of the actual suppliers whom you choose to measure. As you discover what metrics are available or developable and how you really need to determine if the suppliers are meeting your performance expectations, you may need to modify the list.

3. Develop Evaluation Strategy

This milestone (see Table 3.5) involves reviewing the various approaches for evaluating suppliers, such as surveys, assessments, and scorecards. Decisions need to be made about the pros and cons of available approaches in order to choose those that will work best in your company's environment. Part of deciding about evaluation strategies involves identifying potential sources of metrics data. You will need to answer questions such as:

- Will information come directly from suppliers? From internal systems? From internal users or stakeholders?
- Are the tools for collecting this information readily available, or will they need to be created?
- How reliable and accurate are current and potential information sources?
- What is going to work in your company's environment? For example, if you are seeking feedback from internal stakeholders, does your company have the organizational discipline and motivation to complete

Table 3.5 Develop Evaluation Strategy

Tasks	Key Decisions	Challenges
Review, determine evaluation approaches	Decide which tools will work best: RFI, buyer survey, instant feedback, supplier assessment, enterprise metrics	Level of stakeholder participation in surveys
Identify potential sources of metrics data	Best sources for accurate and timely performance information	Reliability, accuracy, and accessibility of sources
Identify integration issues/tasks	Availability and accessibility of information from IT systems	Usability or accessibility of data sources Desired information may require IT integration work
Plan how metrics information will be obtained	Identify metrics sources	Reliability, accuracy, and accessibility of sources Stakeholder cooperation
Select data collection/survey instruments	Choose SPM data collection tools Strategies to obtain stakeholder participation	If survey approaches chosen, level of participation of stakeholders critical

supplier surveys on a regular basis? How will you ensure that surveys are completed regularly?

These are some of the tasks and decisions that will need to be addressed in order to complete the evaluation strategy milestone. This is also the milestone where you will discover what evaluation tools you have and what you will need; whether they need to be developed internally or procured; and what sources of information are available and suitable for your strategy. If your company is a service organization, you may not have an internal business system that is currently producing enough or the right metrics on which to base supplier performance measures, and you will need to explore alternative approaches.

4. Define Performance Expectations

Besides determining which suppliers you want to measure and your overall evaluation strategy, you will need to define your performance expectations—the areas of competency and the performance standards that you expect your suppliers to meet. You will need to delineate the most important and/or critical areas of performance for each segment of your supply base that you wish to measure. You should not start out with the actual metrics, but rather the overall areas of

Table 3.6 Define Performance Expectations

Tasks	Key Decisions	Challenges
Define performance areas most critical to business by segment	Define areas in each segment that need to be measured	Understanding overall challenges to business and impact of suppliers
Define performance expectations by segment	What specific business practices and types of performance does company expect from suppliers within each segment?	Internal knowledge of best practices and relevance to the business
Identify metrics indicative of supplier meeting expectations	Identify potential metrics for each expectation Define actionable metrics	Linking performance expectations with available metrics Ability to find or develop the most pertinent and critical data for metrics

performance. These might be, for example, quality or customer service rather than specific metrics such as on-time delivery or percentage of service calls answered. Ideally, supplier performance expectations should support purchasing strategy and corporate strategy. After defining the supplier performance expectations, you can then identify specific metrics related to the expectations. Keep in mind that as you go through the SPM development process, you may find that you are unable to find or create the specific metrics you desire because you do not currently have sources of information for those metrics. Sources of metrics data is an issue to keep in mind, but it can be dealt with later on. At this stage you are creating the overall structure of the program with specific details to be determined.

Table 3.6 summarizes the key tasks in this milestone, decisions that must be made and some of the challenges.

5. Define KPIs and Scorecards

In this step, you will refine the metrics or KPIs that you have identified in the last step. These KPIs will help you and your suppliers determine how well the suppliers are meeting performance expectations. It is important to have good reasons for choosing particular metrics other than "this is what everyone else is doing" (see the more detailed discussion of metrics development in Chapter 4). Other companies' KPIs and scorecards may not apply as well to your company, particularly since you should be linking metrics to your company's supplier performance expectations. Also, you will need to specify how the KPI is going to be derived, from what source or using what calculation. After identifying the metrics for each supplier segment (i.e., using the segments that are derived from the supplier segmentation step), the next task is determining the acceptable level of performance for various segments and categories of suppliers who are being measured—the baseline—and what should be the performance goal. You want to choose a reasonable number of metrics: enough to cover performance expectations but not too many to track and to review and communicate with suppliers. Too many metrics can be more problematic than not enough, as they can be too time-consuming to derive, track, and act on and ultimately may prove to be meaningless.

Once you have chosen the metrics, you can then design the scorecard. You may need to design scorecards for different categories or commodities, for direct versus indirect suppliers, or for different supplier segments. One size may not fit all. Yet you do not want to create mind-boggling complexity that will require an army of developers to design and a team of data stewards to maintain. Another purpose for defining KPIs is to synchronize them, if possible, with service level agreements in supplier contracts. This puts teeth behind the scorecards and makes it easier to monitor contract compliance. However, many legal considerations mean that your legal department should be involved in putting SLAs into contracts so that you do not violate any laws or use SLAs that are not enforceable. Table 3.7 illustrates the tasks, key decisions, and challenges of defining KPIs and scorecards.

6. Develop Data Collection Instruments

In deciding upon KPIs and scorecards, you will also need to determine how to collect the information that feeds the scorecards. This means figuring out the sources of the information needed and how you are going to get this information. Potential sources include data that your company is already gathering, such as information being collected in corporate information systems, and also information that can be collected directly from suppliers and internal stakeholders using various survey instruments. If surveys will be required, you must decide what types will work best in your environment and see what tools, if any, are currently available in your company for creating surveys and collecting survey data before you create these surveys or supplier assessments. Also, if you decide to assess suppliers using site visits, site visit instruments will be needed. That is, you will need a survey or questionnaire that is specifically designed for gathering information during a supplier site visit. The details of how to develop such an instrument are covered in Chapter 8, "Designing the Process." Data feeds from current systems will need to be identified, as well as any feeds from outside sources (such as financial information or the suppliers' own inputs). You will need to determine the level of effort and resources, both IT and other, that it will take to get any or all of this information into KPIs and scorecards. Also, this is the point at which you may

Table 3.7 Define KPIs and Scorecards

Tasks	Key Decisions	Challenges
Based on performance expectations, identify key metrics and their sources	Which metrics to collect Which metrics sources to use How many metrics to collect Which metrics will most accurately indicate the sources of problems	Either too many or insufficient metrics end up being collected Metrics difficult to obtain Data not accurate Metrics not relevant to what you are trying to accomplish
Set initial baselines and goals by category or segment	Where to set initial goals and baselines	Set baselines and goals either too high or too low May not have the means or system to easily track
Design scorecards	How many scorecard flavors to design	Creating optimal number of scorecards and KPIs so that they can be adequately reviewed and communicated
Align contract metrics with SPM metrics	Which metrics to include in contracts with suppliers	Metrics open to dispute Legal resources required Resources to review and enforce

decide that you wish to review software and services from outside software suppliers, depending upon the needs that have been identified and the scope of the project. If you decide to look at software, you will need to specify requirements for your process and system that the software companies can respond to. To do so means understanding your business requirements as much as possible before bringing in software suppliers. The software selection process is another piece of the overall SPM process that will need to be carefully managed. This is also the point where you can develop more detailed budget estimates to submit for management approval. Table 3.8 summarizes tasks, decisions, and challenges of developing data collection instruments.

7. Plan Transition from Metrics to Action

Since the purpose of measuring supplier performance is to uncover and reduce hidden cost drivers and risks, develop supplier relationships, and find quality and performance opportunities to pursue, companies must plan how they are going to turn the data and information they collect into action and results. Metrics to action planning requires communications with suppliers to share results and to plan improvements, corrective actions, and/or supplier development projects. A plan should be put in place detailing in what manner and how

Table 3.8 Develop Data Collection Instruments

Tasks	Key Decisions	Challenges
Develop standard surveys	RFI, buyer survey, or instant supplier feedback	Stakeholder responsiveness to survey Expertise to develop good surveys
Develop assessment models, as appropriate	Is supplier assessment applicable?	In-house expertise for developing robust models
Develop data feeds from internal/external systems, as required	Are data feeds available and necessary? Are outside software and services needed?	Developing requirements System feeds may require IT resources

often to review performance results with suppliers. Determine whether you will have face-to-face meetings with some suppliers, send them their results, let them view results in a portal, or all of these. Also, when setting baselines and goals for categories of suppliers, you should decide on the outcomes of meeting, not meeting, or exceeding the baselines and goals and put a system in place for recognizing and rewarding the high performers and potentially disengaging with poor performers. Whatever actions are planned, performance expectations and the rules for these actions need to be clearly communicated with suppliers. While these activities will be covered in more detail later, the main point about this part of the planning is that you need to set standards, have consequences for performance, and clearly communicate all of this with suppliers and your organization in order to get the full benefit of supplier performance management. Also, you should set a baseline for tracking your suppliers' performance at the start of the process and then monitor the scores over time to look at the efficacy of the program. All of these decisions can be made by the SPM team at the initiation of the program. Then, once the process is implemented, specific people and functions will have the responsibility for supplier improvement and corrective actions on an ongoing basis. When important supplier performance improvement opportunities arise and are implemented, having the discipline to track and quantify the savings from implementing improvements will demonstrate and provide the real payback of SPM. Progress should be continually communicated with management, depending upon the structure you have put in place, via the process owner, executive sponsor, and procurement council. Metrics to action planning is an essential part of a supplier performance management program, without which SPM has a much lower probability of success within a firm. Without action, a firm will never realize the full return on investment of SPM. And without action, sen-

Table 3.9 Metrics to Action Planning

Tasks	Key Decisions	Challenges
Plan frequency, form of supplier communications	Which suppliers and how often for reviews? How often should suppliers get performance information? In person or electronic?	Organizational discipline to institutionalize and maintain communications
Plan recognition, reward, and disengagement actions	How will the SPM info specifically be used (positive and negative)?	Resources, discipline, and follow through to execute successfully
Develop supplier corrective action and improvement strategy and process	Will suppliers be asked to improve based on SPM info?	Less or unknown ROI for SPM if no improvement plans or process Resources to deploy Capturing the ROI

ior management will question the value of SPM and will not afford it the resources it needs to continue. Table 3.9 summarizes the Metrics to Action Planning milestone.

8. Develop the SPM Business Process

The supplier performance management business process should be consciously developed with a clear plan in mind so that roles and responsibilities for operating and maintaining the system are clear. (See Table 3.10 on the tasks, key decisions, and challenges of developing the business process.) The new or revised process along with any new policies and procedures should be documented and communicated with all people in the organization who are involved in it or impacted by it. Suppliers need to understand the process, too, as they will need to understand new or changed performance expectations, any new rules, and the impact of the process on them. Including selected suppliers in the development of the process will help make it work better and help with supplier buy-in. A new SPM process is a big change both for internal and external stakeholders, and it needs to be viewed as requiring change management. As in any change process, it is not an overnight phenomenon, and there will be pockets of resistance. The process, policies, and procedures around SPM must be integrated into daily work and not be implemented as a bolt-on process that is regarded as "just extra work" and will therefore never be fully addressed.

Table 3.10 Develop SPM Business Process

Tasks	Key Decisions	Challenges
Develop roles, responsibilities	Determine additional responsibilities for SPM	Skills to handle supplier relationship management
Create and document SPM workflow	Best way to deploy SPM process	Resources to develop
Internal/external process communications	Internal—Who needs to know External—Impact on suppliers Effective communication methods	Willingness of stakeholders to adopt and support new process

9. Conduct SPM Pilot

Like the majority of key new initiatives, SPM needs to be rolled out in waves, not implemented according to the "Big Bang" theory. Because multiple functions and stakeholders are involved, it is important to have small successes to start—or at least small failures that you can recoup from—rather than a failed project. SPM is an ongoing and iterative process. It is not necessary or even desirable to have all surveys, all metrics, and all suppliers in place from the first day of implementation. The pilot is a microcosm of the whole project and can be planned at the same time. Table 3.11 shows pilot tasks.

The pilot is the time to test the whole SPM process—data-gathering techniques, use of new KPIs and scorecards, and communications with suppliers who are being measured. It is the time to work the kinks out of the overall process both internally and externally. It may also include testing the use of new outside software or internal software functions that have never been used. The pilot process should have a defined beginning and end. The project team should monitor the process and review the results to see what may need to change or be improved. The scope of the pilot can be as small as rolling out just one scorecard or one survey with five suppliers.

You should create a pilot plan, which includes tasks such as developing pilot goals and critical success factors, choosing pilot suppliers, evaluation strategies, creating the data-gathering tools for the pilot, internal and external communications, training, review of results, with input of stakeholders, and modifications as necessary.

Choosing pilot suppliers is important. You want to choose a sufficient but manageable number in order to test the tools and the process. Here are some considerations in choosing pilot suppliers for SPM. You may wish to choose

- High-performing suppliers who are cooperative and willing to give good input and with whom the relationship is healthy.

Table 3.11 Conduct SPM Pilot

Tasks	Key Decisions	Challenges
Pilot goals	Part of the organization and supply base to include Define success	Proof of concept without too much risk
Timeline	How long to collect pilot data	Data collection takes longer or is more difficult than anticipated
Select suppliers	Cross section, problems, good performers	Supplier cooperation
Review and customize surveys, as necessary	Use most generic data gathering approach or customize to pilot suppliers	Data gathering either too generic or too specific for reuse after pilot
Communications (internal/external)	How best to reach internal/external stakeholders	Lack of support or participation
Train pilot participants	Whom to train	Use of the training immediately after pilot to retain knowledge for implementation
Run pilots and review and monitor results	Pilot goals and critical success factors	Data obtained during pilot not useful or insufficient to make decisions Test of business process viability
Modify as required	Whether modifications are necessary and their impact on full rollout	Prioritization

- Suppliers representing key, strategic, or important categories of spend where the stakes are higher so that you can test the system before full rollout.
- Suppliers with whom you have a high spend relative to others, as these suppliers will probably emerge from your segmentation exercises as ones that you will want to measure regularly.
- Suppliers representing the different types and sources of performance data that will be needed as a result of the evaluation strategies and the data collection methods you have developed. Measuring these suppliers in the pilot will test the methods for and viability of collecting these types of data, give you a chance to correct problems, and will mean less work later on during a fuller rollout.
- Problem suppliers where more performance insight is needed or with whom your company has had problems. Including the squeaky wheel,

difficult suppliers, or less than optimally performing suppliers helps test the system and prepare your people for dealing with difficult situations. Also, it gives you a chance to identify and address improvement opportunities with suppliers at the very beginning of the program and potentially demonstrate immediate ROI. However, don't base an entire pilot on squeaky-wheel suppliers.

- New suppliers who want to solidify their relationship with your company. These are the suppliers who are eager to win more business with your company and want to find ways to please you. These suppliers can be the most open to new ways of doing things, as they have had less history with your company than other suppliers and may be more open and flexible. They can be the source of excellent and honest feedback, both good and bad, on the new process.

Pilot suppliers should be able to participate without risk to their business. It is best to not let the first go-round of data collection count against suppliers. Until you work out the kinks, the information may not be totally valid. Plus, you will make pilot suppliers needlessly nervous about participation. In the case of an assessment that is used for certification or becoming approved, a good approach is to let the score count if the results are clearly positive and not count if they are negative. Then let the suppliers who did not score well in the pilot have another chance at improving their metrics. Or offer them assistance, such as supplier development resources, to help them improve. Actually seeing the results of an evaluation can be alarming or upsetting to some suppliers. Supplier evaluations can create fear and uncertainty. Smaller companies in particular may have a lot of pride about their company, feel very disappointed or embarrassed about a poor score, and want to do better. This can work to both the customer's and supplier's advantage.

The pilot provides a chance to test the deployment of surveys and development of data collection techniques. Because it feels safer, some companies prefer to test information gathering with less critical segments of their supply base, such as visible but noncritical indirect suppliers (i.e., office supplies). Others try to tackle the most critical suppliers first. If you want to truly test the SPM process, it is good to test important segments of suppliers who represent the key suppliers who be measured in the future. It is better to uncover problems, deal with risks, and solidify the SPM process in a pilot phase than to discover them later on during a fuller rollout. It will make later implementation waves easier to deploy.

The pilot offers an opportunity to train a cadre of people who become process champions and power users. Potential areas of training may include the new process and using new reporting or even new software, conducting a site visit, giving performance feedback to suppliers, and how to do supplier development.

After a designated period of time of pilot deployment, you should review the pilot against the original goals and critical success factors to see where changes and improvements need to be made. Feedback needs to come from all categories of stakeholders who are involved, including suppliers. Using a pilot feedback questionnaire can be useful. And listen seriously to the feedback, using it to improve the process. Some suggestions may not be readily used or impractical, but to improve the process that you never considered, it is certain that you will get some excellent suggestions.

This next story is about the use of pilot feedback to strengthen and improve a new supplier evaluation process. Boeing had been dealing with sub-tier issues for a while, as this area has become of increasing concern to the aerospace industry (as well as the government), as it has high quality and safety standards. Before creating the sub-tier assessment, Boeing had gone through a process to gain consensus on what needed to be measured, first within their Supplier Quality organization and also within their Supplier Management organization. To avoid creating two separate sub-tier assessments, supplier manager Charles Ballard brought representatives of the two groups to develop an overall consensus on what to measure. This business model was turned into an assessment that could be deployed down the supply chain and the results rolled up by supply chain or by tier.

So, in a sub-tier supplier assessment pilot done with a group of Boeing suppliers, the pilot suppliers were each asked for their feedback on the process. The assessment, which was done using Emptoris Supplier Assessment software, was done conference room pilot-style. The Boeing pilot project team, who, along with purchasing agents and supplier managers, had previously been trained in the software and the sub-tier assessment process, visited several of their pilot suppliers. At each site, the customer company (Boeing first-tier supplier) plus several of their suppliers (Boeing second-tier suppliers) were gathered either in the same room or remotely conferenced. Boeing presented an introduction to the process and covered what, how, and why they were going to be assessed. They were shown how the software worked. Most of the training covered how it worked and what it was going to be used for, as the actual software was very intuitive for suppliers to use. All participants completed their assessments at the same time. Reports were generated, and the results discussed. Then, both first- and second-tier suppliers gave their feedback during the discussion. Additional feedback was solicited with a questionnaire sent by e-mail to participants. Participants gave Boeing valuable feedback. Deploying this pilot process helped Boeing address problem areas in advance of a rollout. In addition, the pilot helped build buy-in from suppliers, who liked the quick feedback and view of their supply chain's performance that they could get from the software.

Table 3.12 Fully Deploy SPM

Tasks	Key Decisions	Challenges
Select suppliers and categories for phased rollout	Select suppliers Determine which supplier managers should be involved	
Additional internal/external communications as required	Determine how and to whom to communicate effectively	Suppliers may not understand implications of SPM on their status
Adoption planning	Determine additional training needs Ensure stakeholders are supporting program	Resistance to change, largely internally
Deployment across supply base	Set goals for monitoring performance of additional suppliers Decide whether adjustments to process needed	Staying focused on metrics to action process Integrating SPM into daily work

10. Fully Deploy SPM

The last step is full deployment of the SPM process. At this point, the process should have been defined and refined through the pilot. Communication is again critical in this phase, both internally and externally. Suppliers need to understand the implications of the evaluation process on their status and the methods their customer plans to use to give and receive feedback. Internal stakeholders need to understand their roles, responsibilities, and any impact that the new process will have on them. Therefore, adoption planning, tracking, and follow-up are important. What is the use of a good SPM program if few people are using it or even know about it? Inertia and resistance to change rule in many companies and initiatives requiring organizational change can be prone to failure. For example, if you are planning to solicit internal stakeholder feedback on suppliers, these people need to understand clearly how this process is going to work and what is expected of them and why. They may need training as well. It is important to gain support among the stakeholders for the new process and give them an understanding of what's in it for them and why their participation is important for the company. Table 3.12 shows tasks, key decisions, and challenges of full SPM deployment.

Continued communication with the process owner, executive sponsor, and procurement council or steering committee (depending upon the project structure) maintains support through and beyond implementation. Both tracking and communication of progress and results, such as before and after supplier metrics demonstrating ROI—actual improvements, cost savings, risk avoidance, and value added to the company—help validate and sustain the SPM process. Full adoption of the SPM process within the firm can be a big organizational challenge. The process owner will need to support and drive adoption.

In summary, the key critical success factors in implementing a successful SPM process include the following:

- Management buy-in and support
- Alignment with company and organizational goals and objectives
- A defined and good process in place
- Adoption and integrating SPM into daily work
- Communication with suppliers and within the customer organization
- Staying focused on the metrics to action process
- Measurable results

This book has free material available for download from the
Web Added Value™ resource center at *www.jrosspub.com*

4

DEVELOPING AN EVALUATION STRATEGY

SEGMENTING THE SUPPLY BASE

To develop an evaluation strategy, you need to decide which suppliers you wish to measure. Also, of those suppliers you decide to measure, you need to determine what level of evaluation suppliers require, ranging from high-level monitoring to detailed evaluation. Therefore, you will need to segment the supply base. Segmentation means categorizing suppliers for the purposes of allocating the appropriate resources to manage and monitor them. It is an analysis and prioritization process. Some of the segmentation dimensions can include such areas as: risk, cost, quality, delivery, service, technology, product development, responsiveness, and communications. Four-box matrices abound in the literature on supplier segmentation. Unfortunately, there is no one matrix that will apply to every organization or even to one company. The complexities of segmentation are such that one would need multidimensional matrices to address all the issues and risk factors. Some matrices are easy to understand but impractical to implement. Most should be viewed as suggested guidelines and ways to look at the supply base. Supplier segmentation matrices were developed largely for activities such as sourcing negotiations and supply base rationalization or "right sizing." The underlying factor in typical segmentation exercises is switching cost: How dependent are you on a particular supplier or class of suppliers, and how high is the cost or how difficult is it to switch to another supplier? This is the simplest way to view supplier segmentation. However, other considerations such as competition, market factors, suppliers' performance potential, the sophistication of the company's information technology for information-gathering and performance analysis of suppliers, and other less obvious considerations can add to the challenge of segmentation.

Segmentation matrices are applicable to supplier evaluation activities, but you must keep in mind the scope of supplier performance evaluation activities. Unless you have sophisticated tools for gathering and analyzing performance data or plan to buy or develop them, you may be limited in the numbers of suppliers whose performance you can actually track by virtue of your internal resources, both human and information technology. So segmentation exercises do not need to be focused on characterizing your entire supply base, other than to exclude the majority from supplier performance measurement activities—unless you have already done substantial rationalization. It depends on orders of magnitude. A supply base of 300 suppliers will be easier to work with than one with 30,000 suppliers. If you have spend analysis tools, they can be very useful for making the first cut. But not all information needs to come from information systems. Familiarity with the characteristics or attributes of key suppliers gained from working with them will also help in making segmentation decisions.

In relation to performance management activities, segmentation will help uncover the types of information about different categories of suppliers that will be important in understanding and evaluating their performance. A common or typical approach is to examine your supply base by spend and risk. Spend helps narrow down suppliers to the potentially most critical suppliers to your business and on whom you are willing to spend your time and resources. Risk is the degree of exposure the company has to supplier performance failures such as late deliveries, quality defects, warranty problems, service failures, and so on. While some risks are common to many companies, each company will have its own specific types of risks from suppliers. Examples of circumstances that can create risk factors include custom-engineered products, sole-source suppliers, custom tooling, special processing, geo-political instability, and financial instability. Risk can also be defined as "the level of opportunity for adverse effects on value (e.g., deterioration in delivery, lead time, price, or quality)."[1] In regard to risk, if you identify important supplier risk factors that can adversely impact your business, then you can use performance evaluations to uncover those risk factors in individual suppliers so that preventive actions can be taken in advance of problems.

Using a Pareto analysis, look at how many suppliers fall in the top 20 percent of your company's spend. Another way to review the data is to look at the supply base by major category (or commodity), and then review the top 10 to 20 percent

---

1. Bullington, Kimball, Ph.D., *Supply Base Segmentation*, Middle Tennesee State University, Smart Ideas, ISM Nashville.

of suppliers by spend in each category. After identifying the suppliers, preferably organized by category, with which you spend the most money, prioritize the categories by importance. For example, some businesses have direct and indirect suppliers. Direct suppliers' performance typically has a higher impact on the business than indirect, though there are exceptions. In the indirect categories, some companies will see significant spend in office supplies. While office supplies have high visibility within a company since everyone uses them and office products suppliers have become sophisticated in the data they can provide on their own performance, office supplies is not a category with high risk to the business. Thus, the office supplies category may not be a high priority for performance measurement.

In this exercise, you want to identify all suppliers who would be considered strategic or critical to the business. Strategic means that the supplier provides a product or service that adds value to the business and, if the supplier fails, has an impact on the business's customers, operations, and infrastructure. A strategic supplier can add value to its customer's long-term goals. In the distribution business, this could be fleet equipment, such as trucks that have been customized and designed to order for the customer. In semiconductor manufacturing, strategic suppliers might be those who contribute to the technologies of wafer fabrication. In banking, software and hardware suppliers can be strategic. Also, critical suppliers need to be identified. A critical supplier provides a product or service to the business such that if poorly provided or missing, either the business could not operate or customers would be unhappy. For example, for an Internet service company or a software company, a supplier providing customer support would be a critical supplier. Suppliers can be both critical and strategic, as these are not mutually exclusive categories.

Next, we will take a look at a few ways to segment the supply base. The classic supplier segmentation model is Kraljic's portfolio model, which can be found in many textbooks and discussions about supplier segmentation (see Figure 4.1).[2]

Strategic suppliers, as discussed earlier, are important for their high value and impact to their customer's business and its long-term goals. A strategic supplier's value can be in, for example, providing industry expertise, exceeding contractual expectations, and proactively managing costs for their customers. Strategic suppliers are prime candidates for performance evaluation. The term "leverage suppliers," sometimes referred to as collaborative suppliers, implies leveraging volume of purchases with these suppliers, who can potentially have a financial impact on the business through focus on total cost of ownership and good profit margins. Bottleneck suppliers, also called custom suppliers in some segmentation schemes, are not strategic, but supply goods and services on which the dependence of the

---

2. Kraljic, P., "Purchasing Must Become Supply Management," *Harvard Business Review*, 1983, 61 (5), p. 111.

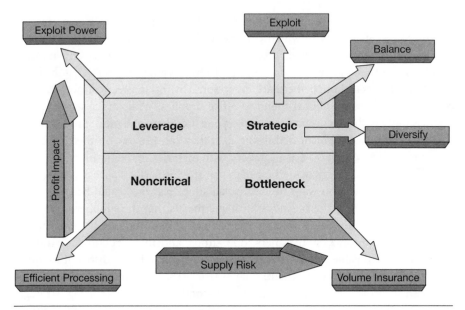

Figure 4.1 Classic supplier segmentation model.

customer is high. Thus, they can create a supply bottleneck if they have problems or fail. These suppliers present potential risk of interruption of supply, which is a consideration for performance monitoring. The lower left quadrant with noncritical suppliers, sometimes called commodity suppliers, is self-explanatory. These suppliers are the easiest to replace, and their products and services are not critical or high risk to the business. This quadrant requires the least attention, other than a focus on operational efficiency in dealing with them. They are the least likely to need much performance management consideration.

The difficulty with segmentation matrices, and the Kraljic one in particular, is that the terms are imprecise, making suppliers hard to categorize. For example, risk and profit impact are important, but there are no guidelines to help quantify these factors. The time one might spend doing this or arguing with colleagues to define and quantify these concepts may not be worthwhile. This is particularly true when segmenting for the purposes of performance measurement and monitoring. Segmentation matrices are useful largely to initiate a thought process and discussion within an organization to identify the important suppliers who should be paid attention to, worked with, and monitored more closely, rather than as a scientific undertaking.

In terms of supplier management and development, the following segmentation matrices offer other ways to categorize suppliers to identify the key or strategic ones. Since it is impossible to show multiple dimensions in one matrix, here

Table 4.1 Supplier Commitment Matrix

	Low Commitment	High Commitment
Low Actual Commitment	Maintain	Plan for improvement
High Actual Commitment	Caution	Maintain

Table 4.2 Supplier Characterization Matrix for Product Development

	Low Spend	High Spend
High Design Input	Target for redesign for standard item	Savings through design input
Low Design Input	Caution	Maintain

Table 4.3 Supplier Characterization Matrix—Spend

	Low Commitment	High Commitment
High Risk	Special attention	Partnership
Low Risk	Transaction	Contract

are matrices that segment suppliers according to categories important to supply management. For example, the matrix in Table 4.1 looks at suppliers' level of commitment to the customer organization. This looks at which suppliers are committed to the customer firm and which are not, but in view of their value, the customer may need to try to increase its suppliers' commitment level. Certain strategic and critical suppliers should be committed to their relationship with the customer firm. Commitment to the relationship, open communications and trust are factors that can help reduce risk. Table 4.2 looks at characterizing suppliers through the lens of product development. This matrix looks exclusively at how suppliers can contribute based solely upon whether or not their product has the potential for redesign. Working with suppliers collaboratively to design new products and services adds enormous value to the customer-supplier relationship. This is just one of many dimensions to consider. Other segmentation matrices can be built around quality, cost, delivery, and communications.

The matrix in Table 4.3 characterizes the attention paid to suppliers in terms of spend and risk.[3] If the risk is high and the spend is low, the customer firm still needs to pay attention to that category of suppliers. With high spend, the need for a stronger relationship or partnership is clear. High-spend, low-risk suppliers require

---

3. Bullington, Kimball, Ph.D., *Supply Base Segmentation II,* Middle Tennessee State University, Smart Ideas, ISM Nashville.

Table 4.4 Supplier Management Actions Matrix

	Collaborative	Strategic
	Focus on lower TCO and promote cost reduction Encourage collaboration Obtain customized, value-added services Aggregate volume with fewer suppliers Sustain competition *Moderate to detailed performance evaluation*	Partner with supplier Focus on availability, quality, reliability Promote customer/supplier collaboration and infosharing Implement improvements and cost savings Best value Need understanding of supplier's industry *Detailed performance evaluation*
	Commodity	**Custom**
	Get the best/lowest price Create competition (auctions) Focus on operational efficiency Volume consolidation Better terms and conditions Less experienced personnel can manage *Least customer oversight*	Basic services Ensure availability Product or service drives value, *not* cost Focus on relationship development Reliability/predictability Need experienced personnel to manage *Monitor service, reliability closely*

Vertical axis (left): Strategic Importance/Investment in Relationship — Focus on Total Cost of Ownership — Low

Horizontal axis: Low ← → High — Dependence on Supplier/Criticality/Difficulty of Switching

less focus on relationship and more on contract terms, as they are not worth spending a lot of resources on and should be dealt with in terms of efficiency.

For the purposes of performance management, a company needs to address how much time and resources to invest in developing and managing a supplier relationship as well as the level of procurement expertise. Instead of single-dimension matrices, Table 4.4 is a supplier management matrix encompassing multiple dimensions on one chart: strategic importance, investment in the relationship, focus on total cost of ownership (TCO) versus dependence on the supplier, criticality of the supplier, and the difficulty of switching. Suggested actions are organized by type of supplier. In this scheme, custom and strategic suppliers have the highest risk to the business and both need monitoring. However, the performance of custom suppliers needs to be monitored because they are critical to the business. They do not typically represent a cost reduction opportunity. Therefore, less detailed types of performance monitoring and measurement are needed. Investment in the relationship and therefore more detailed evaluation are most important for collaborative and strategic suppliers. This matrix also addresses the level of experience needed by supply management personnel: more detailed industry expertise for managing strategic suppliers, less overall experience to manage commodity suppliers. Since a glitch at a custom supplier can bring one's

Table 4.5 Segmentation for Supplier Performance Management Actions

	Collaborative	Strategic
Focus on Total Cost of Ownership (high)	Important to measure Operational performance measures Financial measures Encourage continuous improvement Relationship quality *Medium to highly detailed performance evaluation*	Highest priority to measure Strategic value Relationship quality Contribution to the business Emphasis on continuous improvement *Detailed performance evaluation*
	Commodity	**Custom**
	Lowest priority to measure Focus on operational performance basics Measure internal stakeholder satisfaction *Least customer oversight*	Operational performance measures Service levels Relationship quality Reliability/predictability—avoid surprises *Monitor service, reliability closely*

Vertical axis: Strategic Importance/Investment in Relationship / Focus on Total Cost of Ownership (Low)

Horizontal axis: Low ◄──────► High — Dependence on Supplier/Criticality/Difficulty of Switching

business to a halt, more experienced personnel are needed to manage the performance of these suppliers.

The matrix in Table 4.5 provides general guidelines for what the focus of supplier performance management and measurement should be for the collaborative, strategic, commodity, and custom supplier segments. Since the emphasis with strategic suppliers is on strategic value, the value of the relationship, and contribution to the business, strategic suppliers require more detailed performance evaluation with emphasis on continuous improvement. Continuous improvement is also important for collaborative suppliers. With their financial and operational impact on the business, financial and operational performance measures are important. With custom suppliers, you want continuity of supply and no surprises, so service levels and operational performance measures are useful for this segment of suppliers. Commodity suppliers have the lowest impact on the business but can sometimes have an impact on internal customer satisfaction. If measured, the focus is usually on operational performance basics.

The more strategic and partner-like the relationship between customer and supplier, the more supplier performance depends on noncontractible areas such as innovation, quality improvement, and mutual trust. Supplier relationship management capabilities, such as the ability to share information easily between customers and suppliers to support collaboration, are critical to enabling optimal supplier performance.

In practical terms, a supplier segmentation exercise might be approached by the supplier performance management (SPM) team in the following series of steps:

1. Identify the most important strategies of your company's business to decide on the types of supplier relationships most important to your company.[4]
2. Review your supplier performance expectations at a high level.
3. Look at high-priority or strategically important categories of suppliers. Strategic suppliers would be the highest priority, then collaborative and bottleneck suppliers.
4. Identify the top spend suppliers in those categories. Also, try to identify low-spend strategic or critical suppliers.
5. Identify suppliers with the capability or the potential capability to meet your company's supplier performance expectations and those who are not meeting expectations or who pose a potential risk of failing to meet expectations. If a performance measurement system has not yet been put in place, it may be difficult to identify all suppliers who are not meeting expectations. However, the procurement staff will probably be able to identify the most problematic, potentially problematic, and high-risk suppliers.

Figure 4.2 illustrates some of the considerations in segmenting suppliers for performance management and shows a thought process for taking a first cut at identifying suppliers for performance management initiatives. Following are questions to consider:

- Does the company have a high dependence on this supplier?
- What would be the difficulties with and costs of switching?
- How *strategic* is the product or service to the operation of the business?
- Does the supplier provide value-added services or customizations?
- Is the product or service *critical* to the business?
- Is the supplier sole-source—that is, the only supplier who can provide the product or service?
- Is the supplier single-source—that is, the only supplier used in the category, but others are available?

---

4. Kauffman, Ralph G. and Thomas A. Crimi, "Procurement to Strategic Sourcing: How to Make the Transition," ISM 85th Annual International Conference Proceedings, 2000.

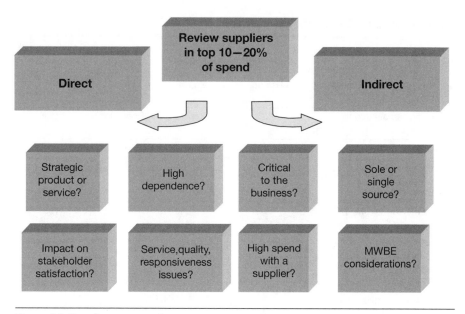

Figure 4.2 Supplier segmentation parameters for performance management.

- Does the product, service, or particular supplier have an important impact on the satisfaction of any important stakeholders, such as customers, employees, shareholders, the community, or other suppliers?
- Are there any MWBE (minority- and women-owned business enterprise) considerations that make switching from a supplier undesirable? Or, does the customer have a particular focus on supplier development for MWBE suppliers?

These questions will help identify the suppliers who are potential measurement candidates. The objective is to make sure that you have identified suppliers who may

- Offer opportunities for adding more value by improved performance.
- Help your company be more competitive in cost, quality, technology, and responsiveness to your customers.
- Create risks that need to be monitored and avoided.

According to a survey from Vantage Partners, customers reported an average of 40 percent more value derived from their most collaborative key suppliers compared to their least collaborative key suppliers.

There are numerous other factors to consider. Table 4.6 shows additional segmentation questions that can be applied to the basic segmentation matrix. These questions can help you think about categories and individual suppliers whose performance may need to be evaluated and provoke discussion within your

Table 4.6 Supplier Segmentation Questions

Segmentation Question	Noncritical	Custom/ Bottleneck	Strategic	Collaborative/ Leverage
Is there an impact on the service provided to customers?	Less so	Yes	Yes	Yes
Is it an item or service that reflects on the company's image?	Yes	Yes	Possible	
Does the product or service impact employee morale?		Yes	Yes	
Is it relatively easier to switch to another supplier?	Yes	No	No	Possible
Does switching involve primarily buyer training?	Yes			Yes
If the company switches to another supplier, will there be an inventory impact?	No	Maybe	Maybe	Maybe
Does switching involve product or service customizations?	No	Yes	Yes	Yes
Are these customizations costly?		No	Yes	No
Are there any other considerations that make switching difficult?		Possibly	Yes	Possibly
Does this supplier provide relatively unique value-added features or services?		Possibly	Yes	Yes
Does this supplier have any impact on external customer satisfaction?	No	Yes	Yes	Yes
Does this supplier have any impact on internal customer satisfaction?	Yes			Possibly
Is predictability of the supplier's ability to provide the product/service critical?		Yes	Yes	Yes
Does the product or service require specific technical expertise to manage?		Maybe	Yes	Maybe
Does this category require supply management sophistication?		Yes	Yes	
Is there relative complexity to the purchase of this product or service?	No	Maybe	Maybe	Maybe
Is the marketplace for the product or service complex?	Maybe	Yes	Maybe	

Table 4.6 Supplier Segmentation Questions (Continued)

Segmentation Question	Noncritical	Custom/ Bottleneck	Strategic	Collaborative/ Leverage
Once this product or service is purchased, does the supplier require oversight?	Little	Some	Yes	Yes
Are there important product and/ or service quality considerations for this item?	No	Yes	Yes	Maybe
Is the supplier integrated into the supply chain? (i.e., contributes to the business in product/service design or value-added services)	No	No	Yes	Maybe
Is the product/service difficult to obtain or scarce?	No	Yes	Maybe	No
Is the choice of suppliers limited?	No	Yes	Maybe	No
Is reliability or predictability of getting the product/service a key consideration?	No	Yes	Yes	Maybe
Is service/product quality critical to the business?	Less so	Yes	Yes	Yes
Is service/product availability critical to the business?	No	Yes	Yes	Yes
Is value more important than price?	No	Yes	Yes	Sometimes
Is price the most important consideration?	Yes	No	No	Important
Is the product/service such that having a good relationship with the supplier would be very important?	No	Fairly important	Yes	Yes
Is the supplier willing to work on continuous improvement opportunities?		Somewhat	Yes	
Are there value-added services that this supplier provides?	Less so	Yes	Yes	Sometimes
Can or does the supplier contribute to product development efforts?	No	No	Yes	No
Has the supplier made significant investments in order to do business with the customer?			Yes	Sometimes

Table 4.7 Evaluation Strategies by Supplier Segments and Industries

Company	Segment	Strategy
Company A (Electronics)	High-value suppliers, based upon spend or performance attributes: Key Approved Restricted	Supplier performance management system
Company B (Banking)	Low-value suppliers Commodity	Procurement cards, ordering process efficiencies
	High-value suppliers Relationship suppliers Strategic suppliers	Supplier development
Company C (Airline)	Segments divided at commodity level: IT, travel, office supplies, employment services	Electronic scorecards
Company D (Insurance)	All segments, grouped by type of relationship: New relationship Established healthy relationship Existing troubled relationship Nontraditional relationship	Two-way assessment

Source: Adapted from "Supplier Relationship and Segmentation Models," Corporate Executive Board, Procurement Strategy Council, December 2002.

organization and the SPM project team. The supplier segmentation exercise helps identify what supplier characteristics, both positive and negative, are important to your company, which suppliers fall into categories or segments according to these characteristics, the strategic value of the relationship, and where to focus supplier evaluation, performance management, and supplier development resources.

Table 4.7 shows an example of potential specific evaluation strategies by segment. These are based upon actual companies in a study done by the Procurement Strategy Council.[5] Note that the financial institution (a bank) focused on ordering process efficiencies for its low-value suppliers and was willing to apply supplier development resources to work with its high-value suppliers. The electronics company focused its efforts largely on its high-value suppliers. This study is interesting for its inclusion of services companies and their SPM strategies, which are seen less often in the literature.

---

5. Adapted from "Supplier Relationship and Segmentation Models," Corporate Executive Board, Procurement Strategy Council, December 2002.

CREATING A SUPPLIER MEASUREMENT STRATEGY

Risk avoidance and the desire for performance improvement are two common reasons for supplier measurement. Poor performance, of course, creates risk. The next step is to look at the segmentation results and create a strategy for performance measurement consistent with the kinds of information you want to uncover. Many companies' first question to me about supplier metrics is this: What metrics do other companies use? We have already discussed the need for alignment of an evaluation strategy with the overall strategy and goals of the organization. The first question should be this: How is the company planning to use the information? That will help determine the types of information on supplier performance to be collected.

Companies collect supplier performance information for many purposes. These purposes fall under three major areas: supplier qualification, supplier classification (for supplier management purposes), and supplier performance improvement. Collecting this performance information may be used to

- Set criteria for new supplier on-boarding.
- Create an approved supplier list.
- Rationalize or right-size current supply base.
- Classify current suppliers to create a preferred supplier program.
- Create a supplier certification program.
- Disengage with low performers.
- Give more business to high performers.
- Identify supplier continuous improvement opportunities.
- Identify supplier development opportunities.
- Bring an internal performance improvement system such as a lean enterprise program or Six Sigma to the supply base.

SUPPLIER QUALIFICATION

In a new supplier qualification process, information is typically gathered directly from a supplier. Depending on the qualification process, information can be gathered via an RFI in an electronic sourcing system, through questionnaires or templates in Word documents or Excel spreadsheets sent electronically (such as by e-mail), and through site visits or on-site audits. The level of detail of the information gathered depends upon how critical or strategic the prospective supplier is to the business. To ensure a robust qualification process, a company needs to go beyond price and evaluate other capabilities and anticipated predictors of good performance and alignment with the customer. Information is gathered typically on capabilities, quality systems, sales, customer references, and financial status. One should get a good understanding of the supplier's product or service quality, responsiveness to customers, as in good customer service, and how well they deliver their product or service, such as meeting delivery or due dates. In the case of a manufacturer, how good is their engineering and technical support? In some cases, a site visit or facility audit of the supplier should be conducted.

A good qualification process should be consistent, efficient and cost-effective, and transparent to internal stakeholders and suppliers. Also, participation from other functions in the qualification process in order for them to apply their specific functional expertise improves the supplier selection process, makes it more robust, and facilitates buy-in among stakeholders. Sometimes tensions between procurement and other functions or business units have a negative impact on supplier selection. Procurement is seen as bureaucratic and focused too much on price. Procurement may see other functions or business units as unconcerned about cost considerations and unaware of alternative sources.[6] Procurement may see the product development function, for example, adding new suppliers without proper qualification and needlessly mushrooming the supplier database of nonapproved suppliers. On the other hand, product development may see procurement as the gatekeepers who do not qualify suppliers for their needs rapidly enough and who lack the expertise to do so. The result may be avoidance between procurement and other functions, where procurement minimizes its involvement and the other functions fail to reach out to procurement. Besides a communications stalemate, the result may be an ever-growing database of unknown and unqualified suppliers.

A supplier qualification process can range from a simple questionnaire that gathers basic information from a supplier to a more detailed process that puts the more critical or strategic suppliers through a more rigorous evaluation. The process of determining what to measure will be covered in the following chapter. For now, I will describe an overall qualification process. Figure 4.3 illustrates the flow of a supplier qualification and approval process, adapted from a telecommunications company's model. In this model, a supplier goes through a self-registration process in a sourcing/supply management system. If there is a need for the supplier, then the supplier is asked to complete a brief self-assessment or evaluation of its capabilities, which includes a risk assessment, the details of which depend on the industry and type of supplier. For example, in a business with global suppliers, risks can relate to corporate social responsibility (CSR) issues, and a customer may need to make sure that the supplier is not using child labor

---

6. Hughes, Jonathan, "Why Your Supplier Relationships Fail to Deliver Their True Value," *Harvard Business Review Supply Chain Strategy*, 2005.

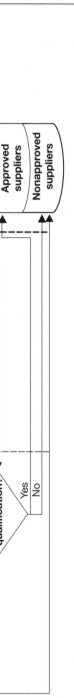

Figure 4.3 Supplier qualification and approval process.

or providing unacceptable working conditions, for example. Quality, financial, and other risks need to be evaluated, depending on the industry.

If the supplier proves adequate in the self-assessment, it can then participate in a more detailed RFI questionnaire or self-assessment and potentially a site visit or detailed audit by the customer for the most critical, strategic suppliers before being approved. Most suppliers do not require either a limited or full site visit. The level of detail of this process depends on the size of the enterprise, available resources, and nature of the supply base. The end result of the qualification process is certain suppliers, whose information is captured at the very beginning of the process and who have met the criteria for their business segment, going from the unapproved to the approved list.

The information gathering during the qualification process can serve as a baseline for future supplier performance evaluation and management activities. Following are some common issues around supplier qualification and creating approved supplier lists:

- The qualification process is haphazard and not consistently followed.
- The qualification process creates an approved supplier list that is inconsistent and not qualified to consistent, robust standards that are aligned with business requirements.
- Departments and company units outside of procurement add or engage suppliers without procurement's knowledge and without a robust qualification process.
- Suppliers are allowed to circumvent the process, even with procurement's knowledge, for expediency.
- Purchasers, including procurement, do not use suppliers from the approved supplier list.
- Purchasers outside of procurement do not know the approved supplier list exists.
- Once suppliers have been qualified and approved, their performance is never reviewed or they are never site-visited again.

The typical result of these situations is that the approved supplier list continues to grow with increasingly unqualified suppliers and thus loses its credibility and usefulness as a qualification tool. Without a good supplier qualification process in place and an approved supplier list recognized, maintained, and consistently used, managing the performance of unapproved but active suppliers becomes more challenging. It enables, even encourages, rogue or maverick spend and the supplier management problems that go with it.

Supplier qualification requires a good business process, good and easy-to-use supplier qualification tools, and organizational communications competencies, cross-functional and cross-business-unit working relationships, and the discipline to clearly define then stick to the process. Also, qualification is only the first step in supplier performance management. Understanding capabilities and performance factors is an ongoing process. Suppliers cannot be reviewed and then their capabilities buried in a time capsule forever, as much can change. If their qualifications are not revisited, the supply base will grow with suppliers whose capabilities and performance have degraded and should no longer be on the approved list. This creates potential risk to the business and ruins the credibility of the approved supplier list. Also, a good qualification process is the entry point for new suppliers. Setting the bar at the appropriate level and maintaining standards is a good way to prevent the supply base from growing with unqualified and risky suppliers or multiple, unproven sources. A weak qualification process allows supplier proliferation and complexity that requires more resources to manage. A good qualification process can also reduce the need for massive rationalization initiatives. However, should a supplier rationalization process be required, a good supplier qualification and evaluation process will make it easier.

EVALUATING CURRENT SUPPLIERS

Qualification gives suppliers the opportunity to perform for and add value to your enterprise. After a supplier is approved, it must continually earn the right to do business with you. We have discussed how to figure out *whom* to measure. Next, we will cover a methodology for figuring out *what* to measure. The depth of the evaluation process depends where the supplier falls in the segmentation exercise. Suppliers who are in the upper right quadrant, the strategic quadrant, require the most thorough evaluation and deserve the most resources to develop the relationship and improve performance. Those who fall in the custom and collaborative quadrants may require less detailed evaluation or simply basic performance monitoring. The commodity quadrant can be left unmeasured or lightly measured, if metrics are readily accessible.

Sources of performance information can include internal business systems, internal stakeholder input, supplier input, supplier site visits or audits, and third-party information sources (such as Dun & Bradstreet, third-party evaluations, and ISO 9001 and other outside party certifications).

Table 4.8 summarizes examples of the sources and types of information that can be gathered from those sources as well as data or information collection mechanisms and techniques.

Internal systems. These can include enterprise management systems such as SAP or Oracle or modules such as ERP, MRP, quality systems, purchasing systems, accounting systems, and even data collection spreadsheets created by individual users. Some internal systems can generate

Table 4.8 Sources and Types of Supplier Performance Information

Source	Examples of Information	Collection Mechanisms
Internal systems and sources (ERP, financial systems)	On-time delivery Call center data on customer complaints Incoming quality In-process quality	Database Spreadsheets Scorecard programs
Internal stakeholders	Supplier responsiveness Service quality Ease of doing business with supplier	Spreadsheets Surveys Data-gathering mechanisms
Suppliers	Inventory turns Business processes and practices information	Surveys Spreadsheets Self-assessments Supplier portals
Site visits	Business processes and practices Specific performance information	Site visit team Assessment software for virtual site visit
Third parties	Dun & Bradstreet Source inspection and supplier quality inspection services Certifications (such as ISO, CSR)	Third-party databases Third-party service companies Outside certifications
Supplier performance management (SPM) or supplier relationship management (SRM) software solutions	Supplier scorecards Detailed business assessments	Enterprise supply management software solutions and tools Supplier evaluation software

KPIs and scorecards. Some companies, such as Toro, RR Donnelley and John Deere, have developed their own custom solutions for gathering data and metrics on supplier performance and gather information from dozens of systems.

Internal stakeholders. Information from stakeholders can be gathered via internal surveys. These can include internal customer satisfaction surveys as well as data gathering mechanisms for collecting feedback from people within the company who have contact with the supplier or use the supplier's services or products. For example, GlaxoSmithKline collects feedback on suppliers from internal stakeholders via an "always on" mechanism. Anyone within the company can provide performance feedback on suppliers at any time (as opposed to responding to a particular feedback survey).

Suppliers. Suppliers can self-assess and self-report information via a software solution, a supplier portal at the customer Web site, customer surveys, spreadsheets, e-mail, or even direct feeds of information from supplier to customer.

Site visits. Customer site visits provide another means to get information directly from suppliers. Also, software solutions can provide a virtual site visit, gathering information in advance, increasing consistency, and reducing the time and resources required by the customer team on-site.

Third parties. Dun & Bradstreet and InfoUSA are common sources of financial information on suppliers. In addition, customers often rely on third-party certifications such as ISO 9001, ISO 14001, and more recently SA 8000, which is the social accountability standard (i.e., corporate social responsibility). Other third-party services include supplier quality site inspection and source inspection services, which have grown in recent years due to the increase in low-cost-country sourcing and the need to ensure that those sources are reliable and meeting customer quality standards.

SUPPLIER PERFORMANCE MANAGEMENT SOLUTIONS

Specific solutions for measuring and managing supplier relationships and supplier performance and collaborating with suppliers are available. These include tools for developing KPIs and scorecards, internal stakeholder surveys, supplier surveys, and supplier business assessment. These solutions are listed separately from other internal IT systems, since they are a niche that specifically addresses supplier performance and supplier relationship management. In addition to the large enterprise management systems providers such as SAP and Oracle, who have some capabilities such as scorecards built into their offerings, Emptoris, Open Ratings, Verticalnet, Hiperos, and Procuri currently provide specific SPM solutions. Technology will be discussed in more detail later.

The number of potential sources for supplier performance information can be either staggering or grossly insufficient, depending upon the type of business. A manufacturing business has much data already at hand in its business systems, while service industries may have less readily available data at their disposal. Just because there is a lot of available data does not mean that this data is useful, accurate, or actionable, so caution needs to be exercised. Gathering performance information from many sources can add complexity, time, and cost to managing performance and must be approached judiciously. It is easy to lose sight of one's ultimate purpose and turn supplier performance management into a massive and expensive data collection exercise. Selection of data sources depends upon what specifically a company needs to measure and for what purpose. Identifying sources of performance information will be required once a company has formulated its performance expectations and evaluation criteria.

SUPPLY BASE SEGMENTS AND TYPES OF INFORMATION

Table 4.9 gives examples of potential types of information to collect and objectives for collecting it—that is, what you are trying to achieve (i.e., reduce total cost of ownership) or risks you are trying to avoid (i.e., avoid supply disruptions) by obtaining this information. The table is organized by supply base segments of collaborative, strategic, custom and commodity.

SUMMARY

So far, the process of developing a supplier evaluation strategy has consisted of the following:

- Segmenting the supply base for purposes of measuring and managing supplier performance
- Deciding which segments to focus on as potential evaluation targets
- Taking a first cut at which suppliers within those segments should be evaluated and why
- Reviewing potential sources of performance information on suppliers
- Reviewing potential objectives that these types of performance data can help meet

In summary, supplier segmentation is an iterative process for analyzing the supply base and categorizing it for the purposes of managing it to derive value and avoid risk and for measurement of supplier performance and performance potential. We are focused on the performance measurement and improvement purposes of segmentation. Once you have identified the suppliers and segments of suppliers to measure, you are ready to develop an evaluation strategy that takes into account the information you need in order to understand your suppliers' performance and the sources of that information.

Table 4.9 Performance Information by Supply Base Segment

Segment	Sample Types of Information	Objectives
Collaborative	Cost, quality, responsiveness, financial	Avoid financial risk. Avoid/reduce cost. Achieve customer satisfaction.
Strategic	Cost, quality, delivery, responsiveness, business practices and processes, technology capabilities, lean assessments, continuous-improvement results	Avoid supply disruptions. Reduce TCO. Increase responsiveness. Add value to customer. Develop new products/services.
Custom	Service, delivery, responsiveness	Avoid supply disruptions and ensure availability.
Commodity	Stakeholder satisfaction, contract compliance measures, fill rates	Customer/stakeholder satisfaction. Reduce transaction costs.

This book has free material available for download from the
Web Added Value™ resource center at *www.jrosspub.com*

5

DETERMINING WHAT
TO MEASURE

INTRODUCTION

Many companies are unsure about what to measure that will help them track supplier performance. Some look to what other companies are measuring. While benchmarking others is a valid approach to gathering information about best practices, it may not lead to alignment with your company's strategies and objectives. Or the types of information others collect may not be as relevant to your particular industry, culture, or size of your company or to the supplier issues that your company is dealing with. Or the information simply may not be readily available. Some companies see what information at their company is readily available to use for measuring suppliers and choose those measurements.

The AMR Research survey of 100 manufacturing companies referenced in Chapter 1 and Figure 1.1 illustrates the issues that many supplier scorecard metrics raise. Many companies are getting at supplier problems in the least dynamic ways: by using lagging indicators that are not future-oriented and represent the consequences of actions previously taken. Lagging indicators focus on results at the end of a time period and describe historical performance.[1] For example, metrics such as inventory levels and rework can be a symptom of many other problems, but a static quantity measured at a point in time may not be particularly revealing or actionable. Lagging indicators tell nothing about future value, such as

---

1. Source: www.balancedscorecard.biz.

investment in customer relationships and long-term capabilities. The supplier is holding too much inventory—now what? And, many companies use metrics that are reactive rather than proactive, preventive, or predictive in nature. This includes the most commonly used trio of: on-time delivery, quality defects, and cost. While good information to know, lagging indicators are limited in the insights that they afford both customer and supplier firms regarding problems and remedies to take. And, it can be difficult and tricky to get guidance on metrics from what other firms are measuring.

Supplier performance measurement is still an evolving area. Performance metrics must be relevant to a company's own goals, strategies, and performance expectations. Performance measurement is a *comprehensive management system*. It is not a collection of "one-off" metrics, borrowed from others, but part of a business process by which a customer firm objectively and often subjectively evaluates the extent to which its suppliers are supporting them in the accomplishment of a specific set of goals and objectives.

CHARACTERISTICS OF MEASUREMENTS

Good measurements for supplier performance should include these characteristics:

- **Meaningful.** Related significantly and directly to the buying organization's strategies and goals, as they are impacted by supplier performance. They measure things that matter.
- **Valuable.** Measure the most important activities of the supplier in relation to both their customer's requirements and their own business success factors, which can and will impact the customer.
- **Balanced.** Include several types of measures, such as the Kaplan and Norton balanced scorecard categories of financial performance, internal operations, innovation and learning, and customer satisfaction. It should look at internal processes and external outcomes. Supplier measurements should give a picture of supplier performance from more than one category and look not just at past performance but at capabilities for future performance. They should also contain leading indicators, not just lagging ones. There is a good discussion of the categories of Kaplan and Norton's balanced scorecard on the Balanced Scorecard Web site.[2]

---

2. "What Is the Balanced Scorecard?" at http://www.balancedscorecard.org/basics/bsc1.html.

- **Linked.** To the customer firm and the supplier responsible for achieving the measure. In the case of supplier performance measures, the supplier is responsible for achieving the measure, enabled by its relationship with buying organization personnel.
- **Practical.** Affordable and easy to retrieve and/or capture data and do not require extensive data cleansing and manipulation beforehand.
- **Comparable.** Can be used to make comparisons with other data over time.
- **Credible.** To the supplier, as the information is based on accurate and reliable data.
- **Timely.** Data can be used and reported on in a reasonable time frame. It is not outdated by the time the supplier sees it.
- **Simple.** Easy to calculate and understand.[3]
- **Robust.** Based upon best practices and current business thought. Also, not skewed to one type of information, such as all lagging indicators.
- **Reasonable number of metrics.** Being practical about measuring performance factors and not measuring too many things that cannot possibly be managed or dealt with.

TYPES OF MEASUREMENTS

Much has been written in the realm of economics about leading and lagging economic indicators. This terminology has also been applied to performance metrics, which includes supplier performance metrics. Companies are looking for leading indicators, which are those that predict or drive bottom-line performance results. Leading indicators are value attributes. Lagging indicators show the operational results. But more typically, companies tend to track the lagging indicators, which are metrics or trends that occur *after* certain activities have already occurred or actions have already been taken. This is, as Bob Rudzki writes in his book, *Beat the Odds*, in Principle 7: Measure Only What You Want to Achieve, like "looking in the rearview mirror. It's useful information about where you've been, but it's dangerous to steer by it."[4] Metrics that show the picture after the fact are much more readily available in operationally oriented business systems. Lagging indicators and investment advice should both be viewed with the same caution: past performance is no guarantee of future results. Lagging indicators are reactive and not predictive and therefore cannot help managers be proactive. Here are some examples in relation to suppliers:

---

3. Adapted from Balanced Scorecard Workshop by Matt H. Evans.
4. Rudzki, Robert A., *Beat the Odds*, J. Ross, 2007, p. 79.

- **Leading indicators.** Supplier performance problems, customer satisfaction, employee turnover at supplier, number of supply chain alliances implemented
- **Lagging indicators.** Accounts payable cycle, quality metrics, inventory turns, scrap, purchase orders processed per employee, calls per customer service employee

Many companies tend to concentrate on the lagging indicators, since they are the easiest to measure and are traditional and typical for many companies. Many of the most commonly used metrics are mostly lagging indicators. With the ever-increasing need to avoid supplier problems and risks, you need as much as possible to look to the future and measure leading indicators, not just lagging ones.

Another category or type of measurements is objective or quantitative versus subjective or qualitative. Quantitative measures are empirical indicators of performance and are based on what is considered "hard" data. Examples of objective or quantitative metrics are transportation costs, scrap and rework, and on-time delivery. Qualitative metrics are based upon opinion and perceptions. Examples are customer complaints and deployment of business practices (such as preventive rather than reactive quality practices) that customer firms can observe either directly, get from internal stakeholders, or obtain from the supplier through supplier business assessments and site visits. Subjective measurements can be quantified into KPIs, just like objective measurements. On the surface, they can look similar. Objectively and subjectively derived KPIs can sit in the same scorecard, where they can provide information on different aspects of performance. There tends to be a prejudice toward using objective rather than subjective measurements, as the assumption is that they are real data, are somehow more accurate, and indicate real performance. However, even objective or quantitative measures can be inaccurate or misrepresent performance. Remember the old saw about lies, damn lies, and statistics? Quantitative measurements are not always scientifically precise, since deriving them is dependent on so many factors, not the least of which is company discipline to ensure data accuracy and on ways of calculating metrics that are consistent, meaningful, and useful. Subjective measurements can offer insight into root causes of problems that objective measurements cannot. Plus, when it comes to providing insights into customer satisfaction and deployment of best practices, objective measurements may fall short. Ideally, a balanced supplier performance scorecard will contain both.

When it comes to qualitative information in supplier evaluation, the concept that "perception is reality" has a lot of truth to it. People rely on mental shortcuts to simplify and evaluate complex information. Putting aside for the moment whether or not quantitative performance data is accurately derived, the ability of the user to analyze and apply the data affects perceptions about the data. Evaluation of quantitative data still involves many elements of perception, depending upon the sources of the data, the data that are chosen, the way the data are shown, the math skills of the person analyzing and interpreting the data, how much they care about the results, and how important the consequences of the results are perceived to be. Working with suppliers is more than a quantitative experience or exercise. There is a human relationship element to it. And with the human element, there are perceptions. So the perceptions about the supplier's capabilities, interactions with the supplier firm, the supplier's perceptions about its own performance—all color the customer firm's perceptions of reality. Qualitative metrics, such as customer satisfaction ratings, service ratings, or a supplier's perceptions about the deployment of its own business practices, play an important role in giving a holistic understanding of supplier performance. They are a desirable element and should not be considered lesser than quantitative metrics or hard data, which themselves are also less than perfect.

CREATING PERFORMANCE EXPECTATIONS

We have already discussed the process for determining what to measure. It starts with understanding corporate goals and strategies, then developing a procurement strategy. The next step in the process of creating good supplier performance metrics, as shown in Figure 5.1, is developing expectations for supplier performance that are linked to your procurement strategy.

Corporate goals can be flowed down the organization to develop supplier performance expectations. A performance expectation is a specific statement of a business practice, process, or policy and/or the results anticipated or required from a supplier's performance or behavior in relation to the customer. Performance expectations should be

- Measurable
- Appropriate to the supplier being measured
- Communicated
- Actionable
- Attainable

A performance expectation can be stated in a qualitative way. But then it can be translated into quantitative metrics or specific business practices. A performance expectation is looking forward rather than backward—at the practices and processes the supplier should have in place to perform well for its customer (and for its other stakeholders). Essentially, these expectations consist of best practices that the customer would like to see the supplier deploy. Quantitative metrics, on the other hand, are measurements that show the results of these efforts and business practices but are not predictive of future performance. Table 5.1 gives some examples of supplier performance expectations in the areas of sourcing, quality, and lean.

Figure 5.1 Supplier performance expectations development hierarchy.

Table 5.1 Strategy Deployment to the Supplier Performance Expectation Level

Topic	Performance expectations
Sourcing	The supplier has a documented source selection system.
	The supplier has an approved supplier list or database.
	The supplier uses an established process and criteria to approve suppliers.
	The supplier uses only those suppliers who are on the approved supplier list.
	Suppliers are evaluated before being added to the approved supplier list.
Quality	The supplier has a process to prevent defective work from moving to the next work area.
	The supplier deploys a proactive rather than reactive approach to quality.
	The supplier has eliminated the need for incoming inspection.
	The supplier works to improve the quality of service it provides to its customers.
Lean	The leadership team at the supplier supports and enables the lean enterprise.
	The supplier has implemented the visual workplace.
	The supplier works to reduce cycle time.

Now let's look at the linkage between corporate and procurement strategies and performance expectations. Figure 5.2 takes a corporate goal and shows an example of strategy deployment by flowing from corporate goals down to the supplier performance expectation level. The corporate goal of improving customer satisfaction by 10 percent translates down to a corporate strategy of using Six Sigma to uncover the causes of customer complaints. Next, the procurement strategy addresses one of the causes of customer complaints uncovered in the Six

Figure 5.2 Strategy deployment to the supplier performance expectation level.

Sigma process: supplier quality escapes. So the supplier performance expectation of having a corrective action in place is derived from the procurement strategy, which ultimately flows down from the corporate goal of improving customer satisfaction and strategy of using Six Sigma analysis to uncover the root causes of customer complaints. The level of detail of the performance expectations can vary. But the objective is the alignment of supplier performance expectations with the procurement strategy and overall company strategy.

For many reasons developing supplier performance expectations via a strategy deployment process may not be practical for many companies. The company goals and strategies may not be formally communicated. Or procurement has never formally tried to align its plan with an overall corporate plan. Or a corporate plan doesn't exist. Perhaps there has never been a procurement plan or strategy. However, the more these expectations are aligned with senior management goals, whether or not the goals are part of a formal plan, the more likely it is that procurement will be supported organizationally and with the resources to manage, measure, and improve supplier performance. Of course, this alignment still needs to be communicated clearly to senior management.

While alignment with corporate strategy is always important and should be strived for, strategy deployment is not the only way to develop supplier performance expectations. Supplier performance expectations can be derived from many types of business and best-practices models, not just a corporate strategy deployment hierarchy. Some of the respected and recognized business models that could be used to develop performance expectations include the Baldrige National Quality Program, ISO 9000-2000 series, the SCOR Model (Supply Chain

Operations Reference) from the Supply Chain Council, and lean enterprise principles and practices.

Baldrige has frequently been used as a high-performance business model or system to drive performance. Its robustness, comprehensiveness, and best practices make it a good tool. Here are its seven categories:

Category 1—Leadership
Category 2—Strategic Planning
Category 3—Customer and Market Focus
Category 4—Measurement, Analysis, and Knowledge Management
Category 5—Workforce Focus
Category 6—Process Management
Category 7—Results[5]

Baldrige is considered a high-performance business system and is well respected and recognized. It could be used to guide the development of performance expectations. It is well designed and publicly available. Its disadvantage is that it may not be aligned with your company's current goals and strategy, though it may be a good future path to pursue. However, some companies use Baldrige as a business planning and continuous-improvement tool. And some require their suppliers to use it as well as a business improvement tool. Cessna Aircraft is an example of this practice. At one time, they asked their growth suppliers to take part in Baldrige training and use it as an evaluation and continuous-improvement tool.[6]

Companies can create performance expectations based upon other business considerations. If a company is adopting a high-performance business model such as lean, Six Sigma, or lean sigma, determining supplier performance expectations will be fairly easy. High-performance business models are typically based upon clear management philosophies and business improvement methodologies. These require alignment throughout the enterprise and ideally with suppliers as well. For example, companies implementing lean enterprise processes internally find that they need the cooperation and alignment of their suppliers to achieve their own goals. One example is the lean business practice of using pull systems, where processes "pull" what they need from the previous step in the process. Pull at the customer means that pull should occur from supplier processes as well; otherwise, inappropriate and costly inventory can build at both customer and supplier. Traditionally, materials from suppliers are "pushed" to the customer less frequently and in larger quantities. Therefore, companies implementing lean will find the development of supplier performance expectations fairly straightfor-

---

5. Malcolm Baldrige Quality Program, "2007 Business and Nonprofit Criteria," pp. 8–9.

6. Avery, Susan, "Cessna Soars," *Purchasing Magazine*, November 4, 2003.

ward, as there are many processes and practices that suppliers will need to adopt in order to convert from push to pull, for example. Similarly, other high-performance business models create performance challenges for the supply chain, as these are rarely self-contained and typically need to extend beyond the customer's own enterprise. Supplier performance expectations and evaluation criteria are readily found within these models.

USING BUSINESS MODELS TO DEVELOP PERFORMANCE EXPECTATIONS

Another approach to developing performance expectations and evaluation criteria is to develop a business model to drive evaluation. Business models are particularly useful for evaluating key suppliers, as you will be interested in not only metrics that show results but also in the more predictive characteristics of evaluation. These will help anticipate risk and tell you a lot more about the root causes of problems that may surface, such as what processes suppliers have in place to create a quality product or service or how they ensure that they do a good job of managing their suppliers. A business model can be made up of topics or functional areas such as quality, product development, supply and inventory management, risk management, and so on. A business model is a set of business practices, processes, and performance expectations that are organized in a hierarchy or outline form. At the bottom of the model hierarchy are precise individual measures or questions and associated quantitative measures that relate to the business topics. Examples of possible topics for business models are Lean Enterprise, High-Performance Enterprise, Corporate Social Responsibility, Sub-Tier Supplier Assessment, and Preferred Supplier Certification. Models can be built based upon third-party systems such as ISO and Baldrige or internal high-performance business systems. This section will show you a process for building a business model and help you think through what to measure.

A business model starts with the topic or area that you wish to measure. Then it is broken down into different levels of subcategories, depending on the detail needed to cover the topic. Essentially, the business model is an outline of the subject being measured. At the lowest level of detail are performance expectations or business practices, which can be measured by either quantitative metrics or qualitative questions. Structuring a business model in this format helps you develop a full and balanced view of the areas that you wish to measure. It will help you measure the areas of supplier performance that are most important to your company and that mesh with your company's goals and strategies. The business model can be used to conduct assessments in the form of KPIs and scorecards, site visits, or

Table 5.2 Business Model Hierarchy

Topic or Category: I. Inventory and Supply	
Element: A. Supply	
Component: 1. Sourcing	
Performance Expectations or Business Practices	1.1 The company has and follows a documented source selection process. 1.2 The company evaluates approved suppliers. 1.3 The company optimizes the supplier base to reduce costs and deliver quality products and services. 1.4 Suppliers are managed by a multifunction team. 1.5 Supply management processes are reviewed and managed for continuous process improvement.
Component: 2. Supplier Quality Processes	
Performance Expectations or Business Practices	2.1 The supplier uses a process for initial approval of its suppliers for the product and/or service being purchased. 2.2 The procurement process includes multifunctional review of company requirements and agreement with suppliers for performance expectations. 2.3 The supplier uses acceptance metrics to demonstrate product or service conformance. 2.4 The supplier has a process for resolving disagreements regarding responsibility for nonconformances (quality problems).

a combination. Scores can be calculated at any level in the business model and rolled up the hierarchy.

Table 5.2 shows part of a business model hierarchy. The top-level topic or category in the hierarchy is Inventory and Supply. The next level down is Supply. The component parts of Supply are Sourcing and Supplier Quality Processes. Each of these is broken down further into performance expectations.

The hierarchy can be created to be more or less detailed. But most important is covering all areas or topics that are and can be impacted by supplier performance. For example, most suppliers will claim to have a source selection process. But upon further examination, many suppliers may have a source selection process, but often the buyers are not fully trained in it or aware of it or they are not following their own processes. Failure in just this one business practice can

Table 5.3 Lean Hierarchy

1. Leadership	1.1 Lean Vision 1.2 Vision Deployment 1.3 Workforce Involvement 1.4 Communication 1.5 Organization
2. Workplace Organization	2.1 Work Cells 2.2 Flow between Cells 2.3 Optimizing Cells 2.4 Local Control of Resources 2.5 Order Status/Communication
3. Materials and Supply	3.1 Sourcing Management 3.2 Inventory Control 3.3 Materials 3.4 Supply Integration
4. Work Process	4.1 Value Stream Mapping 4.2 5S and Visual Workplace 4.3 Setup Reduction 4.4 Quality at the Source 4.5 Standard Work 4.6 Total Productive Maintenance 4.7 Capital Equipment
5. Enabling Practices	5.1 Continuous Improvement 5.2 Team-Based Work 5.3 Lean Metrics

result in a myriad of problems and risks, such as poor-performing suppliers, inappropriate sources, low-price but high-cost suppliers, supply base growing too large to manage, and insufficient spend under management. Not having a defined source selection process or having one that is not adhered to is an example of both a potential risk factor and a cost driver. By specifying performance expectations in sufficient detail, a company can uncover these potential costs and risks

Lean enterprise is an area where many assessment tools have been developed. Table 5.3 contains an example of a lean business model hierarchy with elements and components. Any of the components can be expanded into performance expectations. For example, under Element 5.1, Continuous Improvement, the component is: The supplier works to reduce cycle time. Supplier performance expectations related to this component can be

- The supplier has a plan to reduce cycle time.
- The supplier is achieving significant reductions in cycle times.
- The supplier's employees understand effective cycle time reduction tools and techniques.

- The supplier's cycle time and lead time reduction projects support key customer satisfaction objectives.

By understanding whether and how a company is reducing its cycle time, a customer firm can create supplier performance expectations that support its own goals of responsiveness to customers and customer satisfaction.

If a company is trying to increase velocity at its suppliers to enhance its own flexibility and responsiveness to its customer, it will need to communicate to its suppliers exactly the processes and practices it expects them to have in place in order to reduce their cycle times. The business model approach to assessment can spell out expectations in sufficient detail so that it can be used both as a measurement tool and as an informative and developmental tool for suppliers. Some suppliers may not be aware of the business practices that can help them achieve better business performance, and detailed customer performance expectations may give them insights and information to develop better practices. To the extent that business models can be software-enabled helps make them a more effective and efficient supplier assessment and supplier development tool. My former company, Valuedge, used this approach to develop its supplier assessment software and is now part of Emptoris's supply management software suite.

These are just a few examples of how to create supplier performance expectations that align with customer firm goals by creating a business model and breaking it down into specifics.

USING VALUE STREAM MAPPING TO IDENTIFY PERFORMANCE EXPECTATIONS AND METRICS

Another approach to developing performance metrics is to identify the specific areas where suppliers impact your operations and those of your customer. This can be done by creating a value stream map of your enterprise. Value stream mapping is a graphical representation of the specific activities and processes required to design, order, and provide a specific product or service, from concept to launch, order to delivery, into the hands of the customer. It helps identify which activities add value to the customer and which do not and are considered waste (non-value-added). Much has already been written about value stream mapping, and we will not get into the details here of how to do this.[7]

For example, you can map the order to delivery cycle, a core business process and one that has supplier touch points and customer impact. Break it down into

---

7. For more detail on value stream mapping, see the classic how-to book *Learning to See* by Mike Rother, John Shook, Jim Womack, and Dan Jones. For an administrative or office-oriented book, see *Value Stream Mapping for the Lean Office* by Don Tapping.

its components (source selection, purchase order development, receiving of the supplier order, processing of supplier materials or use of supplier services, and so on), and look at the process steps that occur during it. Stakeholders in each part of the process should be involved in the mapping. Mapping the process steps will help uncover performance expectations and issues between customer and supplier firms that need to be addressed. For example, stakeholders in the process may express concern over:

- The quality of the service they receive from suppliers
- The responsiveness of suppliers to their business needs
- The capabilities and willingness of suppliers to do business electronically
- Compliance with and timely resolution of customer requests for corrective actions
- Compliance with contract service level agreements
- Complaints from customers about products and services that lead back to supplier performance

These are just a few of the many issues that will arise during value stream mapping that can translate into supplier performance expectations and ultimately continuous-improvement actions. The mapping process will help provide a foundation for developing performance metrics. In addition, it can expose waste and non-value-added activities involving the customer and/or the supplier. For key suppliers, the mapping process can be done across both customer and supplier enterprises. This process will also, of course, uncover areas that the customer firm needs to address.

USING BUSINESS DRIVERS TO IDENTIFY PERFORMANCE EXPECTATIONS

Another approach to defining performance expectations is to identify the most important business drivers that impact your company and its customers. These business drivers are typically in the areas of cost, quality, time, and technology/ innovation. Breaking down each of these drivers into supplier impacts and supplier risks can help you identify what to measure.

The business drivers described in this section connect the supply chain management system to marketplace success and to overall company performance and are critical for gaining and maintaining the support for the supplier management.

Cost

For an increasing number of companies, the supply chain has become both the largest single source of cost and largest opportunity for cost reduction and profitability. Hidden cost drivers lie in the supply chain and can ruin profitability and competitiveness of both customers and suppliers. Identifying and removing cost drivers is a key objective of supplier performance management. While cost pressures are always an important concern, they are more a result or side effect of the business processes that drive them. The best way to address cost drivers is improving the business processes that drive cost, both within the customer company and within the supply chain. Reducing cost is, of course, far different from simply getting a better price. Eliminating cost drivers can produce sustainable results and can increase value to the customer. Price reductions may not be sustainable for suppliers. The current situation in the automotive supply chain in the United States illustrates the dangers of pressuring suppliers for price reductions.

Quality

Variability in supplier processes impacts the quality of products and services. In businesses with high supplier content or heavy dependence on supplier services, the supplier quality has a heavy impact. Responsiveness to corrective actions can fall under either quality or customer responsiveness. When supplier failures occur in the field or at the customer, a company's responsiveness to its customers is gated by the capabilities of its suppliers. And when this failure is traced back to a sub-tier supplier, this sub-tier supplier may be unaware who the actual customers of its end products are and of their warranty requirements. Quality is a cost driver. When it is missing, it causes the waste of rework, reshipping, increased inventory, expediting, and customer dissatisfaction. Therefore, important measurements might be quality escapes, in-process quality, and incoming quality.

Service quality is another key area for some companies, especially nonmanufacturing businesses, to measure. For example, Radisson Hotels was measuring four aspects of service quality:

Willingness to return. Percent of customers who indicate that they are willing to return

Percent advocates. Percent of customers who indicate a willingness to recommend Radisson Hotels to others

Percent defectors. Percent of customers who indicate that they are unwilling to return

Percent complaints. Ratio of complaints to room nights[8]

8. Hill, Arthur V., Susan Geurs, Julie M. Hays, George John, David W. Johnson, and Richard A. Swanson, "Service Guarantees and Strategic Service Quality Performance Metrics at Radisson Hotels Worldwide," *Journal of Strategic Performance Measurement*, December 1998, pp. 27–31.

Time

With approximately 40 to 50 percent of cycle time attributable to the supply chain, market responsiveness is very dependent upon supplier performance. Two important areas where suppliers impact cycle time are purchased material lead time and product development cycles.

Purchased material lead time can be the longest portion of cycle time for the buying organization. Therefore, time-based measures such as on-time delivery and supplier lead time are common measures. But equally important is how and whether the supplier continually addresses the improvement of internal cycle time and on-time delivery to customers.

Another aspect of time is responsiveness. How quickly a company can respond to its customers' needs often depends upon the level of responsiveness of its suppliers. Responsiveness measures can include order-to-delivery cycle time, internal customer or stakeholder satisfaction, time to respond to corrective actions, and perceived cooperativeness.

Technology

For many companies getting new products to market rapidly is a key competitive opportunity. Suppliers who are used to support new product development strategies must be qualified and measured not just from a technology capability standpoint but also from understanding of the robustness of their internal product or service development processes. Too often, firms choose development partners without using a formal process and with no criteria beyond good technical capabilities. They neglect to look at the total picture: how the company develops products and services and whether their internal processes and practices are robust and sustainable. With the company's future dependent upon new products and realizing that development suppliers played an important role in future products, The Boeing Company created what they called a development tool to assess the product development capabilities of those suppliers with whom they partner on new product development. Often development engineers choose development suppliers for their technology. The supplier must also possess good internal development processes. The types of suppliers that Boeing targeted with this assessment tool ranged from materials development, total systems development, pilot development, and software development to technologies exploration suppliers. The key objective was to reduce risk in new product development by better understanding business processes and practices at key development suppliers. Some of the areas that were measured included leadership, quality, cost and development processes. Assessment topics under development processes include Alignment, Communications, Affordability, Research and Development (R&D) Processes,

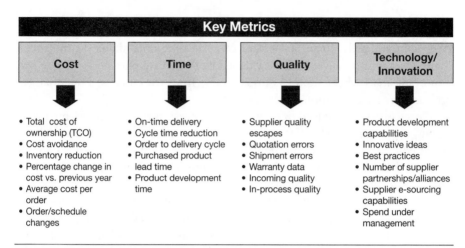

Figure 5.3 Business drivers and metrics.

Lean in Product Definition, Performance and Measures (i.e., customer satisfaction, metrics for making design decisions, cost control, productivity trends).

Figure 5.3 illustrates some of the metrics related to the key business drivers of cost, quality, time, and technology/innovation.

MEASURING TO UNCOVER RISK

Avoiding and mitigating risk are some of the top reasons for measuring supplier performance. Supply chain risk is high on the list of executive concerns right now. Risk is an area where perception often is reality. Some people think that they can estimate risk with a great deal of precision, while others are in denial about risk in order to reduce anxiety about it. The scientific approach is to estimate the chance of an event occurring and its order of magnitude by using probability. Non-scientists—and that includes supply chain managers—tend to focus only on the aspects of risk that they are aware of. All risk assessments are estimates and are based on uncertainty and incomplete data. In spite of the high level of uncertainty, executives tend to prefer quantitative data about risk, believing that it is more certain and more definitive, even though it may be neither definitive nor accurate. Risk mitigation is a high priority with C-level executives. The extent to which supply managers can mitigate risk in the supply chain engenders C-level support in their firms. While the CFO, for example, may be active in developing risk mitigation strategies, senior management usually pays more attention to risk-induced disruptions and failures than to a smoothly operating supply chain. That is, senior management is unlikely to thank its supply managers for a smoothly operating supply chain, but rather to focus on the anomalies.

Supply risks include everything that can disrupt supply. The risks can include financial, political, geographic distance (such as low-cost-county sourcing), long lead times, regulatory issues, scarcity of supply, and the way the leadership at the supplier run the company. Some types of risk are highly uncertain, such as political risks and natural disasters. Others, like financial and business process disruptions, are easier to analyze and predict. The best antidote to risk is information—that is, greater understanding of and insights into the elements of supplier performance along the dimensions just discussed: cost, quality, time, and technology. Therefore, it is important to have cross-functional support and participation in managing supplier risk, as the impact on the company is broader than just on procurement. Some businesses have a harder time seeing the return on investing in disruption avoidance. The benefits are clearer in industries such as aerospace and health care where supply disruptions or problems can put lives at risk.

A March 2007 study by Aberdeen Group, *Supply Risk Increasing while the Market Stands Still*, identifies what the respondents from 210 companies surveyed saw as the top indicators of supply risks to their companies:

- Supplier financial viability
- Supplier credit ratings
- Supply disruptions
- Supply concentration (availability of supply from alternate sources)
- Supplier dependency (percentage of revenue from a single supplier)
- Financial impact of disruptions

The types of risks that were identified do, for the most part, lend themselves to risk mitigation measures. Better understanding of supplier performance and performance capabilities and insights into supplier operations are key risk avoidance strategies. Over 60 percent of the companies surveyed who were considered in the "best in class" category said that a measurement and management program is effective against these top risk indicators. Only 45 percent of the average performers felt these programs are effective. The overall lack of deployment of supplier performance management programs shows that understanding and mitigating supply risk is in its early stages.

During a February 2006 Webcast on managing supply chain risk, AMR Research asked 150 supply chain managers what risks kept them awake at night.[9] The responses fell along these dimensions:

- Supplier disruption (critical supplier failure)—49%
- Logistics failure (e.g., port strike)—17%

9. Hillman, Mark, "Strategies for Managing Supply Chain Risk," *Supply Chain Management Review*, July/August 2006, p. 12.

- Natural disaster event—13%
- Strategic failure (e.g., selling the wrong product in the wrong market)—13%
- Geopolitical event—8%

Better insight into and understanding of the supply base is again the preferred approach. The recommendation was to map the supply base of critical and strategic suppliers so that companies understand risks such as sub-tier risk for key suppliers or a key supplier having too much dependence on one customer. This type of information can come out of good supplier qualification and segmentation processes. These risk factors, along with the leading and lagging indicators that have been thus far suggested, should be assessed and monitored and risk mitigation plans put in place. Assessing for risk factors should be an integral part of supplier qualification and continuing evaluation. Also find out whether your key suppliers have risk assessment and mitigation plans in place and whether they require risk mitigation plans from *their* suppliers. How suppliers manage their suppliers has, in my own experience, been one of the lesser-known and weaker links in the chain and is one of the lower-scoring areas of supplier assessments. Hidden risks further down the supply chain need to be identified and dealt with.

Some approaches to supplier risk mitigation include the following:

- Choose good sources in the first place by using best practice sourcing methods.
- Choose the right supplier performance measures—those that are applicable to your organization and your supply base.
- Be disciplined about measuring supplier performance regularly.
- Develop and grow relationships with important suppliers so that you better understand their business and reduce the chances for the unexpected to occur. Also, look at current relationships to see whether your firm is doing anything to make it difficult for a supplier to stay in business.
- Review supplier contracts for disruption clauses, surge capacity provisions, and other risk-related clauses.[10]
- Identify, create, and implement available risk mitigation strategies and contingency planning.
- Incorporate risk mitigation metrics into the supplier performance management program.
- Adopt technology to enable supplier performance management.

---

10. Pickett, Christopher, "Prepare for Supply Chain Disruptions before They Hit," *Logistics Today*, March 2006.

There has been some emphasis on financial risks—being alerted to a supplier's deteriorating financial condition. Though useful, this is a lagging financial indicator and occurs at a later stage of the problem at a supplier. Insights into the trends of KPIs along the cost, quality, and time dimensions can be predictive of many of the risks, other than geopolitical, global market conditions, and natural disasters. Deteriorating quality and customer service or an increasing cost structure (such as higher inventory, loss on bidding new business) are usually indicative of problems within the supplier and potentially some business performance and financial impact on that supplier. Gaining insights into key suppliers by developing relationships with them helps reduce risk rather than just looking in the rearview mirror at after-the-fact-metrics on their finances.

EVALUATING SUB-TIER SUPPLIERS

An increasingly important area of supplier assessment is sub-tier suppliers or a firm's suppliers' suppliers. Visibility into sub-tier supplier operations is difficult and is a growing concern in industries such as aerospace, automotive, and electronics where the end customer is increasingly the systems integrator and depends upon its supply base to manufacture the components and subsystems that go into the final product. It is also a concern in other industries such as consumer packaged goods and pharmaceuticals, where items are being sourced increasingly from contract manufacturers who manage their own supply bases. Sub-tier supplier problems can be expensive in their impact on the prime and end customers. A low cost item can stop a high value shipment and be costly to remedy.

How can this type of problem be prevented or uncovered early enough to do something about it? Companies need to make sure that their direct suppliers are doing a good job of managing their supplier relationships and communicating with suppliers. But how can the customer firm find out whether their direct suppliers are doing a good job of supply management? What are the risk factors in the supply chain and how do you uncover them and even mitigate them? A comprehensive assessment of your direct suppliers' supply management practices would reveal risk factors in the sub-tier supply chain. It is challenging, however, for customer firms to get visibility into the performance and practices of their suppliers and the tiers below without dispatching armies of assessors to find out and without overstepping your contractual agreements with direct suppliers. Often customer firms have no idea who their sub-tier suppliers are.

The following are examples of general areas of performance expectations to use for evaluating suppliers and their sub-tiers:

- **Contract review and requirements flow down.** Customer contract requirements are understood both within the supplier firm and by their direct suppliers whom they plan to use to provide products and services.

- **Design process.** Suppliers have robust design processes and use good business practices when subcontracting design to their suppliers.
- **Sourcing process.** Supplier firms are using a robust, consistent sourcing process.
- **Contracting process.** This process ensures that contracting with their supply bases is efficient and cost effective.
- **Customer-supplier communications.** Suppliers use good communications processes to enhance their supplier relationships. Wherever possible suppliers share requirements electronically.
- **Risk management.** Suppliers have formal risk management processes in place.
- **Performance management.** Suppliers measure performance and give regular performance feedback to their suppliers.
- **Manufacturing processes.** The manufacturing processes of sub-tier suppliers are documented and controlled.
- **Continuous improvement.** Suppliers work with their suppliers on continuous-improvement activities and share training and best practices.

The challenge for customer firms is how to get an adequate understanding of sub-tier supplier risk factors in order to prevent problems. Many supplier assessments come down to a question of resources. The size of a sub-tier supply chain and the scope of evaluating sub-tier suppliers are potentially vast. So a company has to be willing and able to commit resources to sub-tier assessment, at least for critical products. Making site visits to an entire supply chain is not practical. It is costly for the customers making the visits and the suppliers hosting and responding to the visits. Scaling the process using technology, if possible, is preferable and more likely to be sustainable.

As mentioned in Chapter 3 during the discussion on supplier assessment pilots, Boeing developed a Web-based sub-tier supplier assessment to try to address this challenge. This assessment is capable of pinpointing key risk factors and measuring the performance of an individual supplier, a tier, or an entire supply chain. Its purpose was not to perform an in-depth assessment of every supplier in the chain. It was to ask enough questions in the areas that were considered most critical to success and risk avoidance. The assessment can expose potentially weak sub-tier suppliers and specific risk factors without a need to visit every supplier in the chain. A supplier manager can then determine whether further investigation or action needs to occur. This type of assessment must be done with the cooperation and assistance of the direct customers of sub-tier suppliers in order not to overstep contractual bounds. And, there are issues of confidentiality as well. There is a delicate balance between gathering sufficient information on sub-tier supplier performance to understand risks, strengths and opportunities for improvement and asking for so much information that suppliers are unwilling to take the time to participate. The technology for doing so now exists, but deploying and acting on sub-tier assessments require business discipline and focus.

Evaluating sub-tier suppliers is a notion of increasing importance as outsourcing has become a key strategy for many customer firms as they try to figure out how to understand and monitor sub-tier performance to avoid costly risks, problems, and unpleasant surprises.

MEASURING INDIRECT SUPPLIERS

Because direct materials are tangible, direct material supplier performance is much easier to measure. Also, more information on which to base metrics is immediately available in a company's enterprise system. Direct material can be defined as a purchased good that is required to manufacture a finished good or create a service for a customer. Indirect material can be defined as any purchased good or service that does not become part of the product or service that is delivered to a customer. As previously discussed, many people think that only quantitative measures can be considered objective. KPIs for quantitative measures are understandable and more readily available. However, qualitative measures can be equally useful and are not inherently less valuable or necessarily less accurate than quantitative metrics. In the case of indirect suppliers, qualitative measures may comprise many of the metrics that are both available and meaningful.

Indirect suppliers can be more difficult to measure for several reasons. Data may not be readily available. Elements of their performance are not typically captured in a company's enterprise management system as they are for direct suppliers. There is no incoming inspection or on-time delivery data already resident in the business system or data warehouse. Another issue is spend under management. Frequently and in many organizations, portions of indirect spend are maverick or not under procurement management, and thus more difficult to identify. Poor indirect supplier performance can cause serious problems. Poorly functioning trucks from a fleet supplier can bring operations to a halt. Software suppliers whose product malfunctions can bring your business to a standstill. Outsourced customer support representatives can alienate your customers. Consulting services firms who do a poor job can leave a company without the expected expertise. During the segmentation exercise, you need to identify those indirect suppliers whose performance has the highest impact on your internal and external customers.

Measuring indirect suppliers typically will require a combination of both quantitative and subjective measures. Many indirect suppliers have areas that can be quantified. Productivity measures are one area. Examples are fleet truck breakdowns, office supplier fill rates, employment agency placement rates, and so on. Other quantifiable measures for indirect suppliers are cost savings. Examples are negotiated prices for hotel rates, rental car rates, consulting rates, and legal rates. In creating indirect supplier metrics, you must be careful not to make them too complex, too hard to calculate, or not truly meaningful to the business. Where possible, you should include leading indicators, not just lagging indicators. The metrics should reflect the scope of the service being measured. Prioritization of what to measure is key. Don't measure aspects of a service that are not important to your company and that you won't take any action on. This can occur when metrics are difficult to obtain and companies use metrics because they are readily available, but not meaningful. Another aspect of prioritization is in relation to the actual metrics themselves. Not all metrics are equal, either. You may need to weight metrics according to their relative importance to the business.[11]

Another way to look at developing measurements for indirect suppliers is to identify the important elements of indirect supplier performance that you wish to measure. These elements should relate to the key business drivers of cost, quality, time, and technology/innovation. Some of these may include customer satisfaction, continuous improvement, cost competitiveness, and compliance to contract service level agreements.

Following are questions to consider:

- How do indirect suppliers impact cost?
- How competitive is the indirect supplier's cost?
- How do their products or services affect quality, such as, for example, service quality?
- How good is the supplier's customer service?
- How quickly does the supplier resolve service problems?
- How does the supplier impact the timeliness of the customer company's ability to provide service to its customers?
- Some indirect suppliers provide technology-based services or use technology to give them a competitive edge. How does their technology give competitive advantage to your company?
- Does the supplier demonstrate continuous improvement to resolve issues, reduce costs, and improve performance?
- What is the relative importance or weight of the KPIs?

Another important part of determining what aspects of performance to measure for indirect suppliers is to think about the supplier behaviors and actions that you want to support or enable. For example, if your supplier runs customer call centers for you, you want to measure behaviors and business practices that

11. Crump, Jamie S., "Supplier Performance and Scorecards for Indirect Spend," 90th Annual International Supply Management Conference, May 2005.

will result in their running the call center cost-effectively, but without any ill effects on your customers who are using that call center. In this case you may wish to concentrate on customer satisfaction measures rather than on purchased price variance. Other issues to consider include the following:

- Are the measures and expected performance clear to the supplier?
- Are they meaningful to the supplier's business and to the impact their business has on your company?
- Are they within the supplier's control?

A good way to find out is to include suppliers in the process of developing performance measures and get their input and feedback. This helps avoid miscommunications about performance expectations and disputes over the meaning and relevance of the measures. Including suppliers in the development of performance measures supports supplier buy-in and commitment to the evaluation system. It makes the system more robust and meaningful to suppliers. Otherwise, it can be perceived as just another program being laid on the suppliers that creates extra work, has the potential to cause a loss of business, and does not add value to supplier firms.

After identifying the elements of good performance that relate to your company's objectives and/or relate to the key business drivers, the challenge will be to choose evaluation approaches and methodologies and develop good sources of performance data. Since there may be less information on the indirect supplier immediately available from internal company sources and systems, other sources will need to be considered, such as directly from the supplier and generating internal feedback through surveys. Indirect supplier measures are likely to require feedback from internal stakeholders, more so than direct suppliers do, because of the dearth of metrics regularly collected in enterprise systems on indirect suppliers. The key issues to consider are whether the information desired is useful, relevant, and actionable. Some companies follow the path of least resistance and collect information just because it's available or easy to collect. There are financial considerations as well to data collection. It costs money to develop metrics, and the benefits should be worth the costs. Better to have fewer measures that are meaningful and actionable than too many measures with less value. Too many metrics may create the appearance of a good supplier evaluation program, but may be impossible to deploy effectively both from a customer internal resources and a supplier compliance point of view. The purpose is to support the business and improve performance.

6

EVALUATION APPROACHES

MEASUREMENT METHODOLOGIES

We have looked at potential data sources for supplier performance management such as internal stakeholders at the buying company, transaction data in enterprise systems (financial, quality, shipping, etc), suppliers, and third-party sources of information. We will now discuss different measurement methodologies using these sources and their pros and cons.

SURVEYS OR QUESTIONNAIRES

Surveys have always been a popular way to find out information about suppliers and their performance. Supplier surveys can be used to identify current or potential performance issues and to identify ways to resolve issues between customer and supplier. They provide a structured way for customers to gather both qualitative and quantitative feedback without the interference of personality clashes or defensive behaviors. Surveys can also help identify changes that will provide opportunities to improve key business drivers such as cycle times and quality. Types of surveys include the following:

- **RFI surveys.** Sent to qualify prospective suppliers and can contain questions about performance metrics. These can be done via telephone, mail, or Internet.

- **Quality surveys.** Sent to gather information from suppliers on their quality planning systems and processes, third-party certification, corrective action, tooling, test equipment, cost of quality, quality results, and so on.
- **Supplier surveys.** Sent to gather detailed information about the supplier. Surveys can be done via telephone, mail, Internet, or in-person interviews.

While a common and good way to gather information on supplier performance, surveys have a variety of potential pitfalls. Here are some key elements that will impact the quality of the results.

Deployment Methods

The method of deploying the survey—mail, personal interview, site visits, Internet, electronic files—will impact results. You must choose the most suitable method given budgets, number of suppliers being surveyed, and types and lengths of surveys being deployed. Methods include the following:

1. Hard copies sent through the mail are probably the least effective method in the electronic age. In an era where much business is done electronically, getting a survey by snail mail these days may make it stand out. However, hard-copy surveys are the most inefficient information-gathering method for the customer. This is because compiling the results from multiple suppliers is a manual, time-consuming process. Companies who use paper surveys may find that the paper just collects dust and the results are not used effectively. If you want to analyze, compare, or readily keep the results of multiple surveys, paper surveys are the least effective way to gather the data. This is also true for surveys that are e-mailed as attachments. The same problem exists: how to compile and analyze results. E-mailed surveys have an advantage over paper because the survey can be more readily shared and viewed in the supplier organization, but the compilation problems at the customer end still remain.

2. Telephone surveys are another alternative. They may help enhance the relationship because they are more personal. Also, a skilled interviewer may be able to obtain comments from the supplier that shed more light on their firm. A good interviewer can increase cooperation rates.[1] Disadvantages include the following:

---

1. Scheuren, Fritz, "What Is a Survey?" www.whatisasurvey.info, p. 22.

- Finding the appropriate person at the supplier
- Setting up the telephone meeting with the appropriate person
- Both the customer and supplier finding the time to complete the survey
- Making sure that the supplier participant has all the information at hand (or may need to receive a copy of the survey in advance to do the research)
- Making sure that the interviewer is professional and does not influence or bias the results

In many cases, one person will not be able to answer all questions without research. The survey taker at the customer end should ideally be able to enter the results into a spreadsheet or an information system so that results can be compiled and analyzed. Another pitfall of telephone surveys is that they can reflect the capabilities and biases of customer personnel conducting the survey. Customer personnel can skew the results by helping the supplier give the "right" answers or by interpreting the answers through their own lens—which may or may not be advantageous to either the supplier or the customer. Conducting a supplier survey by telephone is a skill that needs to be taught. Don't assume that anyone can conduct a telephone survey without prior training.

3. Supplier site visits—Surveys or questionnaires are often deployed during site visits. Site visits will be discussed in detail shortly.

Clarity of Purpose

Purposes and uses of supplier surveys must be decided in advance, and communication with suppliers must be clear. Suppliers want to know the rules of the game. Confusion about the purpose of the survey and/or the use of the information will cause suppliers to be concerned about whether and how the survey results will impact the amount of business they get. Lack of understanding about the purpose can adversely impact the amount of cooperation and the openness of the supplier responses.

Clarity of the Survey Instrument

Surveys should be well constructed and well written. Many think that survey development can be done by anyone with knowledge of the subjects to be covered in the survey. This is untrue. Think about the surveys you have been asked to fill out. How many were confusing, long, and difficult? Probably most of them.

Unclear surveys may result in the respondent abandoning the survey process. Also, the results may be less useful.

Clarity of the Questions

Questions must be clear and unambiguous. Otherwise, the respondent may get confused about what exactly is being asked, thus making the results less useful. We will cover specific techniques for developing good questions and question types to avoid in the next chapter.

Time to Complete

The length of time the participants are given to complete the survey is important. Too much time and the respondents may procrastinate. Too little time and they won't be able to get it done. Also, the length of time to complete a survey depends on the length and method of the survey as well, how complicated or difficult it is to respond to, and how much research is involved. Web-based surveys can be more efficient than paper surveys.

Timing of Deployment

In relation to time, try to choose a reasonable completion date, one that is mutually acceptable to the customer and supplier firms. For example, you may get less compliance at the end of a month or a quarter or during a seasonal or industry uptick, depending on the business cycle of the supplier.

Survey Length

This may adversely impact participant completion, depending upon other factors, such as clarity and ease of use, which will aid completion. Respondents are more likely to abandon surveys that are too long or may not put sufficient effort into answering them.

Confidentiality

Some participants may not want to respond honestly or at all to certain types of questions. The company requesting the information must address confidentiality issues with suppliers. Customers and suppliers may have already entered into mutual nondisclosure agreements or confidentiality agreements to protect sensitive financial and product information. There are some suppliers, in particular privately held companies, who will not disclose certain information to their customers or about their own finances. Whether or not there are agreements in place, it is important to treat supplier information confidentially, protecting it both from parties internal to the customer and particularly from the supplier's other customers and the supplier's competitors. It is appropriate for customers to make comparisons of one supplier to others. However, customers must be careful not to divulge confidential or identifying information. Another area of confidentiality issues is in a survey with multiple respondents at a supplier whether the respondents' identity should be kept confidential. In certain companies, employees may fear retribution if they do not answer as they feel their management expects. In some cases, the identity of individuals may need to be kept confidential in order to promote honest responses and protect these individuals. This issue will need to be addressed with the supplier in advance. Confidentiality policies should be discussed with or communicated to suppliers and participants at the supplier in advance of a survey.

Team Experience and Capabilities

For site visits, team members must be chosen carefully for their level of subject matter expertise, their ability to work as a team, their ability to conduct themselves appropriately in front of suppliers, and their ability or potential ability to conduct a good site visit. Even if this expertise exists in the customer firm, training is always important for site visit teams. I was once on a supplier site visit where the quality expert started arguing with the lean expert, telling her to back off and stop trying to tread on his turf. Not only was this incorrect, since quality can be part of lean practices, but it was inappropriate to have this kind of argument in front of supplier personnel.

Communication Strategy

The customer needs to develop a strategy for communicating about the survey to suppliers. There are various methods, such as sending out a letter, setting up a telephone conference call or Web meeting, visiting the supplier, sending out e-mail communications, or a combination of these methods. This is the customer's opportunity to explain the purpose, rationale, and use of the survey and gain the support and participation of the supplier. Equally important is communication with stakeholders within the customer company. Since some stakeholders are currently dealing with suppliers, are impacted by suppliers, or may be asked to give feedback about suppliers, you should make sure that they are in the loop about supplier evaluation surveys. This helps ensure buy-in. And the communication process is essential for keeping management support for the effort, both in the area of planning and survey results. If there is lack of communication with suppliers about surveys, suppliers may not participate or may withhold information. If the internal communication at the customer is not done, then a lot of good work will go unnoticed, unappreciated, and eventually unbudgeted.

Budget

It will probably be necessary to obtain a budget for supplier surveys. The budget may encompass people, travel, and possibly information technology expenses, depending on the types of survey techniques used. Some companies conduct supplier surveys on a small scale and low budget, sometimes even under the corporate radar. But eventually, a good and effective survey program will require visible resources and accountability for results.

Language of the Survey or Questionnaire

Depending upon the composition of the supply base, language may be a consideration. One issue is whether the survey will need to be translated into other languages. In cases where there is a large non-native-speaking population that is part of the organization, you should consider whether you will need feedback from non-native-speaking employees at suppliers and how and even whether you are going to try to get feedback from that population. In many multinational companies, surveys can be in English, as it is considered to be the universal language.

Cultural Background

In addition to language, the cultural background of respondents can also be a challenge. Suppliers are trying to make a good impression and will try to tell you what you want to hear in a survey or site visit and show you what they want you to see on a site visit. They may exaggerate to show their company in the best possible light. How many customers have been welcomed to suppliers with freshly painted floors in the factory? In some cultures, trying to give you the right answer on a survey can become a barrier to finding out what is really going on. This becomes a challenge particularly when the supplier is too far away geographically to easily visit.

An example of cultural differences can be seen in doing business with Chinese companies. To them, the concept of *guan xi*, or the Chinese practice of building and maintaining relationships, is very important. Identifying supplier performance issues can run in direct conflict with accountability for poor performance, as pointing out problems can be seen as endangering the relationship. Chinese management structure is hierarchical. Also, cleanliness and neatness are not priorities, which can be a particular problem for companies pursuing lean and 5S practices (workplace organization). Where one might ask lower-level associates in a business in the United States for input, this would not be considered appropriate in China, as not only would they not be involved in any decision making, they would also fear making their management look bad by citing problems or opportunities for improvement. This makes implementing certain lean and quality practices more challenging.[2]

---

2. Paolini, Anthony, Bekki Leu, and Robert Chinn, "Exporting Lean to China: Know Before You Go," *PRTM Insight*, Vol. 17, No. 2.

Compliance

Suppliers will comply with completing a customer survey if they think the survey is important to their current or future relationship with the customer and if having a relationship with a particular customer is important to their business. That is why the communications piece is so essential. If the survey seems as if it won't "count" or seems like extra, needless paperwork, suppliers will not complete it. If the survey affords incentives, such as an opportunity for winning or increasing business, certification, preferred status, recognition, or some other potential competitive advantage, then suppliers will be cooperative. Alternatively, from a negative customer approach, if not responding to the survey or doing poorly in an evaluation may cause a loss of business, the supplier will also find it important to comply, assuming in all of these cases that the supplier wants to initiate or continue a business relationship with the customer.

Many companies want and need to get feedback on suppliers via internal stakeholder surveys. Internal stakeholders can be a good source of information on supplier performance. Also, having their participation and input includes a broader perspective and increases the chances that good decisions about suppliers can be made, as there will be more information on which to base decisions. In companies where there is little or no quantitative or transactional information in the business system to use to evaluate suppliers, internal stakeholders will be the only available source. For internal stakeholders responding to a supplier survey, their perceived importance of completing supplier surveys is very essential in gaining participation. You want to try to get broad and balanced enough feedback to ensure that more than just complainers and unhappy stakeholders are participating. The purpose, uses, and importance of collecting their feedback must be continually communicated. You must make these surveys convenient and easy to access and complete to get maximum participation. Some companies have considered drawings for small rewards or prizes for internal survey participants. And, you must use stakeholder input in decision making so that they know that their feedback is not gratuitous.

SITE VISITS

Site visits involve deploying a survey at the supplier. Site visits are particularly suited to suppliers whose product or service is considered critical or strategic to the business; suppliers who represent high levels of spend; and suppliers who are sole-source, single-source, or for whom the switching costs are high.

Site visits can take different forms. They may be brief visits of several hours to review specific issues or problems at the supplier or to review specific business process areas. Or, site visits can be comprehensive business reviews of suppliers that are conducted by a cross-functional team from the customer and can last several days.

Another approach is the supplier audit, which is typically a quality-oriented, detailed review of the supplier's operations. An audit involves a set of standards or specifications against which the auditor measures the supplier. An audit team verifies business requirements on-site through inspection, interviews, and review of objective evidence such as documentation, analytical data, records, and samples. Per David Bossert in *The Supplier Management Handbook*, an audit is "examining an activity to see if it was done in accordance to the rules"; it can also mean 100 percent inspection to see "if everything is present and correct."[3]

In contrast to the supplier audit approach to a supplier site visit, there is the supplier business assessment, which differs from a supplier audit but is similar to what Bossert calls a performance audit, which "looks for efficiencies and business results."[4] In a business assessment, the rules are challenged, but, according to Bossert, the underlying principles driving those rules are accepted and not challenged. Also, in a business assessment, assessors review both qualitative and quantitative information to gain an understanding of how the supplier runs its business and to get at the root causes of business issues. A business assessment review is focused less on the detailed quality processes of an audit and more on reviewing the deployment of overall business processes and practices, including enabling behaviors, as discussed in Chapter 2, such as continuous improvement, alignment, and agility.

Also, keep in mind that the term *audit* can be seen by the supplier as more intimidating. This book does not address how to conduct a supplier quality audit, which has been thoroughly covered in the quality literature, particularly by Bossert. An assessment looks at not just business results but the operational inputs that impact the business results. It's a forward-looking view more than a backward view. Also, a business assessment is typically done by a cross-functional team and led by procurement, supplier management, or supplier quality. A supplier audit is usually led by the quality function. (Of course, all of this can vary by company, but this describes the typical approach.) For instance, an example of an audit finding might be that the supplier's quality process is robust, well defined, repeatable, and produces product that is compliant with all contractual and supplier-established requirements and produces the required objective quality evidence to prove compliance to these requirements. A supplier assessment or performance audit result, on the other hand, might be that while the supplier's quality is adequate, the supplier is not working to continually improve its quality

---

3. Bossert, David L., *Supplier Management Handbook*, 1991, p. 4.

4. Bossert, David L., *Supplier Management Handbook*, 1991, p. 9.

processes. Audits are more compliance-oriented and are more common for manufacturing suppliers. Business assessments are more adaptable to different types of supplier businesses, such as service and technology. A business assessment is not better or worse than an audit. It just uses a different approach and has different objectives.

You must decide when a site visit is appropriate and cost-effective. Another consideration is cost. Suppliers within geographic proximity are less expensive to visit from a travel perspective, though from an employee time perspective there are still costs to site visits, but they are less visible. A company may be able to conduct site visits at a lower cost to closer suppliers and may be able to visit more of these suppliers, even if these suppliers do not fall in the critical or high-risk category. Cost also depends on how comprehensive a site visit is. One must weigh costs versus benefits. Whether to conduct a site visit is a decision that should be made by the key stakeholders involved in a sourcing decision (if the purpose of the site visit is for vetting new suppliers) or by the stakeholders responsible for different aspects of supplier performance and quality or who may be directly impacted by the supplier's product or service (for an existing supplier). This may include personnel such as: supply managers, end users, quality, engineering, manufacturing, finance, and lean experts.[5]

The prerequisites for a good site visit include a good, easy-to-use survey or site visit instrument, advance preparation, a well-trained site visit team, good advance communications with the supplier about what to expect, information about how they will be evaluated and the impact of the site visit results on supplier status, and effective post-visit follow-up plans and actions. In the next chapter, we will cover the "how-to" aspects of conducting a good site visit.

To yield the best results, site visit surveys, as in all other surveys, should be well constructed, based upon a robust business model and aligned with the customer's strategy and processes. The survey should be easy to use and flexible enough to accommodate small to larger suppliers. The survey should focus on need-to-know questions, not just nice-to-know. Surveys should remain as consistent from supplier to supplier as possible, as that will make it easier to compare results from year to year or among various suppliers. Also, consistency is much fairer to suppliers, especially when their future business and/or approval or certification status depends upon the site visit. While you want to continually improve the site visit survey, you should try as much as possible to keep it relatively stable in order to preserve comparison data. It is fine to add or delete questions, but frequently changing the overarching topics is not advised. There is also the issue of fairness among competing suppliers, a situation that argues for consistency. You

---

5. Flynn, Tim, "Conducting an Effective Supplier Site Visit," *Inside Supply Management*, October 2002, pp. 42–47.

do not want to make it easier for one supplier to gain approved status than its competitor due to a lack of consistency in the site visit approach and survey.

The site visit team should be well prepared for the visit. It is not a matter of grabbing a few people and telling them they are going to be industrial tourists at some supplier next week. Customer personnel should be prepared with some understanding of the supplier, the purpose of the visit, what their particular role is in the visit, and how they are going to deploy their part of the site visit survey instrument and record results. Site visit teams need to understand that they must be respectful of the supplier, even if they find irregularities or believe that some of the things that supplier does are inadvisable or, in their opinion, backward. On one supplier site visit I participated in, the owner/general manager was prone to making rather outrageous statements in front of the customer team. One of the statements was that he thought that his operators never had an improvement idea and never would have ideas to contribute in the future (as verified by paging the operations manager) and that their jobs could easily be done by trained monkeys. Of course, the site visit team was taken aback, but they maintained their professional demeanor. The company did not get high marks for leadership or employee participation, among other things.

When effective, supplier site visits can facilitate the collection of valuable information and the discovery of potential issues or problems. Site visits can help enable well-informed decisions and improve the overall relationship between customer and supplier firms. As in all survey approaches, the design of the survey instrument itself is critical, as are the relationships of the areas that are being measured to the customer performance expectations. A supplier site visit is an excellent way to gain a better understanding of a potential or current supplier's business beyond the obvious operational metrics such as corporate goals, culture, and management philosophies; understand its current performance; and gauge future performance. The customer team can see first-hand the supplier's business in action and gather information directly from that supplier.

Following are challenges of site visits:

- They can be resource-intensive and difficult to scale.
- If site visits are done without a good, robust, easy-to-use survey instrument, the results can be inconsistent, unusable, or irrelevant.
- You must have people with the knowledge and expertise to conduct a successful site visit. They must have knowledge of and the ability to recognize the business practices, processes, and issues they are looking for. And they must be able to see what's missing at the supplier as well as see through attempts to hide issues. This ability comes both with experience and training.
- Site visits must result in action and follow-up to ensure the return on investment in them.

SCORECARDS

Scorecards are probably the most common method of collecting and displaying supplier performance information. Supplier scorecards are widely used and preferred, since they can show many elements of performance at a glance. Since scorecards typically gather quantitative information, many think that they are a good way to focus on facts for decision making. Scorecards can be a good way to get insights into and manage supplier performance. The benefits of scorecards are that they help organize supplier evaluation data and they are quick and easy to use. Scorecards can be a powerful tool, particularly when scorecard data is displayed as graphs and charts to show time-based trends and is analyzed to show comparisons both with a supplier's previous scores and with other suppliers.

While scorecards may be easy to use, there are many challenges. The biggest challenges are as follows:

- What data or metrics should be on the scorecard?
- Where is the data going to come from?
- How accurate is the data?
- How is it going to be used?

In our discussions of sources for metrics, we discussed potential sources of scorecard data: internal business systems, stakeholders, and suppliers. We also discussed how metrics need to be derived specifically for a company, not copied from others. They need to relate to a company's business objectives and strategies or at least the overall business drivers of cost, quality, time, and technology. Metrics cannot readily be borrowed from others' scorecards, though it is possible that some metrics may be a fit, particularly if another company is in the same business or industry as your company. Figures 6.1, 6.2, and 6.3 show examples of scorecards. The first is in an Excel spreadsheet format. The second was generated within the Emptoris Supplier Performance Management application. The third was adapted from an Allstate scorecard.[6] In Figure 6.1, we see an example of both lagging and leading indicators. This example is not meant to be a guide to what measures should go on a scorecard, as it is full of lagging indicators as well as leading ones, but to illustrate format and the types of measures that some companies use.

Scorecard Case Study

Toro, a leading lawn care products company, illustrates a well-developed scorecard system. Toro has developed its performance system in-house and extracts data from over 25 sources, such as SAP ERP, MS Excel spreadsheets, Access Database,

---

6. Dunn, Christine, "How to Build a Vendor Scorecard," *Computerworld*, May 29, 2006.

Supplier Performance Indices			
	Goal	**Actual**	
Quality PPM	500		
Cost Reductions Submitted	5.00%		Goal missed by greater than 5%
Past-Due Corrective Actions	0		
Cycle Time	3 days		
Procurement Indices			
	Goal	**Actual**	
Supplier On-Time Delivery	97%		
Supplier PPM Quality	400		
Supplier Daily Past Dues	.5%		Goal missed by less than 5%
Purchase Price Variance	2%		
Days on Hand Purchase Inventory	20		
Past-Due Accounts Payable	$1,500,000		
Obsolete Purchased Inventory	$150,000		
Strategic Indices			
	Goal	**Actual**	
Implemented Cost Reductions	$175,000		
Turnover	1.2%		Goal attained
Efficiency Rate	100%		
Cost of Quality	24%		

Figure 6.1 Supplier performance scorecard.

third-party desktop software, and Dun & Bradstreet. It has taken them over 10 years to build this supplier performance system.

At the highest level, Toro tracks three key metrics and weights them in the following way: quality (50 percent), delivery performance (25 percent) and failure cost (25 percent). They use a total cost of ownership (TCO) ratio to determine the failure cost. Some of the components of the numerator of this ratio include quality failure cost, warranty failure cost, rework cost, cost of process rejection, line shutdown cost, cost for products on hold, shipping cost, and product cost. In the denominator is the purchasing cost. Delivery metrics include items such as number of on-time lots and late deliveries. This information feeds into scorecards that are common throughout the enterprise and are universally accessible. Suppliers may also log on to the system and review not only their own scores but the data of other suppliers in the same commodity. Key suppliers also receive a PDF file of their scorecards.

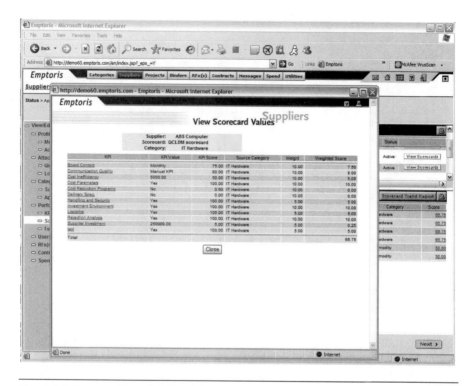

Figure 6.2 Scorecard from SPM module.

Toro tracks its strategic suppliers, which make up about 20 percent of its 1,000 total suppliers. Each buyer manages about 15 to 20 suppliers, residing in about 60 commodity groups. The scorecard process is as follows. First they compile the data, transform it using formulas, and then link it to scorecards. The data is compiled per supplier, per category, and per plant and rolled up to the enterprise level, which enables users to look across plants or drill down at the plant level and also enables senior management views of the information. Stakeholders within the company include management, suppliers, buyers, engineering, advanced quality, product development, plant quality, and service parts group.

Toro strives to collect data that it will take action on. If suppliers have good performance scores, they can earn more business and approved supplier status. Also, suppliers must earn good scores to take part in new product development business. Unsatisfactory performance scores can mean less business. They can also land a supplier on probation with the potential to lose its approved status. With poor performance, there is a corrective action process, which includes determining the root causes of problems, finding and implementing solutions, follow-up, and monitoring.

SUPPLIER PERFORMANCE SCORECARD

	Weighting	1 Does Not Meet	2 Barely Meets	3 Meets	4 Regularly & Consistently Meets	5 Exceeds Requirement	Score
Account Management Responsiveness	35%						
Supplier understands requirements					4		4
Supplier contact has product knowledge					4		4
Supplier communicates effectively		1					1
Supplier provides information on best practices					4		4
Average Score							3.3
Score based upon weighting							5.2
Customer Service and Delivery	25%						
Deliveries are prompt				3			3
Deliveries are complete				3			3
Product and/or service meets expectation					4		4
Supplier resolves issues appropriately					4		4
Supplier meets support commitments					4		4
Average Score							3.6
Score based upon weighting							3.7
Financial	20%						
Supplier provides best value products or services				3			3
Supplier proposals are accurate					4		4
Supplier invoices are accurate					4		4
Supplier strives to reduce costs					4		4
SCORE							3.8
Score based upon weighting							3.0
Relationship	20%						
Supplier strives to meet our requirements						5	5
Supplier willing to go the extra mile					4		4
Overall relationship with supplier is good					4		4
Would do business again with this supplier					4		4
SCORE							4.3
Score based upon weighting							3.0
Total Cumulative Weighted Score							14.9

Supplier: Q3: July 2007 - Sept 2007

How Well Supplier Meets Performance Requirement

Figure 6.3 SPM scorecard.

There are several interesting aspects to Toro's scorecard system. The system is closed-loop—the company collects, shares, and uses its performance information. However, it did not happen overnight. It has taken them over 10 years to develop the many data feeds and calculations in the system. Not every company has the resources to develop vast amounts of information from this many sources, even when the return on investment can be proven and is quite real. Not every company has this many sources of information to tap into.

Challenges of Scorecards

Scorecards can be an excellent way to capture supplier performance. However, there are many challenges and pitfalls.

- **Data collection can take on a life of its own.** You need to be careful that you are not spending more time collecting data than using it. A large printing company that has an elaborate scorecard system that is granular down to the machine feeds and speeds level has the full-time function of "data steward" to manage supplier performance data sources and data manipulation. Capturing large amounts of data requires resources and costs money. Don't lose sight of your ultimate objectives in collecting data and get into a "data for the sake of data" scorecarding process.

- **Relevance of the scorecard data collected.** Companies sometimes collect data because it is readily available, rather than because it is the most relevant and actionable information. This is because relevant and actionable information is not always easy to come by. If the axiom "you manage what you measure" is true, then you may end up managing the wrong things if you are basing scorecards on data that you can easily collect rather than on what you really need to understand and manage.

- **Data integrity.** One of the biggest challenges of scorecards is data integrity. Scorecards are only as reliable as the data that feeds them. When this data comes from internal business systems, the data may be flawed for several reasons. One reason is a lack of organizational discipline in data collection. If you depend upon stakeholders to fill out questionnaires about suppliers, the resulting information can get skewed if only those with complaints or those with high praise participate.

- **Data feeds from disparate systems.** Another problem is in the way metrics are calculated in multiple systems. In the case of companies with ERP systems, there may be multiple ERP systems due to mergers and acquisitions. Each may have its own idiosyncrasies and different ways of calculating the same metric. For example, incoming quality calculations might be based upon shipments or individual lots. Or on-time delivery may be a three-day window in one system and no window in another. Let's take the metrics around customer service calls. At one supplier, each call is counted as a separate incident, while at another, several calls concerning one incident count as one call. Thus, you can end up comparing apples to oranges or having completely unreliable data. If the data is considered unreliable, no one will use it. Yet another area of organizational discipline that can impact metrics and suppliers is whether the activities and interactions with suppliers that form the basis for the metrics are done in a timely and correct fashion. I have seen endless disputes between customers and suppliers regarding on-time delivery where the supplier's shipment sat on the customer's dock for days or even weeks before being entered into the system. This made the supplier appear late, even though it was clearly the customer's fault. Or, suppliers are deemed late with deliveries because the customer visited their business and prevailed upon them to change their order priorities at the last moment.

- **Data that needs cleansing.** As a result of the variations among the ways the same metric is calculated within the same company, data cleansing and recalculation may be necessary to equalize the metrics. This can be challenging and resource-intensive to cleanse and maintain the data.

- **Disputes with suppliers over data integrity.** Issues over data integrity can end up with suppliers disputing how they are being measured. If you are basing supplier decisions upon the metrics in scorecards, suppliers need to understand the basis for the calculations and have some comfort level that the data is correct. If the definition of late is plus-or-minus two days versus no days, suppliers need to understand this. In the area of quality, disputes and finger-pointing can arise over how parts per million (PPM) quality is calculated. I worked with one organization in the semiconductor industry that would spend days each month after getting a quality report card from its key customer trying to refute the calculations. They were trying to prove that some of the quality glitches reported were actually their customer's fault and not theirs and that the overall PPM defect rate was too high. Management would analyze, prepare for the customer meeting, argue with the customer about some of the bases of the PPM calculations, take a beating, and then go back to deal with the quality issues, only to repeat the same cycle the next month. Two issues were apparent.

One is that this exercise took too much time both at the customer and the supplier for too little payback and no systemic improvement. The other is that the supplier was not truly able to get at the root causes of the problems with the data on the report card. The efficacy of this system and the value of the scorecarding done this way are dubious.

- **Punitive use of scorecards.** Customer firms should not use scorecards as punishment for poor performance. This relates to the story just described. It is easy to beat up a supplier with poor scores on the scorecard. The ultimate purpose of the scorecard is to find opportunities for improvement, which also should not be treated as punishment for the supplier. Perhaps some of the reasons for poor scores lie with the customer firm. Or perhaps the supplier was not worth the resources required to do business with it and needed to be replaced rather than continually punished. The scorecard should help give insights into performance that enhance performance and the relationship, not lay the blame on the supplier. Or as the saying goes, fix the problem, not the blame.

- **Scorecards don't tell the whole story.** As the story above illustrates, scorecards don't always help a supplier get at the root causes of problems. They highlight areas for further investigation, but even these issues may be the symptoms and not the actual problems. The underlying causes of supplier problems can run deeper than the results on a scorecard can show. For example, a supplier whose scorecard is showing that its quality scores are declining may not find a quick fix to the problem. One electromechanical supplier in the aerospace industry was showing symptoms of problems. After several years of perfect quality metrics on its scorecard, it suddenly and unexpectedly to everyone experienced a very serious quality problem. The defective product was shipped to its customer, who caught the problem. The customer had a good relationship with this supplier, and had been asking the supplier to adopt lean principles and practices for several years. While the supplier had made some minor changes, it hadn't adopted lean on any scale and was mostly giving lip service to the request. Since nothing appeared really broken, nothing was fixed until the big quality glitch blindsided both customer and supplier. Upon further investigation by the customer, it was evident that the supplier was using inspection rather than prevention as a remedy for quality problems. The supplier was inspecting the product at the end of the process using inspectors, and this method worked well for the supplier in the early stages. As business ramped up because of the supplier's success, the ability of inspectors to catch all the problems was decreasing. Rework was becoming a cottage industry. Finally, the inspectors missed something important. The only symptom that the customer noticed, in retrospect, was that this supplier, who had been very competitive and winning lots of their business, was gradually winning less business because of price. This would not typically have set off alarms. But in analyzing the situation, the customer realized that their large batches and departmental approach to production was causing them to increase their cost structure as well as lose control over quality. The story has a happy ending. The supplier began to truly adopt lean and put preventive quality practices in place of the reactive ones. This story could be told as a lean success story rather than a scorecard failure story. But the point here is that scorecards did not give advance warning of the problems, nor did they give any inkling about the root causes. One could argue that not enough other data, such as leading indicators, was being collected to warn of potential problems. Another important lesson in this story is that the strength of the customer-supplier relationship helped salvage what might otherwise have provoked great business loss for the supplier, had the customer decided to disengage. Both customer and supplier were willing to work together to solve the problem, rather than the customer dumping the supplier at the first big problem or the supplier ignoring the warnings and continue doing things the way they had grown accustomed to doing them.

Start Small and Expand

Don't start by trying to create the ultimate scorecard and measure everything you always wanted to know about suppliers but were afraid to ask. Too many metrics on the scorecard become meaningless and confusing and do not lead to corrective action. The scorecard of a business systems and business process outsourcing company mushroomed to 80 different metrics, far too difficult and resource-intensive to create and far too many metrics to be meaningful or actionable. It's meaningful metrics that are important. Pilot the program with a few metrics and a small cadre of suppliers, refine the process, and expand the program gradually, in waves. Measuring suppliers takes resources. You want to work out the kinks and show results and success before expanding.

Scorecards cannot solve all supplier problems. Some companies believe or perhaps hope that scorecards will be the panacea for poor supplier performance. Scorecards can help provide insight, but they are just a tool and one part of the supplier performance management process.

CERTIFICATION TO THIRD-PARTY STANDARDS

Many companies wonder if certification to third-party standards can be a good evaluation approach or a measure of a supplier meeting recognized requirements. These standards may include ISO 9001, ISO 14001, ISO/TS 16949 (automotive version of ISO), AS 9000 (aerospace version of ISO), or SA 8000 (social accountability standard). Third-party standards can be a baseline or starting point, but can never substitute for ongoing supplier evaluation to specific company requirements.

ISO 9001 and its derivatives have been both praised and maligned. On the positive side, the ISO standard requires a review of business processes for the purposes of documenting them. Some companies use this as an opportunity to look at their processes and improve them. Also, ISO can be the seal of approval and entry ticket into many markets. For others, it is the baseline requirement to get in the game with certain customers who require it.

Many companies are registered to the ISO 9000 series of standards (ISO 9001, ISO 9002, and ISO 9003), and many also require ISO 9000 registration for their suppliers or consider it a positive factor. What is the evidence that ISO 9000 is a useful indicator of company quality and business performance?

Here are some of the issues:

- First, there is the standard itself. Many complain of its excessive documentation requirements and lack of senior management involvement. This can take the focus away from performance to documentation of procedures.
- The standard does not require a connection between internal standards and performance and external end-customer requirements or expectations. The standard is not specific to performance, processes and practices required by the customer firm.
- Conformance to procedures does not guarantee best practice deployment
- ISO 9000 has no requirement for a functioning continuous improvement system. However, the ISO 9000-2000 standard has enhanced this requirement.
- The registration is a binary, yes or no, process that may not reflect actual company performance.
- There are many companies that are registered, but we still have little understanding of how the performance of one registered company, even if the same size and type, compares to another.
- Many executives view ISO 9000 as a necessary hurdle, not a method for improving customer and shareholder value. This means that it is typically a "program" of the quality department and not seen as a broader business improvement model.

- Studies have not yet found a positive correlation between ISO 9000 registration and company performance in sales, profits, and quality.

However, one study has found an avoidance of a decline in return on assets for those companies who do not choose to pursue ISO. The special report "Does ISO 9000 Certification Pay?" concludes that relative "improvements in return on assets (ROA) does not necessarily translate into specific improvements that can be predicted and captured in such a cost-benefit analysis. This is exacerbated by the fact that the performance improvements are not absolute but relative, and contribute to maintaining, rather than improving, financial performance."[7]

What about ISO 9000:2000, the newer standard? This standard (in place since December 2000) represents a significant and positive change in direction. Key changes include requirements such as: focus on end-customer value, executive leadership involvement, continuous improvement, process management, simplified documentation, and stronger supply chain management. Time will tell how companies who become registered to this standard actually perform in the field.

ISO 9000 and its derivatives still remain a necessary entrée into global markets. However, most experts do not recommend it as a substitute for supplier evaluation to a customer's requirements or as the sole method to decide whether to approve or not approve suppliers. ISO 9000 certification is no guarantee of performance.

Another new international standard that has emerged is the SA-8000 standard for Social Accountability, known in many companies as corporate social responsibility. This is not a performance standard in the traditional sense. However, CSR has become an important global movement and is being required by a growing number of international companies. It falls under the category of ethical business practices and represents one piece of the overall picture of supplier evaluation.

THIRD-PARTY INFORMATION

Third-party information has a role to play in supplier evaluation. Some sources include Dun & Bradstreet, InfoUSA, and Hoovers. Another source is proprietary data providers, such as Open Ratings, a D&B company, who collects and analyzes a combination of public information (such as D&B information) and private information on suppliers, collected directly from suppliers by customers. This method, called predictive analytics, tries to predict supply risk, such as future

7. Corbett, Charles J., María J. Montes, David A. Kirsch, and María José Alvarez-Gil, "Does ISO 9000 Certification Pay?" *ISO Management Systems*, July–August 2002, pp. 31–40.

financial viability of suppliers, and alert users to potential supplier problems, such as bankruptcy, union strikes, and quality problems, before they occur.

Issues with Third-Party Information

Third-party information is a good source of information on financial risk, in particular. It is a part of the whole picture in supplier evaluation. The main issues with third-party information are chiefly accuracy and relevance:

- The information can be self-reported to parties with whom the supplier has no relationship and thus can contain inaccuracies.
- Suppliers may not report information to third parties accurately or honestly, fearing or knowing that this information is not confidential.
- Certain algorithms in the way the financial information is reported may be flawed and show conditions that are not accurate. For example, an emerging company may not be cash flow positive, yet it has investment funds available to it. The company may appear less stable than it actually is.
- Information is not always up-to-date.
- How a supplier performs for someone else may not be an indication of how that supplier will perform for your company. The customer-supplier relationship ingredient and the ability to add value can make a difference in performance.
- Financial information from third parties is a lagging rather than leading indicator. Information gathered in relation to your company's specific requirements may be a better indicator and predictor of desired and future performance. For example, if you are collecting information on quality, delivery performance, and cycle time and your supplier starts declining in these areas, financial risk around this supplier is highly likely to be increasing

As long as third-party information and proprietary databases are not the only source of supplier financial and performance information, they can give good insights into the overall supplier performance picture and serve a valuable purpose in mitigating risks.

SUMMARY OF EVALUATION APPROACHES

Table 6.1 summarizes the most common approaches to evaluating suppliers, along with their advantages and challenges.

Table 6.1 Summary of Evaluation Approaches

Method	Advantages	Challenges
Paper questionnaires (mailed or e-mailed documents)	• Can be easy to prepare with no technology involved	• Hard to construct sound information-gathering instruments • Requires knowledge of what to measure • Difficult to deploy • Suppliers procrastinate filling out
Web-based questionnaires (for either internal company surveys of suppliers or for suppliers to complete)	• Easy to deploy • Easier to tally results	• Requires resources to develop • Requires knowledge of what to measure • Compliance issues (internal and external)
Extract information from current systems	• Information already exists • Can use tools within the systems to extract data	• Data integrity • Requires cleansing, massaging, formatting • Issues when extracting from multiple systems/sources • Data integrity disputes with suppliers
Site visits	• "Seeing is believing" • Gain a good understanding of supplier	• Resource intense for both customer and supplier • Requires trained personnel • Can be inconsistent
Certification to third-party standards such as: ISO 9001:2000, ISO/TS 16949:2002, QS9001	• Recognized international standards • Supplier bears the burden of certification	• Conformance to procedures does not guarantee best practice deployment • Can take the focus away from performance to documentation of procedures • Not specific to performance, processes and practices required by the customer
Third-party information	• Access to additional data not available internally or from suppliers • Outside validation	• May not be accurate • May be difficult to determine what to react to

Web Added Value™

This book has free material available for download from the Web Added Value™ resource center at *www.jrosspub.com*

7

USING TECHNOLOGY FOR SUPPLIER EVALUATION

Technology can enable and scale supplier performance management. There are growing numbers of software solutions available to support supplier performance management as part of supplier relationship management. Overall, this software space is supplier relationship management, or SRM. Here are two definitions of SRM:

- The management of the flow of information between suppliers and purchasing organizations and the integration of supplier information in the procurement process by the buyer
- Evolving set of applications enabling enterprises to create a more comprehensive life cycle view of suppliers' operational contribution to the top and bottom lines

SPM, a subset of SRM solutions, can help collect information and track, analyze, and generally give insights into supplier performance. And it can help enable and scale processes that previously may have taken herds of software developers to create and/or armies of people to deploy. SRM solutions come in many varieties—standalone solutions, best of breed as part of sourcing and supply management software, part of a quality management application, and part of ERP (enterprise resource planning). In addition, the PLM (product lifecycle management) vendors are getting into the SRM arena. The companies in these spaces are continually changing, evolving, being acquired, merging, and so on, and the market is in flux. As a class of solutions, supplier performance management is relatively young and still an emerging area. Similarly, the whole practice of supplier performance management is in an earlier stage of adoption than are, for example, sourcing solutions. The purpose of the following discussion is to provide an understanding of the types of software tools and applications that are available for measuring and monitoring supplier performance. It is meant neither as a comprehensive guide nor a specific recommendation about particular solutions providers.

SPM STANDALONE SOLUTIONS

An example of a standalone solution provider is Open Ratings. Open Ratings draws from multiple information sources to help customers avoid supplier risk. These sources are used to provide alerts to customers about changes and risks in their supplier base. Some of these include events such as disasters, criminal proceedings, lawsuits, EPA violations and actions, and credit information. Open Ratings also gathers information from suppliers via assessments and questionnaires as well as performance information from other sources. Open Ratings is now part of Dun & Bradstreet. Another company, Xcitec, provides solutions in several aspects of supplier evaluation—supplier qualification, supplier rating, and supplier development—though it does not provide sourcing solutions. Another newer company is Hiperos, which offers relaionship and compliance management solutions primarily in the indirect supplier space.

Other standalone solutions have either been acquired or gone out of business: Valuedge, Intellimet, and Apexon. For example, Valuedge was acquired by Emptoris and its software integrated into Emptoris's application suite. Intellimet is no longer in business. And Apexon was acquired by Symphony Technology Group. This may indicate that SPM solutions can be more successful integrated into an SRM or full application suite and cannot survive as a standalone application. However, new SPM solutions continue to be introduced (such as The Performance Score and Alere Performance), and it remains to be seen whether these standalone solutions can thrive or survive as the market matures. This area is still the domain of early adopters and market leaders and is probably five years behind the rest of SRM applications.

SUPPLIER RELATIONSHIP MANAGEMENT AS PART OF SUPPLY MANAGEMENT SOLUTIONS

Software vendors focused on the procurement space, such as Emptoris, Ariba, and Verticalnet (now part of BravoSolution), provide SRM applications for sourcing, negotiations, spend analysis, and contract management. Supplier performance management is a natural and logical extension of these sourcing and supplier management platforms. These solutions not only address the issues of understanding supplier performance in the sourcing, qualification, and subsequent onboarding phase for suppliers but naturally extend to the management of current

Table 7.1 Supplier Performance Management Software Capabilities

Capability	Description
Supplier qualification	• Self-registration and qualification surveys
Supplier survey and assessment development and deployment	• Ability to create subjective (qualitative) and objective questions • Secure, electronic deployment • Cross-functional team can rate suppliers
Systematic collection of assessment results	• Results can readily be stored and analyzed • Transform results into KPIs and scorecards
Supplier classification	• Classify approval or certification status of supplier
Stakeholder satisfaction surveys	• Internal stakeholder or customer satisfaction surveys can be developed • Ability to allow feedback on suppliers without sending out a formal survey
Creating KPI formulas	• Create KPI calculations • Performance baselines and goals
Importing KPIs from other systems	• Readily import data from systems such as ERP or a data warehouse to use in scorecards
Rolling up KPIs to scorecards	• Flexibility to build supplier scorecards with KPIs
Sharing scores and results with suppliers within the system	• Suppliers can log on to the system to see their scorecards or assessment results and to keep information about themselves up-to-date
Trend analysis	• Performance tracking • Reporting to look at individual supplier performance scores, trends over time • Comparison of suppliers among each other, within commodities, among customer divisions, etc.
Alerts to supply managers or buyers regarding performance issues	• Alerts regarding performance issues • Notification when supplier falls below or exceeds goals or falls below baseline measures • Notification when supplier completes an evaluation • Notification of scheduled supplier evaluations
Supplier development	• Strengths and weaknesses identification • Potential for supplier development • Management and tracking of corrective action and continuous improvement plans

suppliers and provide tools for understanding ongoing supplier performance. Some of the capabilities or functions that supplier performance software can provide are summarized in Table 7.1.

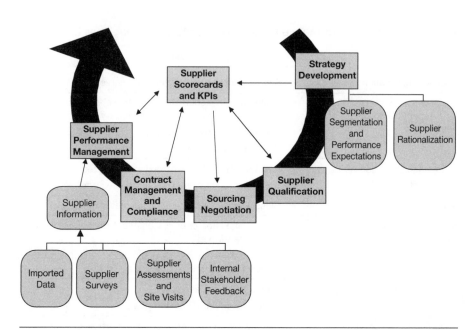

Figure 7.1 Supplier performance data in the procurement process life cycle.

SPM software functionality varies from vendor to vendor, but it typically measures performance through Web-based surveys or importing data from current systems, displays KPIs and scorecards and trend analysis, tracks performance, and sometimes provides supplier development tools, depending upon the vendor. SRM software vendors are quite willing to meet to discuss requirements and to provide a demonstration of their solutions. It is important to have as much clarity as possible on your business requirements, preferably in written form, before meeting with vendors to review software solutions. Also, several analyst firms such as AMR Research and Gartner Consulting publish reports, ratings, and analysis of SRM or SPM solutions.

An advantage of the integration of SPM into sourcing solution suites is the potential for linkage of supplier performance management information to other activities and decision making in the procurement life cycle. This integration gives a more holistic view of supplier performance. And the information and insights about supplier performance that are gleaned and also used at various steps in the procurement and supplier management cycle can enable better decision making about suppliers. Figure 7.1 illustrates how supplier performance data integrates with and is used in the procurement process life cycle. It shows the sources and uses of performance information within sourcing and supply management software applications.

The development of a procurement strategy sets the stage for supplier segmentation and the development of supplier performance expectations—both of which will influence the development of supplier performance KPIs and scorecards. Information for strategy development can be obtained by using analytical tools such as spend analysis. Spend analysis applications can be used to analyze and segment the supply base before developing supplier performance expectations and for figuring out whether the firm is spending money with high performers or low performers (once performance has been measured). During the sourcing process, supplier qualification information can be gathered using software applications for RFI functions. During a sourcing decision where incumbent or current suppliers are bidding, current performance information can be factored into the decision making. SLAs can be put into contracts in a contract management system and tracked in the supplier performance management system. Suppliers can be measured on an ongoing basis. With information from internal business systems, supplier surveys (internal and external), and supplier site visits, KPIs and scorecards can be developed. The SPM system can be used to identify supplier strengths and opportunities, identify supplier development projects, track development or continuous-improvement projects, identify good performers to recognize or reward and poor performers for probation or disengagement—all the types of activities that are being described in this book. The performance information, in turn, can be used to support various functions, as described, in the procurement cycle. Procurement can regularly review the scorecards to determine whether its strategies are being successfully executed and its supplier performance goals are being met.

Table 7.2 summarizes the business functions and software applications in an end-to-end enterprise supply management system and shows how this software can be used to execute the business functions in the procurement life cycle.

QUALITY MANAGEMENT AND COMPLIANCE SOFTWARE

Another category of software solutions that typically provides supplier performance management capabilities is quality management software. Some of the providers of these solutions include Metricstream, EduNeering, and Openpages. These solutions focus on managing the compliance process in mandated regulatory environments such as Sarbanes-Oxley and FDA regulations as well as compliance in initiative-based processes such as Six Sigma, ISO 9000, and supplier quality. In contrast to SRM or SPM software, software for managing supplier quality operates at transaction level and may include collecting and analyzing quality data, tracking quality issues, supplier corrective action request tracking and resolution, supplier chargeback process for nonconformance, supplier audit tracking, and supplier scorecards.

Table 7.2 Using Supplier Performance Information within the Procurement Life Cycle

Business Function	Software Application	Source or Use of Performance Information
Strategy development	• Use spend analytics software to help develop supply chain strategies	• Use for supply base segmentation • Use for Pareto analyses and supplier rationalization
Supplier qualification	• Gather information (RFI) on supplier characteristics during sourcing	• Capture performance characteristics from RFIs
Sourcing negotiations	• RFx • Sourcing optimization tools	• Factor performance of current suppliers into sourcing decision
Contract management and compliance	• Contract management software • Put SLAs in contracts	• Measure performance against SLAs for contract compliance • Create KPIs that correspond with SLAs
Supplier performance management	• SRM software • Supplier performance management software	• Use supplier performance data to manage suppliers • Make decisions in procurement and quality functions • Uncover risks and problems. • Develop mitigation and remediation plans • Identify supplier development projects • Track supplier improvement projects • Identify suppliers for recognition and rewards

Quality management and compliance software focuses at a more detailed level on quality processes than do procurement-oriented supplier performance systems, which have a broader coverage and support more of a balanced scorecard approach.[1] That is, the procurement-based supplier performance software can collect data from quality systems as one of its measurement areas, but it is not its sole focus. Also, quality management and compliance software is targeted at

---

1. The balanced scorecard approach, created and outlined in the book by Robert S. Kaplan and David P. Norton, *The Balanced Scorecard: Translating Strategy into Action*, balances measures of financial performance, internal operations, innovation and learning, and customer satisfaction.

manufacturing environments, not service companies. Procurement-based supplier performance software is part of supply management and sourcing suites and has been targeted largely at the procurement function, which is seen as the owner or facilitator of the supplier relationship in an organization, even though the role of quality is critical in that relationship. Procurement-based SPM is used not only by procurement but by people in functions such as supplier quality, procurement quality, and supplier management, which may reside in either procurement or quality. Quality-based systems target and are used largely by the quality function.

ERP-BASED SUPPLIER PERFORMANCE MANAGEMENT

The major ERP vendors such as Oracle and SAP have supplier performance management capabilities. They are typically contained in their SRM modules. These modules may include functions found in the application suites of the major enterprise supply management vendors (such as Emptoris and Ariba): strategic sourcing, operational procurement, contract management, supplier performance management, and spend analytics. Also included is e-procurement, which has so far been the most successful of the supplier management related software for ERP vendors, since it syncs so closely with their ERP offerings.

Since this area changes rapidly, it is not too useful to try to characterize any detailed offerings. ERP vendors continue to evolve their supply management, sourcing, and procurement offerings. SAP acquired Frictionless, a sourcing software vendor, in 2006 to gain more traction in this area. In general, the SRM offerings of the ERP vendors have stayed 18 months to two years behind the supply management providers of supplier application suites, who focus solely on them. This situation may change with the acquisition of niche vendors. In the area of supplier performance management in particular, the ERP vendors have had supplier scorecard capabilities apart from and before they got into the SRM area.

Depending on specific needs, the ERP vendors do provide SRM solutions. However, one should look at their functionality, cost, and ease of deployment as compared with supply management and standalone SPM vendors. Since we are specifically discussing the supplier performance management capabilities of these SRM solutions, companies should understand and review their specific supplier performance management requirements and understand the evaluation strategies and approaches they would like to use before jumping into the software realm.

SUMMARY

The advantage of using technology as part of managing supplier performance is its ability to scale the evaluation process in a way that is not possible through more manual, resource-intensive means. When well deployed, software can give you the tools to do more with less. An investment in these software tools has a quick payback period, less than a year when properly implemented. The ways that these systems achieve ROI is by reaching a greater portion of your suppliers and giving you actionable insights into these suppliers that help you in the areas previously mentioned: avoid risks or catastrophic events, identify improvement opportunities that save time and money, and eliminate cost drivers (and poor-performing suppliers) that add cost to both your company and to your suppliers and damage market competitiveness.

The key point to keep in mind about SRM solutions is that a company must have both a means of deriving meaningful metrics and a closed-loop, sustainable supplier performance management process in order to gain maximum benefit from a software solution. These capabilities can be developed and do not have to be in place immediately, but the management support needs to be there in order to be successful. Software is an enabling technology that is part of the solution. One approach is to drive the implementation of SPM by buying the software and using consulting experts to support SPM planning and implementation, specifically from a business perspective. Should you decide to go this route, it is important to understand the types of skills that are needed to help you implement SPM. Expertise in how to use the software is the easiest aspect of an SPM implementation. Here is some the expertise that is needed:

- Understanding of the SPM process and how to develop an SPM process that can be successful in your environment
- Change management skills
- Understanding of best practices in order to develop supplier performance expectations and meaningful performance management metrics
- Continuous-improvement methodologies
- Communications skills
- Organizational management skills
- Ability to work successfully with stakeholders with many agendas
- Supplier management and development knowledge

Information technology (IT) solutions today have many capabilities to track and manage supplier performance and supplier development. It is important to create the process and roadmap of where your company wants to go and how you're going to get there before getting into the details of choosing technology solutions. These enabling technologies are made successful by good business processes and will not provide an answer in themselves. Supplier performance management systems are simply an empty shell that needs to be filled with meaningful information supported by good strategies and processes.

8

DESIGNING THE PROCESS

DESIGNING THE SUPPLIER PERFORMANCE MANAGEMENT PROCESS

Supplier evaluation has the greatest chance for success when it is done within a purposefully designed process. Many companies may write policies and procedures, but do not actively consider designing and improving business processes, even as business needs change and evolve. Processes often happen by chance rather than by design. Companies may continue with the current process and bolt on the new one. When implementing software to scale or improve a process, many companies focus on implementing the software as the goal more than designing or redesigning the process that the software is intended to support. When implementing a new supplier survey or a new software application for supplier performance, companies sometimes focus on training a power user in the group to take care of most questions and problems, rather than having the people who work with the suppliers learn the software and the new process. They may neglect to address the actual business process that the software is supposed to support. One medium-size company that I worked with was using supplier surveys, but almost no one at the facility knew about them, including many of the staff in the purchasing and quality departments. They had developed the surveys, but did not drive adoption in the organization with a real process to implement them and use the survey results. Needless to say, they were not getting much in the way of results, as there was no defined process or communications and the supplier assessments were still pretty much a secret. If managing supplier performance has been tangential or an area that either has had little focus or was not optimally deployed, then creating a robust process to manage supplier performance is especially imperative.

Understanding how the supplier performance management process is currently done in your company can be a good step toward creating a new process and designing the future state. Starting with a common understanding of the current state, involving current and potential stakeholders in this new process design is important. If your company is more or less at the greenfield stage, never truly having developed a real or official process, then you will need to identify important stakeholders and get them involved in designing the new process. Observing and understanding the current state is the first step in understanding how to improve it. A good way to do this is to create a process map of the current state to give the stakeholders a common understanding and starting point for the project. For many companies, seeing a visual of current processes helps highlight the inefficiency and waste in those processes and will help them improve.

A current state map can help the project team gain a common understanding of how the supplier performance management process works today and will provide insights in how to improve the process. With the advent and adoption of lean enterprise concepts, many manufacturing companies in particular have become accustomed to creating and using value stream maps and process maps as process improvement tools. But many companies do not have the time, expertise, or inclination to make the effort to create process maps, particularly of administrative processes. By spending a few hours to a day in a conference room, a team composed of key stakeholders and functions involved in the SPM process would be able to come up with a current state process map. The mapping exercise could help them gain a clearer picture and common understanding of their organization's current supplier performance management process.

Figure 8.1 illustrates a business process map of a supplier certification process. Figure 8.2 shows an example of a value stream map. Value stream mapping highlights not only the process but quantifies the non-value-added activities in terms of wasted time and materials.

Components of SPM Business Process

So far we have discussed important steps in developing a supplier performance management process including choosing the team and creating the project organizational structure; creating the SPM plan; developing evaluation strategies; determining supplier performance expectations and measurement criteria; and choosing evaluation approaches, methods, and tools. Once a company has gone through these steps, the foundation is in place for envisioning and designing the future SPM process. At this point, all aspects of the future supplier performance

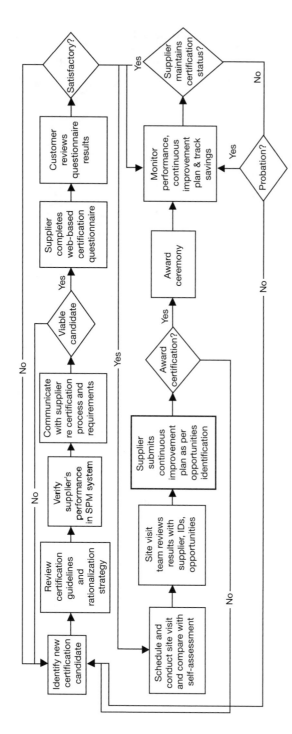

Figure 8.1 Supplier certification process.

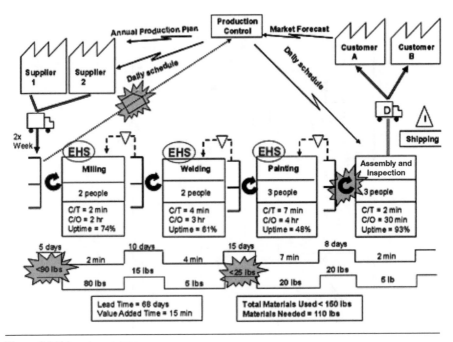

Figure 8.2 Value stream map.

management process will need to be made concrete, specific, detailed, and, preferably, documented. These areas may include:

- Roles and responsibilities, during SPM development and implementation as well as ongoing in the new process
- Categories of evaluation such as approved suppliers, preferred suppliers, and certified suppliers
- Eligibility requirements for evaluation categories
- Criteria for choosing evaluation candidates for each category of evaluation
- Performance expectations and standards
- Performance and process management evaluation criteria and measurements
- Tools for measuring and monitoring performance, such as surveys, information systems, and scorecards
- Approval criteria for current and future suppliers
- Rules for disengagement, such as probationary periods, losing approval status, decertification, and so on
- Goal setting with suppliers

- Performance feedback mechanisms, such as using supplier portals and periodic performance review meetings
- Corrective actions and continuous-improvement expectations
- Risk mitigation expectations
- Recognition, including awards
- Rewards and business opportunities, such as creating expectations about how good performers can obtain long-term contracts and future business
- Periodic review of SPM process

The preceding list shows the building blocks of a supplier performance management process. These topics can also be the basis for documenting the new process. Again using a process map or flowchart of the new or to be process is useful in visualizing, building, and communicating the new process and making sure that it is robust.

Whether a company's process consists of a small scorecard or a suite of evaluation tools, specifically designing the "to be" process, documenting it, and communicating it to internal and external stakeholders will help ensure success.

CREATING SURVEYS

This book has discussed using surveys to gather information from internal stakeholders and suppliers and scorecards to compile metrics gleaned from various sources. Since so many companies rely on surveys to gather information, this section will discuss how to design a good survey instrument. With companies increasingly relying on the results of surveys and questionnaires for supply management, they want to collect information that is accurate, timely, and relevant. A good survey instrument is essential. As mentioned previously, many people think they are good at survey design. With the advent of the Internet age, e-mail, word processing software, online survey tools, and flexible survey tools found in SPM software are readily available, and supplier surveys are usually a do-it-yourself endeavor. If your firm is going to be basing business relationships and the awarding of business on information gathered from surveys, then you should ensure that they are well constructed to obtain the information that is needed. Many problems with the validity and analysis of information can be traced back to the design of the survey.

CONSIDERATIONS FOR DESIGNING SUPPLIER SURVEYS

Be Clear about How the Results Are Going to Be Used

In designing the survey, you need to be unambiguous regarding your goals about what information you need to know and why you need to know it. That is, what are you going to do with the information once you collect it? For example, if you ask a supplier whether they want to talk to their procurement agent more often, less often, or the same, how would you actually use that information? Are you going to look at each supplier and try to calculate how often their purchasing person should contact them? Another example is parts per million defects. If you ask a supplier for their PPMs, are you going to give them the formula for the way you calculate it? What if they calculate PPM a different way? Will you require them to use your formula? What if they don't collect their data in a way where they can calculate it your way? And once you do know their PPM, how will you use the information? Will you set a baseline level of PPM below which their score would count against them or they would lose your business? Or would you offer the supplier help in raising their PPM score? If yes, under what circumstances? These are the types of issues to consider when asking for information.

Be Specific about Calculations

If you are going to be performing calculations on the data that you collect, you need to be very granular and specify the calculations and formulas up front. Examples of this are in how to deal with missing data. If respondents leave questions blank, will the zero be averaged in the results or will it not count against them? Another example is calculating on-time delivery. Does every site in your organization calculate it the same way? Is there a window of time or must the supplier get their delivery to the customer precisely on the expected date? Another example is how to handle the results of asking yes-or-no questions. Are you going to add up the yes's and no's? Or will yes equal 100 percent (or 5 on a scale of 1 to 5) and no equal to zero? Because of this "all or nothing" scoring dilemma, you need to consider whether you will use yes-or-no questions and also how to figure yes-or-no question scores into your results, and how to use the results.

Write Good Questions—How To

There are several techniques for writing good questions and avoiding asking poor questions:

1. *Ask for one piece of information at a time.* Do not ask "two-fer" or "three-fer" questions, as they are too ambiguous. For example, suppose

you ask a yes-or-no question such as "Does your proposal review process include a detailed review of customer contractual and technical requirements?" This question asks two things. If the supplier does not do a detailed review of the contractual requirements but does review the technical requirements in detail, then they can't give you a good answer to the question. "No" means they do neither, which would not be correct. Or take the question, "Do you exchange order, technical, and delivery data with your suppliers electronically?" This question may sound logical on the surface. Upon closer examination, however, you'll note that it asks for many pieces of information and it is impossible to respond accurately unless it's all or nothing. If the supplier exchanges order data but not the other data, yet doesn't do it electronically, how should they answer? Even if ambiguous questions are asked in person, either by phone or during a site visit where they can be clarified, there is still the problem of scoring the answer, since you would still need to enter just one response for one question. While it seems obvious that questions should not be so ambiguous, it is an extremely common occurrence.

2. *Multiple-choice questions should allow for all possible answers.* Otherwise, the respondent will be stymied if the answer he or she is looking for is not on the list or if the question is not applicable to him or her in the first place. Here is an example:

   Our production and office teams working on lean have the following data readily available:
   a. Production efficiency
   b. Inventory levels
   c. Set-up times
   d. Cycle time
   e. Scrap
   f. Non-value-added time

   In this case, the list is not all-inclusive and will not be completely relevant to someone on an office team. If you allow multiple responses, then you may have issues in scoring and tallying responses.

3. *Be cautious in making assumptions about respondents.* Surveys or questionnaires should not presume that a respondent has specific tools or processes in place. For example, suppose you ask a supplier the question:

   Which method do you use to qualify your suppliers before adding them to your approved supplier list (ASL)?
   a. Surveys
   b. Site visits

      c. ISO 9001
      d. Other

What if they don't have an ASL approval process? What if the supplier does not have an ASL? If they answer "other," they are implying an ASL process, which may not be the case. If they answer "other" and you want to know what that is by offering them a blank to fill in, you are then faced with the challenge of tabulating the responses of open-ended questions. Bottom line: First think about whether the question is applicable to and answerable for all suppliers with the wording and choices given. One way to solve this problem is to offer the choice of "Do not have an ASL." Or you can ask qualifying questions first, like "Do you have an approved supplier list?" Even then, they may have it but not use it. So you may need to ask, "Do you use suppliers only from your approved vendor list?" Then you can ask them about the methods they use to qualify suppliers. If they use suppliers both on and off the list, then the issue of how they qualify the suppliers becomes irrelevant in the questionnaire because the ASL is apparently not important to that supplier.

4. *Questions should have mutually exclusive answers from which to choose.* For example:

    Do you have a product development strategy that is
      a. Documented
      b. Informal
      c. Formal
      d. Understood by senior management

If the product development strategy is formal, it may also be documented. And it may be informal and still understood by senior management.

5. *The questions should produce variability of responses.* When no variability occurs in responses, why we asked the question and what we learned from the responses are uncertain. Plus, one cannot perform any statistical analyses on the responses. Here is an example of a question that will not produce variability of response:

    Are the following lean enterprise principles and practices part of your plan? (Yes or No)

      or

    Do you have risk mitigation plans? (Yes or No)

Most suppliers are going to answer yes, especially if they are aware that that is what you, their customer, expects. So it may be pointless to ask the question. You must be far more granular in these types of questions.

6. *The question topics should flow, rather than jump all over.* It is confusing to be asking about quality processes in one question and contract management in the next. It is more comfortable for the respondent to see a flow or logical groups of different topics. It accommodates the most respondents' thought processes and increases responses and completions.

7. *A supplier survey should require little or no research.* The problem with having to do research is that the respondent may not have the time to do the research or may not even know where to find out the answers to survey questions easily. This can reduce survey compliance. It also encourages guessing, which tends to be inaccurate.

8. *Give questions to respondents who will be likely to know the answer.* Asking procurement personnel detailed questions about product development and asking engineering questions about inventory frustrates the respondents and makes them less likely to comply. Since questions on a supplier site visit are usually function-specific, structure a supplier survey so that it can be easily completed by the knowledgeable functions. You can include the option of "don't know" in case the respondent can't answer the question, which in itself is revealing about communications and employee participation and involvement at the supplier. Of course, there are many questions that most respondents at the supplier will or should know. And answering "don't know" can be revealing when one would expect the respondent to know the answer. For example, most respondents should be able to answer questions about customer focus. It pays to be careful about asking the right questions of the right people.

9. *Try to keep questions free of buzzwords, internal jargon, and acronyms.* For example, if you want to use lean terminology in your questions, try to make them understandable without using lean buzzwords. The term "5S" can be referred to as "workplace organization." Or, if you want to use a lean term or a Six Sigma term, be sure to define the term clearly and in layperson's terms, either in a glossary or in a footnote. Your supplier could be doing variation reduction without a full-blown Six Sigma program or workplace organization without 5S. Also, not everyone interprets every term in the same way. Some companies, for example, see lean exclusively as creating work cells on the shop floor. One company that I visited claimed to be deploying

lean "because a while back they got a university professor to put in some work cells." Or at least that is how they attempted to raise their score. So definitions of terms help put customers and suppliers on the same page.

10. *Use simple, clear, and action-oriented sentence structures.* Keeping question sentences in the active voice as much as possible helps ensure clarity. For example, it is better to ask, "Does your company provide your suppliers with timely feedback on their performance?" rather than, "Is timely feedback on performance provided to your suppliers?" Better: "Does your company develop contingency plans for disasters?" Worse: "Are contingency plans developed for disasters?"

11. *When using a Likert scale, keep the scales consistent.* Don't mix response scales in the same survey. Avoid phrasing scaled response questions so that an undesired response scores high on a scale rather than low, especially when the higher number is used to indicate a better score. It can be confusing, particularly when most questions are phrased to elicit a high number for good (i.e., 5) and a low number for bad (i.e., 1). For example, do not ask someone to rate on a 1 to 5 scale a question such as, "Our company changes the schedule of work already released for production to suppliers." The higher the number, in this case, the less desirable the response. This will confuse the calculations. Better phrasing would be, "Our company strives to keep the schedule of work already released to suppliers for production stable." The most important thing is consistency of the scales.

12. *Give the respondent the opportunity to make comments.* Comments, while not part of scoring, are a very rich source of information. In my experience, even with opportunities to make comments, many respondents will not take the time to do so in a supplier survey. Those that do make comments provide valuable insights.

13. *Use response choices to questions that are as clear and unambiguous as possible.* Avoid response choices to questions such as "most," "the majority," and "least." If you want the respondent to make a judgment about order of magnitude or amount, use statements requiring a scaled response.

14. *Be cautious about using branching questions, as they can confuse the respondent.* A branching question directs the respondent to different places in a questionnaire depending upon his or her response to the current question. If you are using software to deploy the questionnaire, are on a site visit, or using the questionnaire over the tele-

phone, then branching will not be a problem. Otherwise, respondents may get confused about what questions they are supposed to skip and which they are expected to answer. An exception is electronic or Web-based questionnaires designed to handle branching.

Ensuring Survey Compliance

The first principle of getting a good response rate is having a survey or questionnaire that is easy to respond to, as just discussed in the section on writing good questions. Long, written surveys sent through the mail or as attachments to an e-mail are the hardest to obtain a good response from. And, from the customer side, they are more work to analyze, since the responses will need to be input into some type of software for analysis. The length of a survey may be less of a factor in getting good response when done via the Web because of its convenience and flexibility. In the case of suppliers knowing that responding to a Web-based survey might shorten or reduce the need for a site visit, they will be motivated to complete it regardless of length. Also, questions can be broken up visually, which helps the respondent get through them more readily. Allowing the respondent to complete the survey in several sittings at his or her convenience rather than all at once helps the respondent fit responding into a busy week and makes completing a longer survey less of a project. The respondent could log on at convenient times and be taken to the point in the survey where they left off. Knowing approximately how far along in the survey a respondent is and how much there is to go helps promote completion. In the Emptoris Supplier Assessment application, for example, respondents see a display at the bottom of each screen that gives them a visual indicator of how much they have completed and how much of the survey remains.

Other ways to ensure questionnaire completion compliance include deadline strategies, communications, follow-up, and incentives. One would use different approaches depending upon whether the respondent was from the supplier organization or whether the respondent is an internal stakeholder in your company.

Following are hints for ensuring compliance:

1. *Set deadlines.* While there is never a perfect time to send out a supplier survey, there are some decidedly less than optimal times. For example, avoid the last week in the month or the last week in a quarter, as most companies are under deadline pressures at those times. When sending out a survey, no matter whether it is internal or external, always set a due date. Make the due date approximately two weeks from the time that the respondents should receive the survey. Give them less time for a very short survey or just a few questions (internal stakeholders). In my experience, I have found that you

need to give respondents enough time to complete a survey, but not so much time that they procrastinate.

2. *Communicate in advance about surveys.* You may be able to schedule surveys at more convenient times for suppliers this way. And, informing people in advance is not only respectful, but it can also help them better understand why completing the survey is important and "WIIFM"(what's in it for me) rather than just sending out an unexpected surprise. For internal stakeholders, you will be continually communicating about SPM and the importance of internal feedback on suppliers, which will help internal response compliance.

3. *Follow-up is essential.* If you have multiple respondents within one company, which is the case in a software-driven supplier assessment and also in larger organizations, you should designate a focal point for the supplier survey who is responsible for ensuring respondent completion. This person can manage the survey at his or her company and be responsible for follow-up with individual respondents. In any case, there will always be respondents who need to be reminded. E-mail is probably the most efficient and effective route, more so than phone calls. You can make the written case for getting it done in a professional manner, and it will sit in the person's e-mail folder as a reminder. Voice mail is a more transient reminder. Plus, leaving long-winded voice mails is less effective than the number of words that can be put in an e-mail without being overbearing or time-consuming, since the recipient can skim the e-mail.

4. *Consider incentives for survey completion, if appropriate.* Internal stakeholders, in particular, may pose the biggest challenge for completing supplier surveys and ratings. While communications about the importance to the company and the benefits of giving supplier feedback are essential in any SPM program requiring such feedback, you don't want to have the feedback skewed toward those who are motivated by complaints. It is better to have a cross section of feedback rather than just the extremes. For internal stakeholders, incentives can be for nominal prizes, such as drawings for dinners or gift certificates—whatever is appropriate in your culture. As for suppliers, there is little to no need for incentives if your SPM program is well-constructed and suppliers see a clear purpose and business incentive for responding to surveys. In fact, offering completion incentives to suppliers may be seen as pushing ethics boundaries.

In summary, getting full compliance on surveys is very important for a successful SPM program, as it is important to have as much information as possible on which to base decisions. Also, compliance reinforces stakeholder buy-in into and support of the SPM process.

Cheating

Measures must be taken to discourage supplier cheating or misrepresentation of capabilities or performance. A supplier views surveys as having high stakes—or at least having some important impact on the relationship or business. And most suppliers naturally want to show themselves in the best possible light. Sometimes a supplier's lack of self-knowledge or knowledge of the information being requested by the customer gets reflected as good performance and capabilities in a survey. That is, the supplier firm is unaware of what it doesn't know and thinks that it is either deploying practices that it is really not or deploying them better than it actually is. Or the supplier may misunderstand what the customer means by particular practices and processes it is looking for or misinterpret the customer's terminology. This may cause "grade inflation." Familiarity with your suppliers will help you readily spot this type of problem. The customer can adjust the results to reflect reality, after first discussing this matter and coming to an understanding with the supplier. Also, a site visit can help both parties recalibrate expectations and results.

However, a small percentage of suppliers will truly try to cheat and answer questions dishonestly in order to look better than they actually are. Misrepresentation can be more of a problem with new suppliers, particularly those who are physically and culturally far from the customer. Misrepresentation of capabilities is a particular issue now with global supply chains and varying cultures. In some cultures, such as in China, a company will be reluctant to report less than optimal information about itself. Potential misrepresentation can be dealt with in several ways:

- In communicating with suppliers about surveys, make a straightforward statement about answering surveys honestly and supplying information that is accurate to the best of their knowledge. You can state that misrepresenting information about their company can result in loss of business.
- Make sure that the responses on your survey instruments can be tested for consistency of answers.
- If you collect operational data on supplier performance, check for consistency with supplier survey results. Quality data should be consistent with quality practices.
- Make it clear that misrepresentation of information will be uncovered and will jeopardize the relationship.

Misrepresentation is a nuisance. It is easy to spot and must be dealt with promptly and directly.

CREATING SCORECARDS

We have discussed the sources of information for scorecards and the pros and cons of using them as a measurement tool. Many organizations choose the KPIs either from looking at what other companies are measuring or from readily available data in their own company. In this section, we will cover a basic process for developing scorecards so that the measures are both aligned with your company's organizational goals and strategies and are actionable.

In Chapter 2 we discussed policy deployment—developing a corporate strategy and flowing it down to the tactical level so that all activities are in alignment. This text assumes that your company has overall strategies and objectives from which measures can be developed, or if not formal strategies, at least informal strategies that can be presumed. Much has been written about how to develop strategies and create strategy maps and will not be covered here. We will focus only on those strategies related to supplier performance that will need to be turned into measures and improvement targets. Lean will be used as an example of a strategy. Here is a description of the process.

Step One: Derive Supplier Measures from Your Supply Management or Procurement Strategy

Figure 8.3 shows a schema for deriving supplier measures or KPIs from corporate strategy. From a statement of corporate strategy, the supply management or procurement strategy is derived or flowed down. In this example, the lean objective is to eliminate waste caused by supplier quality problems. The next step is to outline the objective or objectives for achieving the supply management strategy. Next is the measure, or how success in achieving the strategy will be tracked or what needs to be measured. Then a target for the measure is set. That is, the level of performance or rate of improvement needed to achieve the objective. And finally, there should be a program in place or an action that needs to occur to achieve the objective.

This is where action is specified and linked through the measure up through the objective and strategy. In the case of supply management, the buying company cannot improve supplier quality defects alone, other than possibly through supplier development projects. Operational and other improvements at the supplier are their own responsibility. Supplier action to improve in a particular measurement dimension comes from within, but pressure, motivation, or incentives can be applied from the buy side. In defining metrics, keep in mind the real purpose of the

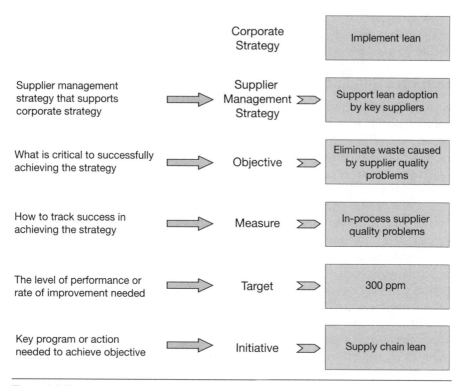

Figure 8.3 From corporate strategy to supply chain initiative.

metric and what problem you are trying to prevent or solve. Supplier measures should relate to customer objectives. In the case of lean, it would be unusual to apply lean metrics to suppliers if the customer was not deploying lean within its own organization, although I have occasionally seen customer firms that expect lean practices at their suppliers that their firm has not yet fully implemented. Many supplier performance metrics can fall under actions or initiatives such as a supplier performance improvement initiative or under customer satisfaction activities.

The point is that measures cannot exist in a vacuum unrelated to strategies and objectives and with no action to back them up. Initiatives typically

- Are sponsored by a leader or executive in the organization
- Require resources or investments in people, funding, and/or technology
- Have designated owners
- Include deliverables or milestones
- Have time parameters or deadlines
- Help enable deployment of your objectives

While measures can be collected apart from activities and initiatives, disconnected or standalone measurements may become pointless or without any clout, as the likelihood of taking action will be slim to none.

Step Two: Structure the Scorecard

Next, you will need to create a scorecard with measures or KPIs, making sure that the components are aligned in order to drive execution of the strategies. Table 8.1 illustrates this method of constructing the scorecard for one goal, achieving full supplier compliance to contracts.

From this are three objectives. One is to increase contract compliance in the area of price—making sure that the customer receives the actual negotiated price. The second is putting specific service level agreements in the contracts. And the last is tracking the SLAs that are put into the contracts. In the actual scorecard, the goal might be the contract compliance scorecard, and the KPIs could be the measurements.

Some scorecards show top-level elements or topics, under which there are various KPIs. Let us take, for example, the following performance areas: financial stability, business performance, delivery, quality management, and technology. Each of these performance areas would break down into different subcategories of performance. But each of these areas is not of equal importance. Perhaps quality, delivery, and technology are more important than the others. This is where weighting should be used to reflect the relative importance of difference performance metrics. Within a particular item on a scorecard, the KPIs that it consists of can be weighted as well. For example, within business performance, the KPIs of compliance to contract and cost reduction efforts may be more important than the KPI of communicating timely information on changes and should be weighted accordingly. Weighting can increase the complexity of the scorecard computations. At the beginning of scorecard development, it may be better to keep weighting simple and confined to the top-level scorecard or not use it initially until the scorecards have been field-tested and/or the SPM process is normalized and stable.

Step Three: Measure the Impact of the Scorecard

After scorecard measurements are put in place, you need to review the results regularly and over time and determine the following:

- To what extent your suppliers are enabling you to meet your objectives
- How far along are your suppliers in reaching the goals that you have mutually set

Scorecards should help you make decisions. Depending upon the results, you may need to rethink some of your approaches for reaching your goals. If performance

Table 8.1 Align Scorecard Components

Goal ➡	Objective ➡	Measurement ➡	Target ➡	Initiative
Achieve full supplier compliance to contracts	Increase supplier contract compliance by 50% over the next three years	Invoice price/ purchase order price	7%—Year 1 10%—Year 2 13%—Year 3	New contract management system
	Put SLAs into all key supplier contracts over three years	Number of key supplier contracts with SLAs	80%—Year 1 90%—Year 2 100%—Year 3	New contract management system
	Measure performance for SLA metrics	Metric #1 On-time delivery (percentage of shipments delivered on promise date)	95%	Supplier performance initiative

results drop, you will need to figure out the root cause or possibly recalibrate your metrics. Perhaps the contracts department has fallen behind in implementing the new contract management system. Or the only trackable SLAs for which your company has data and that you were able to put into the contracts are not producing the anticipated levels of internal customer satisfaction. Reviewing the extent to which you have met the objectives in your plan will help you figure out what else you or your suppliers need to do and will help uncover missing performance indicators or, as objectives evolve, develop new performance expectations. It is a continuous-improvement process.

CONDUCTING SUPPLIER SITE VISITS

Supplier site visits are a good way to verify or validate insights and information about suppliers obtained from other sources such as performance data from internal systems and supplier surveys. They help you gain insights into the ways suppliers run their businesses that are otherwise difficult to obtain. Since site visits require an expenditure of resources, they should be conducted with suppliers with whom a company wishes to uncover cost drivers and reduce costs, increase the value added by the relationship, or develop new products or services. Another reason for conducting a site visit is to narrow the field of contenders to make a final supplier selection. Site visits need to have clear objectives and follow-up actions.

HOW TO CONDUCT A GOOD SITE VISIT

Site visits require preparation in the following areas:

Select the Right Suppliers

Selection criteria for choosing suppliers to site-visit were covered in Chapter 4 in the discussion about the site visit as an evaluation strategy. But to summarize briefly, the typical reasons suppliers are selected for site visits is because of a high level of spend with the supplier, the supplier is a critical source of supply, or the supplier is a limited source of supply for a particular item. Collaborative product development suppliers are also targets for site visits because of their strategic importance to a customer firm. Typically companies use site visits with current suppliers, but this method is also used to qualify a new supplier who is supplying a product or service that currently is or expected to be important to the company.

Develop and Use a Good Site Visit Instrument

The quality and usefulness of the results depend largely on what information you gain from the site visit. And the information you gain from a site visit depends heavily on what types of information you ask for, how you ask for it, and how it's used. Site visits should not be impromptu, free-form, or inconsistent outings. The principles outlined in the section on survey and scorecard development apply to site visit instruments. The extent to which the questions on the site visit instrument are linked to your organization's established goals and objectives will make site visits productive tools that give meaningful insights and produce actionable results.

Select and Prepare the Site Visit Team

When you are clear on the goals of a site visit, you can then staff the site visit accordingly. Some site visits, such as those that address specific issues such as quality, may have a smaller scope and may not require a team. But for many site visits, you are trying to get information from multiple functions at the supplier firm. Or, the company's investment in a particular supplier and scope of the visit may be large enough to warrant a multifunction team. This means that your team may need to be knowledgeable about multiple areas such as quality, finance, engineering, and/or high-performance systems such as lean or Six Sigma. You may need to use either experts in particular functional areas or people with multifunction expertise. Just make sure that you are clear on the site visit objectives and requirements and have the right resources lined up. And give these resources sufficient advance notice about the supplier, the site visit purpose and details. If you do use a multifunction site visit team, you must be careful not to have each team member so focused on their area of expertise that they miss the big picture at the suppliers or have turf battles among themselves about whose area something really is. For example, people in the quality function may think that the world revolves around quality, and people in financial functions may have a financial audit mind-set. Regrouping periodically as a team during the site visit and reviewing findings and issues together helps look at the overall business processes at the supplier and helps overcome the tendency toward a stovepipe or functional approach—or what I like to call the blind man and the elephant approach. That is, depending on what part of the elephant you're looking at, you think it's a different beast.

However, just because someone has expertise in a particular area does not mean that he or she necessarily knows how to conduct a site visit. Site visit team preparation means training the team on the following:

- The objectives of the site visit.
- The content and use of the site visit instrument, obtaining information on-site, and how to interpret results.
- How to conduct an interview to gain information (i.e., put the associate at ease, stick to the site visit instrument to get consistent results at each supplier, avoid jumping to conclusions in advance, and don't "lead the witness"). Role playing about different situations at the supplier can be good preparation.
- Conduct at the supplier (i.e., respect and ethics).
- Giving feedback to suppliers.

Before specific site visits, the team should review any pre-visit information or surveys from the supplier in order to prepare.

You want to be sure to select individuals who will be certain to give a *very positive impression* of your company to the supplier. Figure 8.4 shows some of the attributes of a site visit team. A positive attitude, sincerity, and simple courtesy and respect toward the supplier and toward fellow team members are qualities that help enable that positive impression—and a useful result.

You want to avoid inappropriate and unethical behaviors from site visit team members that are at best embarrassing and at worst can jeopardize or ruin the relationship. Some inappropriate behaviors are accepting meals and gifts from the supplier and socializing with the supplier—such as golf tournaments, baseball tickets, and so on. Accepting a box lunch while on-site during the visit is OK, but going out for an expensive dinner paid for by the supplier is not. The usual ethics

Site Visit Team Member

- Excellent communication skills
- Knowledge of best practices
- Ability to assess processes
- Positive image
- Team player
- Coach/trainer
- Ethical
- Objective
- Fair

Figure 8.4 Site visit team member attributes.

and gifts policies apply, either those put forward by ISM or by your own company's purchasing ethics policy.[1] If you do not have such a policy, you should consider adopting one. You do not want to give the impression that the supplier is unethically influencing the relationship to get business or that the customer is actually allowing the supplier to do so.

When using a team to do site visits, utilize a team leader, someone who is in charge of the site visit from the preparation and communication through the visit and follow-up with the supplier. This person should be familiar with or needs to become familiar with the supplier being visited. If this person is not the manager of the supplier relationship, then he or she must work very closely with that person. Figure 8.5 outlines the major attributes and responsibilities of a site visit team leader.

Communicate with Suppliers before the Site Visit

Suppliers need to understand in advance the particulars of the site visit: who, what, why, when, and how. This information should be communicated to the senior management or owner of the business. The information should include the following:

- Why is the site visit being conducted?
- When is the site visit?
- How long is the site visit?
- Who is going to conduct the site visit?
- What are the expectations about what is going to happen during the site visit, what the customer firm expects, and what the site visit means for the supplier firm?
- How can the supplier prepare for the site visit?

---

1. Refer to ISM's Principles and Standards of Purchasing Practice for ethics guidelines.

Site Visit Team Leader

Attributes

- Experience and ability as a leader
- Excellent facilitator
- Respected both by team members and supplier
- Willingness to be a leader and accept leadership responsibilities
- Has the capabilities and knowledge of a team member

Responsibilities

- Chooses team members
- Reviews supplier data and prior assessments or site visits
- Ensures team has reviewed supplier info before the site visit
- Coordinates communication and site visit activities with supplier
- Conducts team meetings
- Coordinates travel plans
- Leads site visit activities at supplier
- Ensures follow-up actions are monitored and completed

Figure 8.5 Attributes and responsibilities of site visit leader.

- What people at the supplier firm need to be available during the site visit?
- How is the supplier going to be evaluated?
- How will the site visit impact future business with the customer?

This type of information can be communicated in a letter or via an Internet meeting between the customer and supplier. If site visiting is new to your company, you are changing your site visit approach, or you are implementing a new program, such as supplier certification, it is very important to communicate in advance with the supplier. To the extent that you can give a supplier details about the process and your expectations, the better prepared and less apprehensive they will be. Advance communication gives you and the suppliers an opportunity for dialogue and makes the site visit process go more smoothly. A hastily planned site visit can be a waste of time and may allow the team only to scratch the surface in understanding the supplier's capabilities.[2]

Some companies send suppliers a pre-visit questionnaire so that they can get an understanding of the supplier and preliminary view of strengths and opportunities, and they can see what areas might require more time than others. Others use a Web-based questionnaire in order to gather as much information as possible before a site visit, or avoid a site visit altogether for certain suppliers.

2. Flynn, Tim, "Conducting an Effective Supplier Site Visit," *Inside Supply Management,* October 2002, pp. 42–47.

Conducting the Site Visit

There are several approaches to gathering information using a site visit instrument. The typical approach is using a survey and collecting comprehensively the information in the survey from interviews with supplier personnel via word processing or spreadsheets on laptops taken to the site or simply taking manual notes on a paper printout of the survey. Another approach is the Web-based or virtual site visit where the detailed survey instrument is deployed in advance and the site visit is used to clarify inconsistent answers and probe more deeply into the lower-scoring areas of the assessment. Figure 8.6 shows an example of communications about a Web-based supplier assessment sent to the key contact or senior management at the supplier site. With some advance information from the supplier, you can plan how much time your team members want to spend with specific individuals and what areas of the company they may wish to look at in more depth. The downside for the supplier is the time and effort it takes to fill out a pre-visit questionnaire and then go over some of the same questions again during the site visit. A Web-based questionnaire makes this task easier for the supplier. With a comprehensive Web-based questionnaire, the customer firm can focus on low-scoring, inconsistent, or problem areas during the site visit, as they can see in advance which areas will need further investigation and which areas will require less attention.

On-site the team can get information and also ask for evidence for the answers that they are given. For example, if the supplier says that they have a particular policy or procedure in place, it can be viewed. Or if they claim to have employee training, then the records can be reviewed. Suppliers can try to cheat or misrepresent on a site visit as they can on a survey. Customer firm personnel who do site visits must be knowledgeable and savvy enough to see through attempts to mislead or manipulate the team. Suppliers may try to keep the team from seeing particular areas or prevent them from speaking with the associates instead of management. Typically, supplier management will try to control what the site visit team will be told, whom they will speak with, and what they will see. The supplier wants to make a good impression and reap whatever advantages they can get from doing well on the site visit. Site visit team members need to look beyond the surface and know how to find out whether the supplier is giving lip service or is truly doing what they say they are. Part of this is establishing trust with the supplier and part is being good at doing site visits—knowing what to look for and how to look for it. Table 8.2 shows a sample site visit agenda.

Before a site visit, the site visit team should have completed its preparation, team training, review of any pre-visit questionnaires from the supplier, supplier's performance trends, dollars of spend with the supplier, and scorecards, and you should have briefed the supplier in advance on what to expect during the site visit. The actual site visit is an opportunity to confirm previously gathered information

Your customer is seeking to improve its ability to manage and work with suppliers, better understand their performance, and work to improve the products and services you offer your customers. As part of this effort, your customer has developed a Web-based supplier self-assessment tool. This is designed to make the site visit process quicker and easier both for your company and for your customer.

The Scope of the Self-Assessment and Reporting

The scope of the self-assessment includes these four areas: Production, Quality, Leadership, and Material and Supply. Reporting of the results will be provided on these four categories. Reports will include overall scores in the four tools, more detailed breakouts of scores, and a Strengths and Opportunities analysis. These reports will be generated and you will receive them as soon as the participants at your site have all completed their portions of the assessment.

Selecting Participants

The more participants we have from your company, the better. Larger numbers mean that the results will be more accurate and may result in a shorter site visit from your customer. In addition, you want to be sure that people from all functions/levels in your company participate. This means representatives from senior management, middle management and supervisors, and front-line personnel from all areas of the company: shop floor, support services, customer service, and so on.

- Company/site leader (e.g., president, CEO, general manager, owner, business unit manager) and all of his or her direct reports, and, to the extent possible, representatives from the following functions:
- Quality, Materials, Purchasing, Manufacturing Operations, Manufacturing Engineering, Design Engineering, Sales, Customer Service, Finance, Human Resources, Information Technology (MIS)

There are different sets of questions in the self-assessment depending on your functional area (e.g., Purchasing, Manufacturing Engineering, etc.). You may designate more than one function for one individual, as the assessment is able to combine functional areas in the questions.

No individual responses will be reported, except as anonymous data. Your answers will only be used in combination with other respondents. Typically an assessment takes between two to three hours to complete your part. No research is required.

Figure 8.6 Sample communication with supplier.

and other impressions of supplier performance. Also, do not bring a list of complaints to review at the site visit, as reviewing complaints is not the purpose and trying to do so sets a bad tone. The site visit should be a sharing of information between customer and supplier with the purpose of establishing, solidifying, or deepening the relationship; gaining a better understanding of the value that the relationship adds to both companies; solving problems; and identifying actions for continuous improvement. Before the site visit, confirm the dress code. If you wish to put the supplier at ease, you may not want to show up as "the suits" in a casual workplace—or dress too casually in a more formal environment. Business casual is usually acceptable for site visits.

During the site visit, customer team members should be actively listening during the information gathering and not be prescriptive, judgmental, or critical.

Table 8.2 Site Visit Agenda

1. Welcome and introductions
2. Overview of agenda for the day and assessment process
3. Supplier overview of business, operations
4. Facility tour
5. Assessment interviews
6. Consensus with interviewees
7. Assessment scoring
8. Customer site visit team meeting and consensus
9. Meeting with senior management
10. Continuous improvement/corrective action plan

They should try to put supplier associates at ease. Do not use your company's practices as examples or tell the supplier that "the way we do it" is the way they should be doing it. If there are specific things that you have asked the supplier to do and you do not see evidence of them, then you can mention these items in your meeting at the end of the visit. The interviewer should make eye contact, take notes, and keep the interviews on track. Be respectful of suppliers' time by setting a schedule, budgeting your time, and sticking to the schedule. You do not need to verify everything. Sampling is sufficient. Try to be balanced. Do not look only for problems, but for supplier strengths as well, as these strengths are an important base on which to build improvements. And finding strengths sets a more positive tone with the supplier, rather than making the supplier feel that you are only there to criticize and find fault. Adhere to the philosophy (from Sun Tzu in *The Art of War*) that "victory comes from finding opportunities in problems." Identified and specific opportunities for improvement are the key outputs of the site visit. They will help the supplier find specific ways to improve and can add value not only to your company's relationship with the supplier but to the supplier's overall business performance.

When interviewing a functional person during the site visit, try to come to a consensus or agreement about your observations or findings, potential scoring of their area, and opportunities for improvement before the final meeting with management. You do not want to be at odds with the supplier's staff, nor do you want to spring any surprises on the supplier that have not first been discussed with the participants in the site visit. The site visit team meeting and consensus before the final meeting with supplier management are also important. This helps the team look at the supplier both holistically and functionally, so that the results and recommendations do not become "a bunch of trees looking for a forest."

At the final meeting with management at the end of the site visit, team members should give brief summaries of the site visit assessment results and the team leader should present overall results. The meeting should not conclude until next steps and the time frame for submission of improvement plans or corrective actions are discussed. Designate one person at the supplier to collect any outstanding information that the supplier has agreed to provide to the team. Developing the evaluation during the site visit is ideal, since the visit is fresh in the team's mind and most questions can get answered while the team is on-site. A well-constructed, easy-to-use site visit instrument enables a quicker evaluation. However, you may need more time to develop a formal evaluation of the site visit than time allows during the visit. In this case, be sure to set up a follow-up meeting or call for this evaluation while you are still at the site visit.

Site Visit Follow-Up

We have discussed how critical follow-up is to a site visit and that some kind of actions must result. In some companies, these are corrective actions, and there is typically a process or system in place for tracking and completing corrective actions. In quality terms, corrective actions are taken to eliminate a nonconformity. Continuous-improvement plans are broader in scope and can address both immediate corrective actions and longer-term, systematic improvement activities.

The following is a sample outline for a supplier continuous-improvement plan:

1. *Goals.* Key goals for the improvement efforts
   Examples:
   • To reduce the total cost of the product or service
   • To improve quality of the product or service
   • To reduce the lead time to deliver the product or service
   • To improve ability to deliver the product or service on time
2. *Listing and description of specific projects and events that will work towards the goals.* For example, employee training, 5S activities to improve workplace order and organization in administrative areas, Six Sigma projects to improve first time yield
3. *Metrics.* Include the current baseline, goals, and progress made towards the goals
4. *Projected schedule.* Specific projects, events, and tasks shown on a timeline, with projected conclusion dates

Table 8.3 gives an example of a supplier improvement plan with site visit recommendations and the supplier response.

Table 8.3 Excerpt from Supplier Improvement Plan

Area: Material and Inventory Control Systems Opportunities	
Customer Site Visit Recommendation	**Supplier Response**
Strive to increase inventory turns. As the actual product cells are created, drive inventory to the cell level rather than module level. Figuring out the next steps for milling is critical for success. Decentralize or pull production.	Initiated by the financial department, a project was started to reduce working capital. One aspect of the project is the reduction of inventory. First results of this project and implementation of business rules within the logistic department are expected mid-2007. The logistic support department of Operations is directly involved in the working capital project. **Target date:** April 2008 **Responsible:** VP Financial and VP Operations
Consider using the company wiki to create a limited-scope repository for information arising from team solutions or problem solving. It is good for maintaining and tracking information, and it may become a valuable tool to assist in resolving common problems.	An investigation of the quality system is being conducted to improve possibility of analysis and trends. This should give means for a more proactive approach and a more accessible database. We are already working with a database of documents written to address issues of certain products or processes. We will look into using the wiki. **Target date:** June 2008 **Responsible:** VP Quality

There are many formats to use for developing improvement plans. You may want to develop an improvement plan template to give suppliers or let them use their own format if they already have one.

Cost of a Site Visit and ROI

Site visits can be expensive and resource-intensive. Table 8.4 shows an example of estimated costs for a site visit, assuming an existing process and tools and three team members. This table is a guideline for estimating the cost of site visits. This estimate may be high or low for the types and scope of site visits your company is considering or already does, depending on whether you send a team for a few days or one person for one day.

The question is this: What's the payback? When site visits are well done, the ROI can be substantial and rapid. Opportunities for improvement that are

Table 8.4 Estimated Costs for a Site Visit

Type of Expense	Amount	Cost
Preparations	2 person days*	$742
Travel time	6 person days	$2226
Living expenses	Travel, hotel, meals**	$2400
Time on-site	6 person days	$2226
Post-site visit review and actions	2 person days	$742
	Total	$8162

* Estimate $60K salary plus 30% OH X 210 working days/yr = $371 per day.
** Estimate $800 per person.

addressed in the supplier's continuous-improvement plan are likely to pay back the cost of the visit many times over. The ROI will be there if you and your suppliers find ways to: improve quality and reduce your company's rework or reduce warranty costs because of better supplier quality, reduce your inventory because you do not need to keep "just in case" inventory to allow for supplier glitches, reduce downtime for your system because your supplier has put in place methods to reduce software bugs, or your supplier improves its service levels to you—the examples are many. The site visit team should be able to find opportunities for cost reduction and operational improvements that will more than fund the visit. You and your supplier should track the opportunities on the resulting improvement plans and calculate the value when possible.

A supplier visit should result in improved supplier performance and outcomes such as the following:

- A comprehensive understanding of a supplier's business and technology capabilities
- The supplier gaining a better understanding of your company's strategic directions and business requirements
- Specific improvement action items, typically for both parties
- Stronger personal relationships between managers at each company
- ROI: identifying and implementing improvements in cost, quality, and responsiveness

Of course, you should quantify and track the ROI that comes from supplier improvement and report to management on a periodic basis to make the site visit process and its real operational and financial benefits visible to management.

9

MEASURING AND MANAGING SUPPLIER PERFORMANCE

COMMUNICATING WITH SUPPLIERS ABOUT PERFORMANCE

We have emphasized the importance of communications about the evaluation process to both internal and external stakeholders. With the system, tools and process for evaluating supplier performance in place, you need a framework and process for communications and feedback about performance expectations and requirements in order to achieve consistent results. Performance feedback should be a two-way flow of communication between customer and supplier, not just a one-way flow from customer to supplier. Figure 9.1 illustrates the flow of performance expectations and requirements to the supplier firm and goods and services to the customer firm, with performance feedback flowing both ways.

Since customers can cause so many supplier performance problems, the voice of the supplier needs to be considered and incorporated into the communications. Requirements flow-down is a big challenge in industries with complex products and also in new product development. It can be like a game of telephone or whisper down the lane. By the time the requirements flow down the supply chain, they may not match very closely what was originally intended by the customer. During the quoting process, a two-way dialogue between customer and supplier helps avoid flow-down distortion. When defining requirements, customers may rely heavily on supplier expertise or not rely on it enough. Either way,

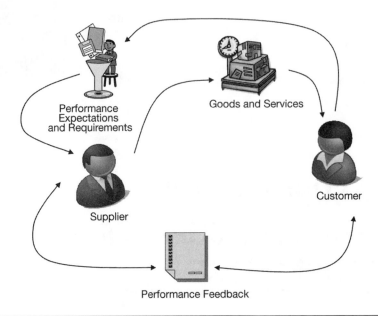

Figure 9.1 Customer-supplier feedback process.

without well-defined requirements and a mutual fine-tuning and communication of requirements and performance expectations, the supplier may not deliver what the customer needs and be blamed for poor performance, even in instances where it is clearly the customer's fault. Avoid problems later by communicating both up front and continually during the relationship.

SUPPLIER PERFORMANCE FEEDBACK

Formal Performance Feedback

Whatever method you use to collect information on supplier performance, you must develop a formal means to share this information with suppliers regularly and to allow time for mutual discussion of this information.

- *KPI and scorecard distribution.* Suppliers for whom you have scorecard information need to be able to see the results on a regular basis—at least monthly or quarterly, depending upon the type of supplier. Key or critical suppliers should see their metrics at least monthly. A good way to share metrics is to have a supplier portal or a means for suppliers to look at their own scorecards on demand and electronically. If your company does not have that capability, then scorecards can be

Table 9.1 Why Companies Don't Share Scorecards with Suppliers

Issue	Possible Action
Concern that the data on the scorecards are not accurate or defensible	Review data sources. Develop means to cleanse data.
Unsure whether the metrics on the scorecards are really relevant	Review metrics in relation to performance expectations and goals.
Too many supplier scorecards. The customer is concerned that there is insufficient time or resources to speak with supplier about scorecards.	Review if the right suppliers are being measured or if too many are being measured. Systematize the feedback process.
Too many metrics on the scorecards and not enough meaningful ones	Look at reducing the number of metrics to the most relevant or important ones.
No policies or actions developed for using scorecard results, so sharing seems futile	Develop baselines, goals, and actions Share results even before actions are developed, but pursue a better process.
Unclear about how to use the scorecards	Rethink metrics. Training

sent electronically (by e-mail). But however you do it, share the results. Don't generate supplier scorecards or report cards without sharing them regularly. Some companies spend more effort generating data than actually sharing the information. Table 9.1 summarizes some of the reasons why some companies are not sharing their scorecards with suppliers and suggests possible solutions to these problems.

- *Supplier performance or business review meetings.* For key, strategic, and critical suppliers, hold formal performance or business review meetings. These differ in scope from routine performance discussions. Depending on the nature of the relationship with the supplier, you may wish to broaden the scope of these meetings from performance reviews to business reviews. A business review would cover more topics than a performance review and would be done with suppliers who are partners, product development, or alliance suppliers. A business review would include sharing information from both customer and supplier to align current business priorities, to discuss technology trends and share new business opportunities, and to discuss future trends and needs, goals, and overall business strategies. For example, Pitney Bowes forms relationships between the top management of its company and the top 5 percent of its suppliers, which includes the suppliers it relies upon for critical technology, contract manufacturing capabilities, or some key OEM (original equipment manufacturer) products. Pitney Bowes does business reviews with these top suppliers. "The supplier business review is an essential element of an effective SRM process for Pitney Bowes," Michael Dempsey, vice president of global direct procurement, explains. "There is no better forum to discuss the topics that are most critical to our short- and long-term success. It's a great opportunity for us to work with suppliers to evaluate our progress against our business priorities and, if necessary, make corrections in course and speed to adjust to marketplace dynamics."[1] A business review between customer and supplier requires senior managers from both organizations, depending upon the size of the supplier and the size of its customer, because the overall business is being discussed and the scope is larger than procurement concerns. In the case of small suppliers, the owner or general manager would attend with senior management team members. For larger suppliers, more senior-level managers might attend. A business review of this scope might occur on a yearly basis.

The performance review is a piece of the overall business review. Performance reviews can be conducted apart from business reviews and are meetings that can provide an opportunity to discuss performance measurements, set goals, discuss acceptable and unacceptable performance, understand the rewards of good performance and the consequences of not meeting performance goals, and discuss progress against goals.

Setting goals and discussing performance can be sensitive for suppliers. In some cases the feedback may not be received well by supplier top management and may result in punitive action toward supplier middle management.[2] Goal setting should focus on performance areas that are important to the buying company and are meaningful to the supplier. The selected performance areas should be able to be measured in a way that seems fair, accurate, and understandable. Working to set goals is a continual process, as goals and expectations will change on both the sell side and the buy side over time. Performance review meetings are used to review progress against goals and discuss opportunities for improvement. The performance review meeting is a good time to discuss the status of corrective actions and continuous-improvement plans. Table 9.2 summarizes the dos and don'ts of supplier performance reviews. The meeting and its goals should be

1. Avery, Susan, "Supplier Relationship Management: Pathways to Convergence," *Purchasing*, April 5, 2007.
2. Wehr, William S., C.P.M., "Managing Supplier Partnerships," 83rd Annual International Conference Proceedings, 1998.

Table 9.2 Supplier Performance Review Dos and Don'ts

Do	Don't
Plan and publish the agenda in advance	Waste your and your supplier's time with an unplanned meeting.
Provide the scorecard, survey, or assessment results to the supplier in advance, if possible, or allow supplier real-time access to information via the Web.	Give them the scorecard to the supplier only at the review meeting.
Be positive and constructive.	Be negative and critical.
Be specific about what the supplier needs to do to meet your expectations.	Make promises or threats that you don't plan to follow through on.
Address the facts as much as possible.	Be emotional and draw conclusions about performance without evidence.
Address performance problems as an opportunity for improvement and supplier development.	Look at performance problems as failings or act as if you view the supplier as a failure.
Work with the supplier to find solutions to performance problems.	Tell the supplier how to run his or her business.
Make suggestions about resources to help with particular problems or about potential approaches to solve problems.	Dictate how the supplier should solve the problem or expect that solutions that worked for your company will work for the supplier.
Be clear on the outcomes of meeting or exceeding the performance goals and the consequences of not meeting them.	Be vague about what will happen if the supplier meets or does not meet performance goals or make veiled threats.
Express appreciation for the supplier's efforts.	Make the supplier feel that no amount of effort will please the customer.
State observations based upon the performance data.	State observations as immutable facts.
Convey negative news or messages in person or on the phone.	Fire the supplier by e-mail.
Own up to your company's part of a problem.	Blame the supplier for problems caused by your company.
Treat critical or key suppliers like valued partners.	Treat suppliers like "just a vendor."

planned in advance with a published agenda that is adhered to as much as possible during the meeting so that the supplier can prepare. Also, the tone should be positive and the supplier treated professionally and as a valued partner. Facts should be addressed as much as possible. If your company is causing problems, take responsibility for your company's part. The goal should be to find common ground and agree upon solutions to problems.

Frequency of performance review meetings depends on several factors:

- *How frequently performance data on the supplier is updated and available for review.* If you update scorecards or survey data regularly, such as weekly, monthly, and so on, then the information is available for review. Some companies are able to keep the information updated in real time.

- *Whether or not the supplier falls into the key or critical category, is considered a partner or alliance supplier, or is certified or preferred, or whether you have a high spend with that supplier.* All suppliers are not created equal. There is no sense in spending time with suppliers whose impact on your business is low.

- *How many suppliers you want, need, or are able to meet with.* The number of suppliers you do performance reviews with may depend upon your resources.

- *Whether the supplier is having specific performance issues that need to be regularly monitored and addressed.* If a supplier is having performance issues, then more frequent meetings may be required to monitor the situation, to review corrective actions, or to see what assistance the supplier might need. These meetings can also be conducted at the supplier. Once performance issues have been resolved, then you can go back to regular, but fewer meetings.

- *What stage the relationship is in.* In the initial stages of engaging with a supplier, the buying company may wish to develop and nurture the new relationship and thus meet more often. With longer-term, more established, and stable suppliers, less frequent reviews may be required. Frequency may depend upon the criticality of the goods or services supplied and any current issues that might impact the frequency of review meetings.

Informal Performance Feedback

There are many ways to give informal feedback. Calling a supplier after noticing an improvement or good service helps demonstrate that you value your supplier and are aware of their efforts to improve. Of course, not all performance feedback is going to be positive, and you will need to discuss the problems that will inevitably arise. Even when bad things occur, it is better to focus on how to prevent problems from recurring rather than to focus only on the problem itself. In looking at the causes of supplier problems, many of them lie, in part, with the customer. Offering to do your part to remove any obstacles to help the supplier is a constructive approach. The expectation is that the supplier will do what is necessary to solve their contribution to the problem. Sometimes there are circumstances that may prevent a supplier from ever meeting the metric and need to be taken into account. A few examples are described in "Help Your Supplier Help You" by David Hannon in *Purchasing* (May 4, 2006). One example is a Japanese supplier to Synetics Solutions in Portland, Oregon, an airflow and automation systems developer. The supplier's on-time delivery percent was consistently at an unacceptable 20 percent. Then the customer discovered that this supplier was located four hours from a major hub and that the product had to be shipped to the hub before being shipped to the United States. After the customer took this situation into account, the supplier was able to meet the on-time delivery goal of 90 percent. The point is that open and honest communication about issues rather than only formal or even no communication helps build trust, solve problems, strengthen relationships, and improve performance.

Customer Performance Feedback

A best practice in SPM is measuring the customer's performance in relation to supporting the needs of the supplier. Since supplier performance is dependent, in part, on the supply management systems and capabilities of the customer, as outlined in the supply chain management framework in Chapter 2, having the customer ask its suppliers about its own performance as a customer is the natural next step. The goal is to find out how good a customer you are and where you need to improve to better enable your suppliers' performance. Sometimes these are known as supplier satisfaction surveys. If you solicit feedback on your performance as a customer, be prepared to act on the results. Asking for feedback and then ignoring it is destructive to your credibility and not good for the relationship with the supplier. It is sometimes hard for customers to listen to suppliers telling them how they are screwing up. Traditionally, the customer is supposed to know it all and be the big "C" in the relationship, imparting wisdom and sending payments to the supplier for services rendered. Admitting that you need to change to improve the relationship or to help the supplier do a better job for you is not easy for some customer firms. Sometimes the areas in your company with the greatest opportunities for improvement are not within your span of control. Or perhaps your company does not have a culture of continuous improvement. Focus first on the areas that can be improved and over which you have or your boss has some control or influence.

Supplier satisfaction or feedback surveys can be either stand-alone or part of a supplier performance survey. As in gathering information on supplier performance, it is important to get feedback from more than one function. Go beyond the sales rep and survey all the functions at the supplier who deal with your company, such as accounting, order entry, materials, quality, manufacturing, engineering,

IT, contracts, and so on. In constructing the survey, think about what you would want your customers to ask your company in a similar survey—the areas where your customers cause you problems. Satisfied suppliers can help companies achieve high customer satisfaction. Three main components affecting supplier satisfaction are a cooperative culture, commitment to supplier satisfaction, and constructive controversy.[3] And according to Genna, customer satisfaction results in increased business.[4] Having suppliers who want to do business with you and who do a good job for you will directly impact your bottom line. In a buyer's market, supplier satisfaction seems less important and is often ignored as customer firms take advantage of their leverage over supplier firms. Given the cyclical nature of business, there will inevitably be a seller's market. When the seller's market occurs, poor treatment of suppliers will come home to roost and those sellers who have treated their suppliers less professionally or more opportunistically or even violated trust will have more problems with suppliers going the extra mile or wanting to do business with them.

Table 9.3 is a sample customer satisfaction survey and shows some examples of the types of questions that you may want to ask suppliers about your performance as a customer.[5] This list is intended to give ideas about potential topics to cover, not about the question structure. Questions can be structured as scaled responses. You should also allow comments to capture the specifics that can be missed in a survey and that add to the richness of the responses.

When I was working for a distribution company as Director of Total Quality Management, my group initiated a customer satisfaction feedback process. We approached our key customers to get feedback on our performance and areas for improvement. This was done through a questionnaire and then a follow-up meeting. Not only did we understand our customers' needs much better, but the process also helped strengthen the relationships with these key customers, who were impressed that a supplier was taking the initiative to improve its service and customer satisfaction. The customers, in turn, shared their views of how they could become a better customer. Our program became part of a Harvard Business School film called *People, Service, Success: Listening to Customers*.

If your firm is aware of the qualities of being a good customer and strives to be a good customer, relationships with and performance of suppliers will be strengthened commensurately.

---

3. Wong, Alfred, "Integrating Supplier Satisfaction with Customer Satisfaction," *Total Quality Management*, 2000, Vol. 11, Nos. 4/5 and 6, pp. S427–S432.

4. Genna, A., Suppliers Are Key to Giving Customers What They Want, *Purchasing*, 1997, Vol. 123, pp. 33–34.

5. Some questions adapted from Patricia C. La Londe and Janet R Raddatz, "Tools for Improving Customer-Supplier Relationships," *Journal for Quality & Participation*, Fall 2002, Vol. 25, No. 3, pp. 12–18.

Table 9.3 Supplier Satisfaction Survey—Sample Questions

1. To what extent are we meeting your expectations?

2. To what extent do we communicate our performance expectations to you?

3. To what extent do we treat you as a valued partner?

4. To what extent do we provide you with the information that you need in order to give us a quote or pricing?

5. To what extent do you want to participate in the product or service design process?

6. Is there any type of technical assistance that you would like us to provide?

7. Is there any training that you would like us to provide?

8. Is the feedback we provide to you adequate?

9. How frequently would you like us to provide you with feedback?

10. To what extent do we provide you with clear technical information?

11. To what extent do we give you adequate lead time to provide us with products or services?

12. How accurate are our forecasts to you?

13. To what extent do we conduct our relationship with you in a professional manner?

14. To what extent do you believe that we treat you fairly?

15. To what extent are we responsive to your needs?

16. How easy are we to deal with as a customer?

Supplier Conferences

A supplier conference or supplier day brings together key suppliers for the purposes of communications, education, and team building. Companies typically communicate goals, performance expectations, and objectives and introduce quality, cost reduction, and continuous-improvement initiatives into the supply base. Some companies invite outside speakers to present on supplier development and performance improvement topics of interest, such as lean and Six Sigma. Depending on the number of suppliers involved, some companies provide time at supplier days for individual meetings with company contacts to review individual supplier performance goals and objectives. Many companies recognize high performers at supplier day conferences. To be successful, a supplier day requires executive support and involvement, a budget, and careful advance planning. The next chapter describes in detail how to plan and run a successful supplier recognition day, which is a more specialized type of supplier day. That type of event is specifically to recognize the highest-performing suppliers. Tables 9.4 and 9.5 illustrate examples of typical supplier conference or supplier day agendas and topics. A supplier

Table 9.4 Supplier Conference Agenda

8:00–9:00	Breakfast	
9:00–9:15	Introduction and review agenda	VP Procurement
9:15–10:00	Review of customer firm	President
10:00–10:30	Expectations of suppliers and supplier handbook	VP Procurement
10:30–10:50	Break	
10:50–11:30	Supplier quality processes	VP Quality
11:30–11:50	New product introduction process	VP Product Development
11:50–12:20	Sourcing and supply chain management process	VP Supply Chain
12:30–13:30	Lunch	
13:30–17:00	One-on-one meetings with suppliers	

Table 9.5 Typical Supplier Day Agenda

CEO overview
Challenges
Accomplishments
Future business directions
Supplier initiatives
Procurement initiatives
Breakout meetings and tours
Supplier recognition

conference is a chance to align a customer firm's corporate and purchasing goals with the supply base. It can also be a time to introduce new initiatives to suppliers. Supplier conferences afford an opportunity to communicate business results, customer firm strategies, and supplier performance expectations, as well as solidify relationships with key suppliers. A supplier day can be a good time for the customer firm to listen to suppliers' feedback on the customer on better ways to do things and achieve cost savings, thereby improving performance and adding value to relationships. A supplier day also may involve good meals, recreational activities, and socializing and networking.

Colgate-Palmolive, for example, has used supplier days to introduce new suppliers to the company. They invite these suppliers to visit so that they can meet key people in the organization and give employees a chance to meet the new suppliers.[6] Other companies, such as Northrop Grumman, hold an annual supplier day conference where they give out supplier awards based upon scorecard achievements. Medical device manufacturer Medrad, a 2003 winner of the Malcolm Baldrige National Quality Award, holds an annual supplier day conference for its key suppliers. It also invites key service providers and development partners to participate. The conference provides suppliers with new product information, quality assessments and initiatives, and purchasing initiatives. One year a new supplier cost reduction idea program was started and introduced at the supplier day. This program ended up providing Medrad with over $300,000 worth of savings after just the first six months. After breakout sessions and a tour, Medrad recognizes suppliers for their accomplishments.[7]

When well-conceived and planned, supplier days can be a valuable tool for communications and strengthening relationships with important suppliers. Without a clear purpose and thorough planning, they can be counterproductive for both customer and supplier. Poor planning was evident at a supplier day at a lighting manufacturer where I was a guest speaker. A company representative spent an hour going over the specifications for their new corrective action system that had not yet been implemented. The presentation was far too detailed for the level of supplier executives who had been invited to attend and who may have preferred to have this presentation given to a lower-level employee. Another example of a poorly executed supplier day was at an electronics firm. One of the goals of the day was to tell the suppliers that the company was embarking on supplier rationalization. The company told the suppliers, "Look to the left. Look to the right. One of you will be gone next year." No details were given regarding how these decisions were actually going to be made. This announcement did not help foster trust and good relations with the suppliers, particularly with the ones that would be left standing after the cuts.

When properly planned and well done, a supplier day will provide rapid payback on the investment. Showcasing high-performing suppliers can inspire others to achieve greater improvements and success themselves. The educational and networking aspects of a supplier day can help suppliers gain new ideas for improvements and cost reductions or inspire them to pursue these opportunities. A customer firm can also learn new ideas from suppliers that will help the firm save time and money. A supplier day can demonstrate that a customer firm considers its key suppliers valued partners and thus can help strengthen relationships.

6. Atkinson, William, "Colgate Palmolive's Council Strategy Drives Diversity Efforts," *Purchasing*, June 15, 2006.

7. Atkinson, William, "Medrad Knows How to Treat Suppliers," *Purchasing*, October 21, 2004.

CHANGING SUPPLIER BEHAVIOR AND PERFORMANCE

Suppliers may behave in ways that customer firms find difficult to understand and to deal with. Likewise, suppliers find customers equally frustrating and inscrutable. Attitudes and behaviors on both sides of the relationship can be a barrier to realizing the value from the relationship and obtaining expected performance. Fine-tuning the supplier base and working with fewer suppliers may mean that suppliers have greater leverage over their customers than they have previously. Also, both customer and supplier firms are under pressure to reduce costs in the short term, sometimes at the expense of larger opportunities in the long term. This can create stresses and behavioral difficulties in the relationship.

What do suppliers do that can adversely impact relationships with their customers? The results of a survey conducted by Vantage Partners indicated some of these behaviors as reported by customer firms as well as customer behaviors according to supplier firms.[8] Table 9.6 summarizes some of these mutual views of one another about how each behaves in its own interest. Both customers and suppliers are observing the most limiting behaviors each others' firms as driven by short-term issues—revenue or savings. Each sees the other as not offering sufficient transparency and also lacking internal alignment and coordination. With the inclination to see the other as the main contributor to problems, working together smoothly can be a challenge. Since the customer is initiating the relationship in most cases, the customer needs to understand and overcome some of the limiting factors, including those caused by the customer's own firm, in order to develop a productive, mutually beneficial relationship and obtain high performance from suppliers. The customer firm has the opportunity and responsibility to "be the change it wishes to see" (Mahatma Gandhi).

SPM, when properly done, is a change management initiative, both internally at the customer firm and externally at the supplier firm. A supplier may not be accustomed to having its performance put under the microscope by an outside business and then receiving feedback that may be hard to accept. In customer-supplier relationships, companies will invariably have suppliers whose performance needs improvement and/or whose attitudes or behaviors are less than optimal. Some customers may alternately plead or threaten. Neither approach may work. Here are some possible reasons:

- The customer has not made its performance expectations clear.
- The supplier is unclear about how it is being measured.

---

8. Hughes, Jonathan, "Leveraging Relationships to Drive Performance," 2007 Supplier Relationship Management Conference, The Conference Board.

Table 9.6 Customers' and Suppliers' Views of Each Other

Supplier Behaviors According to Customers	Customer Behaviors According to Suppliers
1. Focus on short-term revenue and margin by supplier executives	1. Focus on short-term, easily quantifiable savings
2. Unwillingness to enter "at-risk" arrangements	2. Lack of internal alignment at the customer
3. Lack of internal coordination	3. Lack of clarity about needs and priorities of the customer
4. Internal focus on short-term sales instead of building long-term partnerships	4. Late involvement of suppliers
5. Not offering enough transparency	5. Lack of respect for supplier expertise
6. Supplier-sided contract language	6. Unwillingness to make long-term commitments
7. Using information about customers as negotiation leverage	7. Overly rigid RFPs and bidding process
8. Making unrealistic commitments to win business	8. Use of one-sided contract language
	9. Not enough access to senior management
	10. Limited access to personnel outside of procurement

Source: Adapted from Vantage Partners: Hughes, Jonathan, "Leveraging Relationships to Drive Performance," 2007 Supplier Relationship Management Conference, The Conference Board.

- The supplier does not understand or the customer does not have incentives for good performance or specific consequences for poor performance.
- The supplier may not know what's causing the problem.
- The supplier does not have the capabilities or the resources to solve the problem.
- Trust between customer and supplier is lacking.
- Ethics issues exist.
- There are culture clashes between customer and supplier.
- A disconnect between quality systems is causing problems.
- A supplier is not accountable for its performance.
- The customer is responsible for a large part of the problem (and thus the supplier cannot solve the problem).
- The supplier feels that the customer is making unreasonable demands.

Some of these problems may not be soluble. Many of the above problems that arise between customer and supplier are attributable to communications issues:

poor communications about requirements, the purpose of performance metrics, metrics calculation, measurement methods and uses, incentives, and consequences of metrics. With clear rules of engagement for performance measurement, a common understanding of one another's needs, and a system for communication, and mutual feedback in place, supplier attitudes and performance can improve.

MANAGING AND MEASURING FOR SUPPLIER RISK

Managing supplier risk is currently one of the hottest topics in supply management. This is due to several issues: globalization, outsourcing, and just-in-time practices. Supply disruptions are costly and can have many consequences, such as unhappy customers, business lost to competitors, lawsuits, loss to the stock price, and penalty clauses. But according to the ongoing A.T. Kearney "Assessment of Excellence in Procurement" study, preparing for risk is more talk than action.[9] When it comes to risk in the supply chain, companies need to expect the unexpected. Risks in the supply chain from strikes, natural disasters, transportation glitches, unanticipated market shifts (such as increases in commodity prices), and political problems can impact any company. According to the A.T. Kearney study, the nature of supply risks has been changing to governance issues, intellectual property theft, and terror. For example, intellectual property theft in the Far East has been an ongoing problem and difficult for companies to protect themselves against. In the area of corporate governance, when companies do not clearly specify requirements to suppliers and then do not adequately disclose failures of performance to their senior management or even board of directors, they can leave themselves open to loss. The question is whether companies are trying to anticipate the unanticipated and put contingency plans in place. Companies need to put in place supply risk plans for themselves as part of an overall corporate risk strategy. As part of the supplier segmentation process, they should define the types of commodities and suppliers who should have risk management plans in place. While probably all suppliers should have risk management plans, not all suppliers pose a risk to a specific customer. Then, these buying companies need to require that their key or critical suppliers develop their own supply risk strategies and contingency plans. Evaluation of key suppliers should include ensuring that they have risk strategies and risk mitigation plans. Examples of companies who require risk management strategies and plans from their suppliers include Boeing and Peugeot Citroën. Boeing has long required risk mitigation plans from its

---

9. A.T. Kearney, "Creating Value through Strategic Supply Management," http://www.atkearney.com/ shared_res/pdf/AEP_2004_S.pdf.

preferred suppliers. Peugeot Citroën requires suppliers to put plans in place in the areas of corporate social responsibility and environmental requirements.

SUPPLY RISK PLANNING

Throughout this book, the importance of supplier performance management strategies originating from overall corporate strategies has been emphasized. This is also true for supply risk management. While supply risk management can and should be driven by procurement, it works best as part of an overall corporate risk strategy. With corporate visibility and support, there will be more attention paid, resources allocated, and action taken regarding risk. Supplier risk is not just a procurement concern and can significantly impact the well-being and interests of the corporation. Cross-functional participation in supplier risk measurement and management is important, since elements of risk come from different disciplines that can contribute their areas of expertise. For example, environmental risk may require legal and engineering input, finance has expertise in financial risk, and so on. Not all the factors that can impact supplier risk are under the control of procurement (or the corporation, for that matter). Also, overall corporate strategies can increase the probability of supply risk. For example, senior management in an instrumentation company decided that the way that procurement was going to reduce costs was by making a radical shift from U.S. suppliers to mostly low-cost-country procurement within one year. No analysis was done as to whether this was operationally feasible or desirable. This was a dictate from corporate designed to save money. Procurement felt that they were taking on sudden and unreasonable risk with this strategy, but they had no say in the decision. This case may sound extreme, but chasing low-cost-country sourcing to reduce cost has become commonplace. What is problematic in this scenario is the lack of risk planning and the disconnect between corporate strategy and procurement.

Figure 9.2 illustrates a process for planning for and mitigating supply risk.

Identify the Potential Risks

If available, review your corporate risk strategy to see what areas of risk the company is preparing for and what areas may be important in creating a supply risk strategy. Then take a look at potential supply risks for your company. Review such areas as types of risk, vulnerabilities to those risks, high-risk commodities or categories, and types of suppliers with critical risk potential.

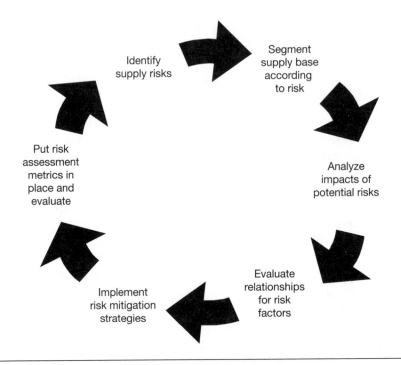

Figure 9.2 Supplier risk assessment and mitigation process.

Segment the Supply Base According to Risk

Look at all types of suppliers who have risk potential, such as, depending on your business, direct material suppliers, suppliers of important services, and transportation suppliers. For example, if disruption of transportation is a risk, then look at third-party logistics and carriers. Or if loss of intellectual property is a risk, identify the most likely segment of suppliers (for example, by geographic location or by type of relationship, such as product development suppliers). If you are using single- or sole-sourcing, look at those suppliers and assess the potential risk. If you have implemented lean and have suppliers delivering products just-in-time, review the trade-offs between supply disruption and using additional sources or carrying additional inventory.

Analyze the Potential Impacts of Risks

Look at how likely and how often the identified risks might occur and the severity of the consequences. In many cases, prevention is not possible and recovery from risk events is the only course of action. Then look at your company's vulnerability to those risks. Identified risks that are not preventable must be looked at in terms of how subject they are to mitigation. That is, can you do anything about lessening the severity or impact of them if these risks do occur?[10] Understanding potential impacts of risks is the first step.

Evaluate Your Contribution to Supplier Risk

Perhaps your company is creating potential areas of risk for suppliers. Examples of a customer creating risk factors for some suppliers include long payment cycles, less than lead time orders, requiring suppliers to hold inventory, the customer making up too high a percentage of a supplier's business, and a low level of mutual trust. These strategies create short-term gain for the customer but can ultimately prove very risky to the survival of the supplier.

Implement Risk Mitigation Strategies

Look at the potential risk mitigation strategies that are available to and feasible for your company. Not all risks can be mitigated. And risk planning can be complex, depending on the characteristics and complexity of a company's supply chain. While predicting risk is challenging and mitigating all risks may not be practical, awareness of and planning for potential impacts as well as planning responses to cope with the impacts are important for protecting your company. Here again, alignment with corporate risk strategies and plans and a cross-functional approach are important success factors.

Make Supplier Risk a Part of Your Performance Management System

Once you have identified the types of risks, the supplier segments, and potential risk factors to measure and monitor, risk metrics should become part of your SPM system. Measure supplier segments for risk factors identified as having the potential for interruption of supply and disruption of your company's business. The most practical way to measure for risk is using information technology so that you can monitor all critical suppliers more easily and more regularly and be proactive about warning signs.

There are other approaches to mitigating supplier risk. Some of these include the following:

- Contracting with alternate sources for critical commodities or areas more open to risk.

---

10. Global Risks 2007, report from the World Economic Forum, p. 22.

- Monitoring supplier financial viability, performance history, and maturity of supplier designs
- Drafting a business interruption plan to identify potential alternate sources whenever a sole source is selected. This plan should include specifically defined processes and procedures to ensure the restoration of core business processes and critical business services in a timely manner.
- Insurance solutions such as hedging contracts, where there is a predetermined price that will be paid for a given product amount regardless of what the actual market value of that product might be at the time it is delivered to the customer.
- Using inventory buffers at risk points in the supply chain.
- Using supply chain visibility software solutions to help get inventory and material visibility throughout the supply chain and to do failure planning.

Many risks cannot be anticipated with any certainty. Even risks with low probabilities of occurring can produce huge consequences. Some risk factors in the supply base can be identified and prevented. Awareness is the first step.

10

RECOGNITION AND REWARDS

FROM METRICS TO ACTION

An SPM process will be most effective when it results in action. The performance measurement process typically has some positive impact on supplier performance just by suppliers knowing that they are being tracked and measured. Just by being measured, suppliers tend to rise to the occasion and improve, reportedly from 5 percent to as much as 25 percent.[1] But allowing the process to proceed without being proactive is to leave much of the ROI on the table. And being proactive means developing a closed-loop performance system along the lines of the classic continuous-improvement model: Plan-Do-Check-Act (PDCA). Figure 10.1 illustrates the PDCA model as it applies to the SPM process.

So far in this book we have discussed the Plan, Do, and Check phases of SPM. Now we will focus on Act. Types of actions include the following:

- Feedback and supplier reviews
- Setting up a performance tier or supplier certification system with different benefit levels depending upon the tier or level
- Recognizing higher performers
- Rewarding higher performers
- Helping lower performers
- Probation
- Rationalizing supply base by disengaging with lower performers

---

1. Source: Aberdeen Group.

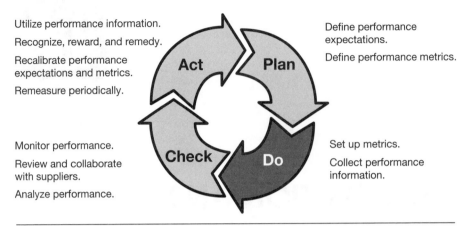

Utilize performance information.
Recognize, reward, and remedy.
Recalibrate performance expectations and metrics.
Remeasure periodically.

Define performance expectations.
Define performance metrics.

Monitor performance.
Review and collaborate with suppliers.
Analyze performance.

Set up metrics.
Collect performance information.

Figure 10.1 Supplier performance management process.

SUPPLIER PERFORMANCE INCENTIVES

To develop supplier performance incentives, you must first develop a structure for evaluating and categorizing performance. That is, you should decide on what incentives, rewards, or awards you will give suppliers, depending upon what performance levels they achieve. These can be structured to reflect ranges of scores, specific criteria, and/or levels of approval or certification. Depending upon the size of the company, its experience with and level of sophistication in supplier performance management, and the complexity and supplier impact on its products and services, performance incentive programs can range from small and simple to large and complex. Companies choose paths ranging from giving suppliers appreciation plaques to developing a supplier qualification and certification process with varying levels of recognition and reward. Whatever path a company chooses, there are several things to keep in mind. Management support in the form of resources and a budget is likely to be required to develop a performance incentive program. Also, a high degree of organizational commitment is essential. Involvement and support of multiple functions will be necessary, since the scope will go beyond procurement or quality alone. For example, if procurement is initiating supplier performance incentives, it will need executive involvement and support in the award or reward process, internal stakeholders to help develop the SPM process and decide on recognition and reward criteria, resources to deploy the process, and possible involvement of public relations to publicize the outcomes. Also, incentives for suppliers can fall into the area of non-contractibles—that is, suppliers make investments that are not on a contract and in addition are asked to do such things as be responsive and innovative, and share confidential information.

What motivates a supplier to want to do this? In most cases, the answer is: more business, less or no competition for business, and longer-term contracts. To look at this simplistically, the idea is that the customer relinquishes some bargaining power and the supplier makes investments for which it is not directly compensated other than through winning additional business. More business can be as a result of meeting performance expectations as determined in a supplier evaluation program or by attaining a formal status, such as preferred or certified, which can also be determined by supplier evaluation.

SUPPLIER RECOGNITION

Supplier recognition programs, when done right, are a good way to motivate suppliers and encourage performance. A well-executed, public supplier recognition program sends a message to your suppliers that you are serious about recognizing excellent performance. The expense of a supplier recognition program can generate a return on investment in several ways. The most visible ROI comes from suppliers' performance improvement. With suppliers striving to be recognized and thus improving performance to do so, both their internal costs and the customer's costs of poor supplier performance can decrease. While the publicity generated among your suppliers by the program is an intangible, it can show that the customer is paying attention to its suppliers' performance and is therefore a lower-risk supplier to its own customers. And for suppliers, the customer "seal of approval" can be a marketing tool to win more business from other customers. A supplier's ability to meet certain standards to win a recognition award from one customer can help make them a supplier of choice for other companies.

Understanding the benefits of recognition can help motivate and raise the standards for your entire supply base. Supplier recognition can have internal benefits to your organization as well. It shows that there is more to supply management than simply negotiating agreements with suppliers. After the contract has been signed, deal execution and supplier performance reflect both on suppliers and on procurement and demonstrate the impact on the entire organization. Also, as has been emphasized in this book so far, other stakeholders besides procurement are involved in supplier performance management programs. Likewise, a well-deployed recognition program involves internal stakeholders in the process and helps sustain their support for procurement and supplier performance management.

A supplier recognition program may seem like a no-brainer. However, there are challenges and pitfalls. This event is high visibility and high impact, both internally and externally, and requires upper management support and participation both from procurement and corporate. Planning for the event requires good project management skills. And the planning process, especially the first time, can be lengthy. You should allow a time horizon of nine months to a year, and that is assuming that you already have a supplier assessment process in place from which to derive the selection criteria. You will need even more time if your organization is starting from a point of no evaluation process.

SUPPLIER RECOGNITION READINESS

I was approached by someone who was eager to plan a supplier recognition day for her company and who asked me whether it seemed reasonable to hold the event in November (it was May when we spoke), as her boss wanted it before the end of the year. It turned out that this company had not even begun to measure supplier performance. Not only did the company have no idea what to measure, but it had not thought about the link between what kind of performance it was looking for and which suppliers it might recognize. When this was pointed out, the person then asked if I would suggest a few KPIs, as the boss had the staff "under the gun" to plan this recognition event. The chances of this company successfully planning any meaningful supplier awards in the stated time frame seemed pretty slim. This story illustrates the lack of understanding and readiness, which I have found to be more common than not, about where a company needs to be in order even to begin to plan supplier recognition. It is the culmination or outgrowth of supplier performance management, not the first step in the process.

So what needs to be in place before embarking on a supplier recognition event? First is having data or information on supplier performance on which to base the selection criteria. Then there needs to be internal agreement on the actual selection criteria for recognition. Another is a company culture that supports the concept of recognition and reward. Some companies do not value the contribution of their employees in the form of employee recognition. For those companies, suddenly wanting to start recognizing outside suppliers is counter to the culture, and supplier recognition just may not be a cultural fit. Company culture also tempers the view of the role of purchasing and of suppliers. Are suppliers viewed as valued partners, or is the view of them more traditional, as adversaries and problem causers, not problem solvers? Supplier recognition will be counter-culture in this type of environment. Recognition must be aligned with the way your company manages, measures, and treats suppliers. If your company has not articulated performance expectations, views suppliers as "just vendors," and treats suppliers poorly or inconsistently most of the time, or is appearing to pay lip service to supplier recognition, then a recognition event is not going to remedy the situation, and it will not make suppliers think better of your company. It is likely to have the opposite effect. Suppliers will be quick to notice the inconsistencies between talk and action and may end up displaying the same inconsistencies by paying lip service to requests for change or improvement.

Attitudes toward procurement are important. Is procurement seen as adding value to the company and not just generating cost? If procurement's role has remained fairly traditional and procurement is viewed as lower status, only as buyers, and not as a strategic, value-adding function, then senior management may not want to be associated with or involved in supplier recognition. And without their support, supplier recognition will be difficult to deploy and have little positive impact on supplier performance and behavior.

DEVELOPING A SUPPLIER RECOGNITION PROCESS

The structure and participants of a supplier recognition project are similar to that used in a supplier performance management process. The actual structure depends upon the size of the company and the structure in place to make decisions at the executive level about procurement and supplier management. The procurement council or supply management steering team initiates the process. It approves the budget and chooses a selection committee or team to choose nominees. The selection team uses input and nominations from internal stakeholders such as procurement and other users. The procurement council makes policy decisions and reviews the recommendations from the selection committee regarding decision-making criteria and approval of suppliers selected. The procurement council would typically host the recognition event, with participation from other members of senior management. The selection committee is responsible for the following:

- Developing and communicating the supplier recognition process throughout the organization
- Establishing the selection criteria
- Choosing the winners from the nominations, subject to final approval of the procurement council

Establishing the selection criteria for the award should be taken very seriously. You may have more or fewer suppliers each year who can meet the criteria, which makes them more meaningful. You should not just give out awards gratuitously because you need to have a certain number of suppliers win no matter what. It is good to develop criteria that will enable different categories of suppliers to be eligible and win. Since, for example, you may not be scoring service suppliers in exactly the same way as direct suppliers, you may need to modify the criteria

Table 10.1 Supplier Recognition Program—Performance Criteria Points Chart

Category	Points
Growth	30
Reporting and Payment Standards	30
Customer Savings/Competitive Pricing	20
Healthcare Business Summit Sponsorship and Support	15
Environmental Excellence Activities	5
Electronic Catalog Integrity	10
Utilization of Vendor Support Tools	10
Support of Implementation Team	20
Utilization of Marketing Support and Contract Launch Tools	5
Outreach Programs (Diversity and Emergency Preparedness) Support*	5
Charitable Giving in Support of Health Care*	5
TOTAL POINTS	**155**
***BONUS POINTS**	**10**

Source: MedAssets, Inc. http://scs.medassets.com/HBS07/files/SupplierRecognitionProgram.pdf.

accordingly. Or you may have different categories of awards such as most innovative, best practices, or best new product. It is better not to concentrate criteria and awards on only one category or type of supplier. This gives a wide range of your suppliers a shot at winning and encourages excellence and some competition among a wide range in your supply base, such as smaller and larger companies, direct suppliers, service suppliers, minority- and women-owned business enterprises (MWBEs), and so on. Also, the selection criteria should reflect the types of performance standards that have a high impact on your company.

As an example, Table 10.1 shows the performance criteria for supplier recognition awards by MedAssets.[2] There are four levels of supplier awards (bronze, silver, gold, and platinum), depending on total points for different criteria. Suppliers are chosen for recognition awards based upon a point system. Based upon scores, suppliers are eligible for awards. Award winners are recognized at its Healthcare Business Summit, with additional recognition communicated to customers, the supplier community, and internally throughout the year.

In a good supplier recognition process, internal stakeholders nominate suppliers to the selection committee based upon clear nomination guidelines and criteria. In one scenario, the stakeholders may nominate suppliers meeting the criteria and with whom they have a relationship and/or whose products or serv-

---

2. MedAssets, Inc. provides technology services to hospitals to help them improve margins.

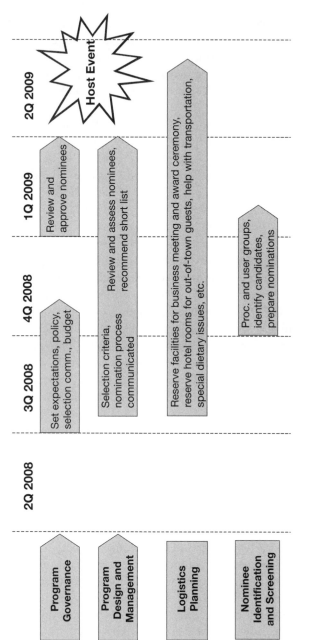

Planning for your first event should begin at least 9–12 months in advance.

Figure 10.2 Supplier recognition planning timeline for the first year.

ices they are familiar with. They inform suppliers of their nomination and the selection decision. Other companies use a rating points system.

Figure 10.2 shows a suggested timeline for planning a supplier recognition event for the first time. It illustrates the major tasks involved and shows that planning for a firm's first supplier recognition event should begin at least 9 to 12 months in advance. In addition to the internal process of developing criteria, nominating, and selecting the candidates, there are logistics planning and marketing/public relations components.

Make supplier recognition a special event away from the distractions of the office by holding it in an off-site facility, like a hotel, which will then require advance booking and logistics planning. Recognition events can be stand-alone or part of a supplier conference event. There are pros and cons to stand-alone versus part of a supplier conference. An advantage of stand-alone is the extra attention from your company, particularly from senior management, that award suppliers can get by having the event focus entirely on them. Also, you are more likely to attract senior management's attention because they are involved in planning the event and selecting suppliers; the awards will be part of company publicity, which they in turn will want to be part of; and the event will require the senior management in the supplier organization, which also helps encourage your senior management's participation. On the other hand, holding the supplier recognition during a supplier day publicly sets the bar high for the other suppliers in attendance and can create more interest in competing to win recognition, especially if the advantages of the award are clear to all. However, it may not allow the award winners as much time with their customer's senior management as a smaller event might allow. Also, some companies have a problem with their suppliers sending sales reps to supplier conferences, despite attempts to limit that practice. This reduces the effectiveness and prestige of the event. Of course, supplier recognition can take place both at a separate recognition event and at a supplier conference.

If senior executives from both customer and supplier are going to be involved, it is best to keep the event fairly short—guests arrive and attend a dinner reception the night before the meeting, attend the meeting in the morning, and then adjourn after lunch. The event can begin with a business meeting, ideally led by the CEO, president, or owner. Having the CEO run the business meeting demonstrates the importance of the supplier's achievement and sends a message both to the rest of the customer company and to the suppliers about the important role the suppliers play in its success. The CEO can give an overview of business conditions, trends, future plans, and challenges in the industry that are or will impact the bottom line. Participants from the customer side can include executives from the supplier, customer corporate executives, business unit executives (if applicable), and procurement council members. The award ceremony can follow the business meeting that other invited guests can attend, such as supplier relationship managers and other employees. After the CEO or president's overview, there can be an open discussion among supplier and customer executives. This is a good time to discuss the ways that suppliers see the challenges, such as cost, globalization, risk, and so on, and how they are addressing them.

To maximize the value and impact of the awards ceremony, it should include an explanation of the selection process and the specific reasons why each supplier present was selected to win the award, including any quantitative or qualitative specifics about their performance. Also, publicity after the awards is an important part of the process to maximize the impact in your supply base and encourage others to strive for the recognition. In striving for the recognition, many suppliers are going to improve their performance, and the impacts on their customers will be positive. Positive publicity is also good for your company and for your suppliers. The trade press is always looking for success stories and may even contact you or some of your supplier honorees to write additional articles profiling them. While every company's communications department may have their own publicity approaches, here are some suggestions:

- Send a press release to your target geographic regions (where you have customers and/or suppliers) regarding the supplier awards.
- Encourage each supplier winner to do their own press release. Give each supplier the verbiage and template on which to base their release. This multiplies the good publicity at no cost, adding value to customer and supplier.
- Present the award again at the supplier facility so that its employees can take part in celebrating their success.
- Take out a full page ad in one or more magazines.
- Develop color brochures explaining the program and do a mailing with a cover letter to your supply base.

The cost of this program, including publicity and the event itself, can run from $25,000 to $50,000, according to Bob Rudzki of Greybeard Advisors and former CPO of Pittsburgh Steel and Bayer, who contributed to this chapter and who has developed and conducted supplier recognition programs for his former employers. While this may seem like a large outlay, the measurable benefits and paybacks can rapidly outweigh the costs. Bob has seen further improvements from the award winners and improvements from other suppliers striving for recognition. One supplier who wanted to be selected in the second year of the program generated over $1,000,000 in new cost reductions, creating a 20 times ROI of $50,000. All of this further reinforces the value of supplier recognition to senior management.

To summarize, here are some of the key elements of a successful recognition program:

- Customer and supplier upper-level management commitment and involvement in the recognition process

- Costs and benefits understood
- Establishment of a budget
- Good project management of the entire recognition process from conception to deployment
- A performance evaluation system on which to base the recognition
- Recognition aligned with the supplier evaluation system
- Clear specification of award criteria and supplier eligibility
- Input and feedback from internal stakeholders on potential supplier candidates
- Periodic evaluation and improvement of the recognition program

SUPPLIER CERTIFICATION

Supplier certification is a process for measuring suppliers against a set of criteria and awarding status and privileges for achieving specific levels of performance and/or having industry or customer-recognized best practices in place. It is a strategy for continuous improvement of supplier performance and reliability and also risk reduction. And, in the context of supplier performance management, certification can provide incentives and a path to more rewards for the supplier. Typically rewards for a certified supplier can include first consideration for new business, visibility and recognition by the customer, and systematic improvements that can increase the supplier's overall performance and profit margins. As part of an overall supplier performance management program, supplier certification can provide ROI and benefits to the customer.

Supplier certification benefits to the customer include reduction in total cost, more favorable supply contracts, supplier productivity gains, improvement in the quality of goods and services, continuous improvement in supplier performance, a path to higher standards for all suppliers, and improved competitive advantage for both customer and supplier. In a multi-site environment, a certification program can help ensure consistency among locations. Benefits to the supplier are more business/increased sales as a preferred source; positive, long-term relationship with the customer; less customer oversight; industry recognition; access to supplier development resources; and gaining competitive advantage by being able to provide higher quality goods and services at a lower total cost (through performance improvement efforts).

A supplier who has been certified should perform at a level where its products and/or services do not need to be checked or reviewed for quality and regularly meet customer requirements and performance expectations. Supplier certification is usually considered the top level of supplier performance. A certification program usually evolves after a firm has already put in place basic supplier approval processes and performance standards. Companies who certify suppliers follow many variations on the certification theme, from one to multiple levels of certification. Suppliers can be approved, which means that they meet the minimum qualifications as a source and you can do business with them. The next level is preferred, which implies a source exceeds the minimum, requires less quality review, and attains a level of performance that makes you want to do more business with them than the approved suppliers. The top level is certified. For some companies, preferred suppliers are the same as certified suppliers. For others, the preferred designation means that the supplier is in the process of becoming certified. According to the classic book on supplier certification, *Supplier Certification: A Continuous Improvement Strategy*, in most companies with a certification process, only about 10 percent of approved suppliers become certified.[3] I have seen similar statistics more recently through my observation of companies with certification processes. It makes sense to apply the resources to the top cadre of suppliers. Plus, most suppliers will either be incapable of or not interested in reaching the highest level of certification. A previous chapter detailed how to conduct a site visit. While site visits are part of a certification process, they are used for supplier evaluation and continuous improvement and for other reasons such as approval, qualification, quality assurance, and partnering.

Certification has traditionally been the purview of large manufacturing companies, since it began as a way to ensure the quality of manufactured products and it required resources that limited the process to mostly larger companies. Since its origins in the quality function, both smaller companies and service-oriented organizations have adapted the audit-oriented aspects of supplier certification and simplified the process to work in their environments. Certification is no longer strictly a quality assurance tool. It can be used to certify suppliers in specific areas, such as corporate social responsibility, diversity, and lean. Or, some companies may consider a formal supplier approval or qualification process as certification, do not use a site visit, and require only some initial profile information forms and subsequent ongoing tracking of performance metrics.

There are three approaches to supplier certification: certification by a customer, third-party certification such as ISO 9000-2000, and self-certification by the supplier. Some companies use elements of all three methods. Boeing is an example of this. Its process has included some supplier self-assessment (done over the Web), assessment that is done by Boeing staff, and information system tracking of metrics, with some additional consideration given for having achieved third-party certification, such as ISO or AQS. Other variations on certification include certification of processes instead of products. Helix Technology

---

3. Bossert, James L., John O. Brown, and Richard A. Maass, *Supplier Certification: A Continuous Improvement Strategy*, ASQ, 1990, p. 7.

Corporation, now part of Brooks Automation, was a semiconductor equipment manufacturer who would certify supplier processes rather than certify the supplier. It would focus on the process to make the specific products it was procuring from a supplier, the philosophy being that high-quality products result from high-performing, robust processes.

DEVELOPING A SUPPLIER CERTIFICATION PROCESS

Supplier certification is another process in the toolkit of supplier performance management. Developing a supplier certification process is similar to developing a performance management process, with aspects of it specific to certification. Here is an overview of a step-by-step approach. It can be developed with the idea of certifying any type of supplier—service or manufacturing. In this discussion of developing a process, there are a few assumptions. First, this is not the only performance management tool that a company plans to use and likely not the first one that a firm would develop. We are assuming that some kind of supplier performance management system is already in place, such as KPIs and scorecards. Supplier certification is usually not done as the first step in creating a supplier evaluation process, but as a next step using higher standards than ordinary supplier evaluation in order to choose and then focus on the best of the best. Certification programs require resources and high commitment on the part of the customer in order to be successful. It is a next step in a progression to developing a high-performing supply chain and not typically a place to begin.

Following are the suggested steps for developing and maintaining a certification process. It is similar to developing an overall supplier performance management system.

Obtain Senior Management Support

You will need to develop a business case with a cost/benefit analysis and ROI. Management may see supplier certification purely as an expense and not a value-added process. Part of the challenge is that the certification process may take time to develop and deploy and require patience from senior management, which does not always have the stamina and attention span for long-term undertakings that require an outlay of resources. Management will need to understand that certification cannot happen overnight, so the expectations about the time frame for results need to be properly set. Depending on the size of the company and number of suppliers who will undergo certification, developing the certification process and producing the first certified suppliers could take a year. Then, once suppliers begin to be certified, it may take another year before there is significant measurable impact. Management support includes obtaining a budget in return for making a clear business case for certification.

Choose the Project Team

You will need to set up a team and a project structure, just as in overall SPM. You can use the same structure or even the same participants described in Chapter 3, with a steering committee, executive sponsor, process owner, and project team composed of internal and external stakeholders. However, depending upon your organization and the nature of the certification, you may decide not to use a procurement council as the main decision-making body, since senior management in the quality function may also need to be involved. Some companies have managers responsible for procurement quality and supplier quality as part of a procurement council or supply management council. The terminology for the decision-making body may vary, such as supply chain steering team or supply management steering committee, and so on. Whatever term is used, all impacted functions need decision-making input at a senior level in the form of a steering committee or council to ensure that certification processes are not developed at lower levels in a vacuum. Regarding stakeholder participation, getting supplier involvement early in the development of the process is important for creating a certification that is a reasonable, easy-to-use, and valuable performance improvement process for suppliers. Suppliers will need to understand the benefits to them of becoming certified and also help you develop additional benefits in order to get on board with the process.

Develop Certification Goals

The project team develops the goals for the process, criteria for selection of supplier candidates for certification, and the criteria for the actual certification. Considerations include goals of certification for your company; supplier performance goals, especially as they relate to overall company goals and strategies; selection criteria for certification candidates; criteria for levels and types of certification, as applicable; incentives/rewards for certified suppliers; and benefits for the customer.

Develop Certification Process

Decisions need to be made about the types of information that will need to be collected to meet the goals of the process and how information will be collected—sources and collection methods, frequency of data collection and site visits, and frequency of performance reviews with certified suppliers. You should also develop processes for: maintaining certification, dealing with suppliers whose performance degrades, making decisions about whether to give suppliers a period of time to improve and retain their status, and whether or not supplier development resources would be offered to help the supplier. Also, decisions need to be made about under what conditions a supplier would lose certification status. Other areas needing development are probation, de-certification, and re-certification criteria and processes. Many companies with a certification process will try to help the supplier stay certified so long as the supplier is motivated to do so and works with its customer to correct problems and issues. Decisions must be made about periodic review: how often the customer will review the metrics, conduct site visits, meet for performance reviews, and review continuous-improvement plans and progress against them with the supplier.

Develop Performance Measures

The project team needs to develop the actual certification instrument, whether that is a survey, Web-based data collection, or a combination. The data collection must translate into performance measures and a system of scoring the supplier to determine attainment of certification status. Typical areas that are considered important criteria for certifying a supplier and that can vary depending on the business of the supplier include the following:

- Zero defects, either product- or non-product-related, for a given period of time. This can range from product quality rejections from a manufacturing supplier to software bugs from an IT supplier. Time ranges for maintaining these performance levels can be anywhere from six months to two years.
- No negative incidents for a designated period of time (i.e., customer complaints, lack of responsiveness, in-process rejections, late deliveries).
- Passing an on-site business or quality review.
- Quality system exists and is documented.
- Processes are stable and in control.

Performance measures and certification criteria should not be based only upon the lagging indicators of incidents and metrics that measure past performance but also on leading indicators. Good processes and good business practices are leading indicators. So are enabling behaviors (as described in Chapter 2). These can be determined in site visits and through well-constructed survey instruments.

Here is an example of the elements of Rockwell Collins' performance measurement to determine its preferred suppliers:

1. Past performance

Table 10.2 Preferred Supplier Certification Business Process Assessment Elements

Leadership	Quality	Production Processes	Cost	Technology	Support
Organization	Management	Alignment, communications, and affordability	Estimating and reporting	Organization, development, and production readiness	Logistics planning
Company integration	Control		Accounting system		Product support
	Assurance	Production system enablers			
External supplier management		Performance and measures	Inventory and supplier cost management	Design development	
			Project cost management		

Source: The Boeing Company

    2. Technology learning curve position of both supplier products and manufacturing processes
    3. Supplier business practices maturity
    4. Supplier business cost structural analysis
    5. Supplier environmental impact and responsiveness[4]

Rockwell Collins' performance expectations overall categories for preferred suppliers are mutual working relationship strategies, technology, quality, responsiveness, delivery, cost of ownership, and environmental responsibility. Performance information is updated on a monthly basis, and suppliers can access their own information through a supplier portal. Rockwell Collins selects 100 top preferred suppliers for recognition at an annual supplier conference, by invitation only. One supplier from the top 100 is chosen for the President's Award on the basis of most fully meeting the performance criteria.

    Table 10.2 gives an example of performance expectations for preferred suppliers from Boeing. Its Preferred Supplier Certification (PSC), recognized as a best-in-class process, has been undergoing some changes. In its original form, it took into account three areas to achieve certification:

---

4. Rockwell Collins, "Our Process" Web page. Available at http://www.rockwellcollins.com/suppliers/Process/index.html.

- Ongoing quantitative metrics in quality, on-time delivery, affordability, and customer satisfaction.
- Detailed quality evaluation.
- Business process assessment (elements of which are shown in Table 10.2). This assessment is based upon the supplier's meeting rigorous and detailed expectations in every one of the six elements (or "tools"). These scores are derived from a combination of a detailed Web-based self-assessment based upon the six elements (or fewer, depending upon the type of supplier) and a Boeing site visit assessment to verify the self-assessment.

Criteria for becoming a preferred supplier included specified levels of performance in ongoing quantitative metrics and scores on the business process assessment. Scores from the site visit along with specified performance levels in the quantitative metrics determine the level of certification the supplier could achieve: bronze, silver, or gold. As an example, a gold supplier needed to achieve 100 percent on-time delivery and 100 percent quality acceptance in a 12-month period as well as meet rigorous cost reduction targets. A supplier could move up the scale from bronze to gold (or the other way around). Besides being a prestigious achievement for the supplier, preferred supplier certification entitled suppliers to more business and access to supplier development resources. Besides Preferred Supplier Certification, Boeing added other areas of assessment. Since a lean supply chain was important to the company, there were lean assessments for suppliers. New product development was another critical area for the future growth of the company, particularly collaborative product development with suppliers. So a development assessment for development suppliers was created.

At Eastman Kodak, certification is part of their SQP (Supplier Quality Process). Also, as discussed previously, not all data for metrics are readily available for performance measurement, nor are all areas trackable or controllable. The team must figure out what areas at suppliers can be reasonably measured, tracked and improved.

Continuous Improvement/Corrective Action

A key purpose and goal of the certification process is continuous improvement. Certification sets performance standards that suppliers will be striving to meet, maintain, and exceed. Certification metrics and site visits will uncover both supplier strengths and opportunities for improvement. You and your suppliers will not get the full benefits from certification unless these opportunities are tracked and pursued. And to maintain continued internal support for certification, maintain supplier buy-in, and demonstrate the business case, you should be tracking

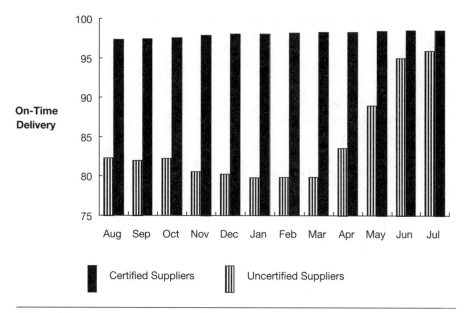

Figure 10.3 Impact of certification on supplier delivery performance.

the before and after metrics of improvement projects and quantify the financial impacts, if possible. This clearly demonstrates the return on investment of supplier certification. Other useful metrics are performance comparisons of certified versus noncertified supplier performance tracked over time. Figure 10.3 shows a significant difference in delivery performance between certified and noncertified suppliers.

Another example of ROI comes from Novartis, whose certification program delivered increasing savings, primarily in the area of inspection and testing costs and also storage costs, starting at a $200,000 savings the first year and reaching an annual savings of $1.3M by the sixth year of the program.[5] Rockwell Collins, on the other hand, was able to reduce supplier lead times by 23 percent and reduce shortages by 30 percent within a two-year period.

Rollout

Implementation planning or rollout should include a pilot of the certification process and its information collection tools to assess effectiveness and whether it is sufficiently supplier-friendly to ensure participation and compliance. As part of

---

5. Alfred T. (Ted) Ericson, C.P.M., "The Successful Merger of Two Supplier Certification Processes," ISM Annual Conference, 2000.

Table 10.3 Certification Team Training Agenda

Background information

Benefits of the process to customer and supplier

Certification requirements

Certification process

Using SPM software to support the process

Certification team responsibilities

- Site visit process
- Planning and preparation
- On-site activities
- Process evaluation
- Scoring guidelines
- Giving feedback to supplier

Follow-up, performance monitoring, and continuous improvement

Summary

the pilot process, the individuals who are going to be conducting certification should be identified and trained, as necessary, in the certification process, the certification tools, conducting certification site visits, use of software supporting the certification process, and giving feedback to suppliers. Table 10.3 shows a sample training agenda for preparing the certification team for the rollout.

During the pilot and subsequent rollout, certification project team members and suppliers and management who are involved in the process need to be kept informed about the status of the project. Once the first suppliers have gone through the process in a pilot mode, there should be internal reviews of the pilots and critiques, and feedback should be gathered from team members and internal stakeholders and from suppliers. Suppliers, for example, can be asked for feedback with questions such as:

- Did you understand the purpose of this assessment?
- Were the questions clear?
- How long did the assessment take to complete?
- Were you able to answer most of the questions?
- Were the questions relevant to your company?
- Was the feedback useful to your company?
- How do you think that your customer should respond to the supplier strengths and opportunities that come out of the assessment?
- Do you think that continuous-improvement planning should result from this assessment?

- How can the assessment itself be approved?
- How can the assessment process be approved?

This information should be used to improve the process before full implementation. Feedback on the certification process should be solicited on an ongoing basis for continuous improvement of the certification process.

Recognize Certified Suppliers

There are several ways to recognize preferred or certified suppliers. The obvious and most common way is to celebrate the actual attainment of certification. Many customers hold an award ceremony at the supplier. While the format of this may vary, it is effective to have a senior management person representing the customer give the award to the president or general manager of the company in front of its employees to highlight the importance of the achievement. Types of awards include plaques and banners. While these may seem ordinary, the pride of the employees at companies receiving the recognition is further supported by visible signs of their achievement. Employees do not take these awards lightly. And when the certification award is hard-won and has been difficult to attain, certification is all the more motivating to employees. Many customers and their newly certified suppliers issue a joint press release. As discussed earlier, suppliers can be recognized as a group at a special recognition event or as part of an overall supplier day. The main goals are to celebrate excellence, improve and support competitiveness of the supply base, encourage continuous improvement, and communicate the achievement internally and to the rest of the supplier community to inspire others toward performance improvement. Recognition can also be given to top suppliers in the community of certified suppliers, not just newly certified suppliers—to the best of the best.

SUPPLIER SELF-ASSESSMENT

Supplier self-assessment can be effective as part of an overall qualification or certification process. It is not as effective deployed as a stand-alone approach, though it can be used as a supplier development tool by highlighting areas of opportunity for improvement that a supplier can then choose to pursue (or not pursue). A good self-assessment can be educational for some suppliers. Using stand-alone self-assessment allows customer firms to reach suppliers to whom it would not ordinarily directly apply its resources. This is particularly true if the self-assessment tool is Web-based and requires little or no intervention from the customer. Some highly motivated supplier firms will seize this opportunity to improve and to show initiative to the customer firm. One supplier that I dealt with was excited to use a self-assessment process because they considered it to be free business consulting. Self-assessment has the advantage of reducing some of the expenses associated with certification by having the supplier do the work of filling out detailed questionnaires regarding its capabilities, processes, and practices without full on-site verification. The disadvantage is the potential for misrepresentation of capabilities or misunderstanding of the customer's questions or expectations on the questionnaire so that the supplier presents capabilities that the customer discovers later do not meet requirements. To the extent that the customer can communicate requirements and expectations clearly to the supplier and the supplier can understand these requirements and prove that it can meet them when it delivers products and services, then self-assessment can be a valuable component in an overall certification or qualification process. With well-designed surveys or questionnaires, a good two-way flow of information and communications, and a desire to make the relationship work, self-assessment can be successful. The customer can soon discover whether the supplier purposely misrepresents itself or exaggerates its capabilities. It is certainly better not to engage with those sorts of businesses in the first place, if possible, by weeding them out with some qualification work. When well deployed, supplier self-assessment can be used to help reduce the time needed on site visits. It can also be used as a supplier development tool to help suppliers understand strengths and opportunities for continuous improvement. High-achieving suppliers in particular will view self-assessment as an opportunity for improvement.

In summary, supplier certification can be a complex and costly undertaking. And while the benefits and payback just discussed may be apparent to procurement and quality staff, they may be less obvious to senior management, whose support is important before developing and during a certification process. And as the process progresses, it is important to have established a measurement baseline and track supplier performance improvements and cost savings against the baseline to continually make the business case clear to all stakeholders. Certification requires resources to develop the process, visit suppliers, track ongoing performance, and then maintain and redeploy on an ongoing basis. Also, the customer doing the certification must have the staff with the knowledge, skills, and tools to successfully evaluate suppliers. There is also the potential disconnect between the areas being evaluated at the supplier and the customer's own internal processes and capabilities. Could the certifying company meet its own requirements? And is the certifying company asking more of its suppliers than it asks of itself? Leading by example is more effective for getting results.

DISENGAGING WITH POOR PERFORMERS

We have discussed how to measure performance and develop recognition and rewards for good performance and certification programs as a pathway to supplier performance excellence. But not all suppliers are on the path to business excellence. Some will need to be disengaged, or put less politely, fired. There are many reasons why companies need to disengage with suppliers and they are not always due to poor supplier performance. Sometimes the need to disengage is involuntary, such as in a merger or acquisition, a bankruptcy, or a change in the customer's business that no longer requires certain types of products and services. In other cases, price may be the overarching issue causing the need to stop using the supplier (though sometimes high prices can stem from performance issues internally at the supplier).

In this book, supplier performance is the issue at hand. And as we discussed, supplier performance is a two-way street. Sometimes the customer shares some of the blame for the supplier's performance and the disintegration of the relationship from trust to lack of trust. The customer may not live up to its commitments to the supplier. While the supplier manager or procurement person has made promises, he or she may have been unable to get internal people to live up to them. For example, the customer firm may be paying the supplier very late, and is hurting its cash flow and operations to the point where the supplier cannot meet performance expectations. Or, in other cases, the supplier's performance metrics may have failed to meet expectations or the baseline metrics set by the customer—and hopefully previously communicated to and agreed upon by the supplier. The customer has begged and pleaded, issued warnings, maybe even given the supplier a probationary period to improve. But for whatever reason, the improvement does not occur. Or perhaps the customer has said nothing at all, assuming that either the poor performance was obvious to the supplier or that the supplier knew the rules of performance in advance. One of the key issues in a breakup of this sort is communications. The customer may not have clearly conveyed performance expectations, how the supplier was being measured or what that meant in terms of the relationship. Or perhaps the buyer was too busy to communicate and the supplier never asked or even knew about the customer's dissatisfaction. What next? How does a customer firm disengage with a supplier in a professional manner, without creating hostility or burning bridges?

Relationships with suppliers can be like marriage and breaking up something like a divorce. How well the breakup goes depends upon how the conflict is managed and how clear the rules of engagement were in the first place (i.e., the contract). There is going to be conflict, but avoiding hostility and accusations and showing respect will help. As in any business relationship, it is better to remain business-like and pleasant and avoid burning any bridges.

Table 10.4 Ways to End a Supplier Relationship

The High Road	The Low Road
Warn the supplier in advance.	Take the supplier completely by surprise.
Make the disengagement clear by notifying the supplier both verbally and in writing. If possible, meet in person.	Just stop ordering from the supplier and avoid actually telling them that their services are no longer needed. Don't answer the phone or return the supplier's calls.
Be clear on the reasons for disengagement.	Never tell the supplier the real reasons why. After all, it is too hard to give them the bad news and you don't have to work with them anymore.
Be respectful and professional. Let the supplier know that it is just business and not personal.	Berate the supplier for their poor performance and other previous crimes against the customer.
Review the contract terms for giving notice.	Get your company in legal trouble by violating the notice clauses.
Work out settlement plans for disposition of inventory and completing any outstanding orders.	Try to stick the supplier with as much inventory as possible.
Figure out an exit plan together and settle any payments with them or their suppliers rapidly.	String them out on the money you owe them, as you'll never have to deal with the supplier again anyway.
Give the supplier a reasonable time frame for a transition.	Dump the supplier immediately with no transition.

Table 10.4 summarizes some of the good and bad ways to end a relationship with a supplier.[6]

The reasons for problem suppliers are numerous and so are approaches to handling different situations. When remediation efforts either fail or are not desirable, the relationship should be ended in as orderly and professional a fashion as possible, with minimal disruption to both the customer and supplier firms.

Sometimes, however, customer firms do not end relationships with poorly performing suppliers and allow the problems to linger. There are several possible reasons poorly performing suppliers are not disengaged:

- There is a lack of monitoring or awareness of poor supplier performance.
- A personal bond between a procurement person and the supplier may cause the customer representative to have difficulty either recognizing poor performance or to be reluctant to end the relationship.

---

6. Adapted from Susan Scott, "Ending Supplier Relationships without Hostility," presented at the 86th Annual ISM Conference, 2001.

- The relationship may sometimes persist due to unethical behavior, such as inappropriate gifts.

If the customer has a supplier performance management system in place with performance expectations, performance results, rewards, and consequences clearly communicated with suppliers, some of the mystery and distrust that can come from unclear rules and uncommunicated expectations will be dispelled, except for business situations (bankruptcies, acquisitions) where the relationship must be ended for reasons other than performance.

SUMMARY

There are measurable benefits of supplier recognition and meeting high performance standards. Setting the performance bar high for suppliers and recognizing excellent performance can result in tangible improvements and measurable ROI that impact both customer and supplier firms and add value to the relationship.

Web
Added
Value™

11

SUPPLIER DEVELOPMENT

With the main objective for measuring supplier performance to improve performance, the challenge is getting from performance measurement to performance improvement. As has been often quoted, good suppliers are made, not born. Few companies start out excellent. But excellence can be nurtured when there is a desire or passion to pursue it. This is called supplier development. According to the ISM (Institute of Supply Management) glossary, supplier development is defined as "a systematic effort to create and maintain a network of competent suppliers, and to improve various supplier capabilities that are necessary for the purchasing organization to meet its competitive challenges." Supplier performance management, when well deployed, can offer actionable insights into supplier capabilities and competencies and can help both customers and suppliers focus on the most essential and impactful opportunities for supplier development.

Not every supplier is going to have the ability or the desire to make that journey. Pursuing improvement opportunities requires giving and accepting constructive (hopefully) criticism, willingness to change, and potentially doing things differently than the way the supplier has always done them. This requires change management and the skills that enable it. We will discuss barriers to change at suppliers and ways to overcome them. And not every customer has the insights to know what is causing problems. Many companies do not have the resources—time, money, or staff—to work with suppliers on improvements. While many customers send their own staff to work at the supplier's site on improvement projects or even pay for all or part of a consulting engagement at the supplier, there are other ways to help suppliers. The customer can enable supplier performance improvement activities, whether through education or connecting the supplier to resources or to other companies who have dealt with similar challenges. We will address creative, less resource-intense approaches to helping suppliers pursue opportunities for improvement and methods for helping motivate suppliers and enabling change. We will also cover how to use systematic processes, usually specific corporate initiatives being implemented at the customer, such as lean and Six Sigma, as supplier development methodologies and opportunities.

WHY DEVELOP SUPPLIERS

Development of key or critical suppliers has come to be seen as an option as increased outsourcing of products and services has resulted in increased dependency on outside suppliers' performance, quality, cost, responsiveness, and technology. Another factor is supplier rationalization or "right-sizing" initiatives. In weeding out poor performers and reducing the size of the supply base, you will still have suppliers who are average to good, but need to do more to be great. Dependence on fewer sources, while still a viable strategy for simplifying processes and reducing the costs and waste associated with managing too many suppliers, can mean fewer alternatives in case of problems. A high dependence on outside suppliers can make it risky, difficult, and costly to find and change to new sources. It takes time and resources to find, qualify, and on-board new suppliers and then to develop a reliable, trusting, and productive relationship. There are pitfalls and risks along the way, as there are few perfect suppliers. Also, there may be limited choices in the categories where you have a need. These factors lead many companies to choose to pursue supplier development rather than supplier replacement.

CHOOSING WHICH SUPPLIERS TO DEVELOP

Because supplier development involves resources, such as money and/or time at both the customer and supplier, and requires a commitment to the relationship with a supplier, the decision should be strategic, not reactive.[1] The following are some strategies for choosing supplier development targets. The different types of supplier situations are not mutually exclusive.

- Choose suppliers with whom the customer's spend is high relative to overall spend. This can result from high spend on a low volume of items or from services or indirect spend. Or high spend can result from high volume. High spend can mean high impact in terms of cost reductions.

---

1. Hartley, Janet L., "Supplier Development: Customers as a Catalyst of Process Change," *Business Horizons*, July–August, 1996.

- Choose strategically important suppliers, whether or not their purchase dollars are high. These can include suppliers who build to specific customer specifications. Development suppliers who may be doing collaborative product or service development can also fall into the strategically important category.
- Choose suppliers with whom the customer plans to have a long-term relationship. You do not want to apply resources to a company that you will need to drop due to market or product shifts.
- Choose suppliers who are weaker than their competitors, if ultimately you want to create a more cost competitive situation.

CHOOSING SUPPLIER DEVELOPMENT APPROACHES

In a study that was published in 2002 in the *Journal of Supply Chain Management*, Janet Harley and Daniel Krause explored whether there were differences between service firms' and product firms' approaches to supplier development.[2] They defined supplier development as:

- *Supplier assessment.* Evaluation, certification and feedback
- *Competitive pressure.* Using multiple suppliers or the threat of switching to another supplier
- *Supplier incentives.* Increased business, promise of future business, and recognition and rewards
- *Direct involvement activities.* Mutual site visits, training, and investment

The authors discovered that both service and product companies did all the above types of supplier development. However, service firms relied on putting competitive pressures on suppliers far more than did any product firms. That is, they had several suppliers compete for business to achieve price reductions. Also, service firms were more concerned than product firms about improving suppliers' financial position. Product companies, on the other hand, were more likely to use supplier assessment, incentives, and direct involvement than service companies. Both kinds of firms focused more on improving actual supplier performance in the areas of cost, delivery, service performance, and quality (less interest in quality by service firms) than the more strategic goal of improving capabilities (such as management, technical, and product development).

---

2. Krause, Daniel R., and Scannell, Thomas V., "Supplier Development Practices: Product- and Service-Based Industry Comparisons, *Journal of Supply Chain Management*, Spring 2002, Vol. 38, No. 2, p. 13.

We have discussed so far the use of supplier assessment techniques—evaluation, certification, and feedback as methods to improve supplier performance. We have also emphasized the need for taking action with incentives (increased business, the opportunity for additional business, and recognition) and consequences (probation, disengagement) as an important part of an evaluation process. The following are supplier development approaches using direct involvement.

Training

Providing training is a straightforward way to help suppliers. There are many ways to provide training:

1. *Provide training and education programs to suppliers, either at the customer or supplier site.* This is an effective way to introduce new initiatives and raise awareness on specific methodologies, such as lean, Six Sigma, and high-performance business systems. It is also effective for introducing specific methods and techniques, such as continuous improvement tools, value stream mapping, 5S (workplace organization), and so on. When I was running the New England Suppliers Institute, we provided supplier training for specific customers. We also conducted public workshops on topics chosen by customer firms with their suppliers in mind. Examples of the topics were "Pull Systems for the Machining Job Shop," "Purchasing Basics for Small Manufacturers," and "The Visual Workplace." Customers would market these workshops to their suppliers and in some cases make attendance mandatory or highly recommended. Another interesting aspect of these workshops was that the suppliers who attended had not all been invited by just one customer but by several customer firms, which provided some additional encouragement. Thus, these suppliers could see that it was not just their own customer who thought that adopting lean and performance improvement technologies was a good idea.
2. *Invite suppliers to customer internal training at the customer site.* That is, when your company is having a training session for its own staff that would be useful for suppliers, you can put aside some slots for supplier personnel so they can attend. This is a lower cost way to provide good training to key supplier personnel. I have seen supplier personnel get lean and Six Sigma Black Belt training at their customers so that they could go back and begin to deploy these practices at their own companies.

3. *Give suppliers the names of specific resources for them to engage for training.* Or give them information on public workshops available in their area. Many U.S. states have workforce development agencies that provide funding and/or on-site workforce training services to companies at a reasonable cost. In addition, for U.S. manufacturing companies, for example, the Manufacturing Extension Partnership (MEP) funded in part by NIST and state governments provides training and consulting resources to small to medium-size manufacturing firms. MEP's mission is to make SMEs more competitive, and it has a wide range of supplier development offerings. With affiliates in every state in the United States, the MEPs work with SMEs individually or with the customer firm to coordinate supplier development programs and activities.

4. *Use supplier role models.* Use suppliers who have successfully implemented the desired improvements or high performance as role models. It is the "if they can do it, I can do it" approach. Suppliers think that sure, my customer can do these things because they are big and have more resources. The customer, on the other hand, thinks that it should be easier for the suppliers to implement the changes because they are smaller, less bureaucratic, and more agile. Typically suppliers may resist directives and prescriptive measures from their large customers. But seeing other suppliers like them who are enjoying success is more powerful than any exhortations from the customer. At New England Suppliers Institute (NESI), we found the role model approach very successful in convincing small job shop suppliers to take on the significant change that adopting lean manufacturing required. Rather than using the typical customer firm directive about adopting a new change or system, we used peer pressure through supplier role models. A standard feature of our workshops on lean was a guest presentation from a supplier who had been successful in implementing lean processes and practices. The president or owner from the supplier firm would give the presentation and would talk about the challenges and issues and would show before and after pictures and before and after metrics and ROI. The supplier firms giving the presentations represented the types of shops in attendance—machining and electromechanical job shops. They were willing to disclose the costs and the significant ROI of implementing lean as well as the problems they encountered along the way. These suppliers, who were practitioners of and evangelists for positive change, would graciously offer to let the participants

come visit their shops. This approach was very powerful and compelling to peer companies, many of whose owners and presidents attended the workshops and then began their own lean journeys as a result of these role model presentations. And some of those who voiced the biggest initial opposition to the concepts turned into NESI's biggest proponents. Another interesting phenomenon was that these small manufacturing companies were willing to pay for lean consultants because the ROI was so compelling. Companies were able to get off extended lines of credit because their cash flow improved so much. The results had a positive operational and financial impact on both suppliers and their customers. Typical results, which are common in lean implementations, were as follows:

- Productivity increased 30 percent annually
- Defects reduced by 20 percent
- Lead times reduced by 90 percent
- Inventory reduced by 75 percent
- On-time delivery almost 100 percent

Consulting and Technical Assistance

Providing consulting or technical assistance directly to suppliers is an effective way to help suppliers with improvement initiatives. There are two kinds of approaches. The first is to help a supplier solve specific problems. The second is to help the supplier develop capabilities for improvement.

Targeted Assistance to Solve Specific Problems

This approach to supplier development is the most common. This method has been termed "results-oriented supplier development" or targeted supplier development. This approach is typically driven by the buying company, the changes are typically technical, and the development process lasts a short time.[3] Customers send resources, either from their own firm or an outside consultant, to suppliers to help them solve particular problems that arise, such as specific quality problems, delivery problems, cost issues, value engineering, production problems, and so on. The buyer-driven approach can be efficient for the buying company when it puts together a team trained to focus on improving specific types of issues. The company deploys the team to a selected group of suppliers; the team works on

---

3. Hartley, Janet, and Gwen Jones, "Process-Oriented Supplier Development: Building the Capability for Change," *Journal of Supply Chain Management*, Summer 1997, Vol. 33, No. 3, p. 24.

specific types of projects, finishes, and moves on to the next. Or, the buying firm has individuals with particular skill sets, such as quality staff, who are sent to a supplier to fix specific problems that fit in with their particular skills. Some companies have dedicated supplier development teams that do nothing else but supplier development (though these teams may do more than provide targeted assistance).

There are many advantages to targeted assistance. First, it is a quick hit. A supplier problem that is adversely impacting the customer can get solved rapidly. This means there is immediate return on investment to both the customer and the supplier, even if no further efforts are pursued. Because they are specific and technical in nature, targeted development projects often do not require management or organizational change at the supplier to implement, a potential barrier in more systemic change. Because the issue may already come to light during supplier performance evaluations and the information needed to analyze the specific problem is quantitative or technical in nature, it can be easier to work with the supplier without the supplier feeling that the customer is treading on sensitive turf. In addition, an outside firm, particularly a customer who can model the changes it is seeking from the supplier, often has more clout to suggest improvements that are more difficult to make than relying on changes from within. A supplier may be more willing to quickly adopt changes suggested from the customer that don't rock the boat, but afford measurable, rapid improvement. Another advantage of targeted assistance is that success breeds success for both parties. The supplier organization will experience success, which can help build support and momentum within the supplier for future improvement efforts. The customer firm also enjoys results of a supplier problem solved and a quick and visible return on its investment in the supplier. Additional support for supplier development within the customer organization can be built upon the successes of supplier development projects.

What are the disadvantages of this approach? The biggest challenge is that such targeted improvements may not be sustainable. More systemic changes may need to be made to ensure improvements are more than a "one-off." Also, the short-term nature of targeted improvements means that employees may not have a chance to learn the skills they need to make more improvements and sustain those improvements. The need for basic skills in the workforce to bring about and sustain improvements became obvious to me when I was Director of Total Quality at a distribution company where the president and founder hired me to start the function and implement total quality management (TQM). We thought we could just jump in and make the changes that both the data and the employees so clearly indicated needed to occur. The employees were excited and ready to embrace TQM. But we found that employees had never worked on improvement projects and needed to learn the most basic skills before any continuous improvement could occur. This was without taking into account that there were significant, overall changes that were required to create a culture that supported continuous improvement. The workforce needed to be trained in such areas as how to conduct a meeting and how to work as a team before we could even start to train them in continuous improvement tools and techniques. In many companies, English and basic literacy in the workforce is a need and a challenge. Even though improvements may be specific and targeted, people issues may arise and the improvements may require organizational changes to sustain. For example, if a quality problem is addressed by changing a work process so that the associates are responsible for the quality of their work before moving it to the next work process, this can change the nature of their jobs and that of their supervisor or inspectors who thought they were responsible for quality. Another issue is that improvements that have the potential to save money can sometimes mean eliminating jobs, redefining functions, or redeploying the workforce. These important issues require supplier management awareness, buy-in, and attention. Not addressing job elimination or workforce job security policies in advance can create resistance within the supplier organization to making the changes that a supplier development project may require. Another potential problem and policy issue for the supplier firm in bringing about change at the supplier is how the process is integrated into daily work. If improvement is treated as more work to be done after the "regular work" is completed and the employees are not given improvement time within their regular work time, then the chances of bringing about the change are reduced. Continuous improvement will be viewed as an additional task to get done as time permits and not part of the way work is done.

The types of targeted improvement projects that are most likely to be successful and sustainable are those that are limited in scope, mostly technical in nature (not organizational projects or requiring organizational change), and require little follow-up to sustain.

Help Suppliers Build Their Own Capabilities for Improvement

Teach a supplier how to develop itself. Initial training and guidance in continuous improvement techniques or other business improvement methodologies can encourage and help willing suppliers to get their own improvement processes started. If the business case is compelling and the benefits to the supplier firms clear, they may be willing to continue on their own with improvement initiatives and processes. New England Suppliers Institute (NESI) worked with a large manufacturer that wanted its key suppliers, which consisted of mostly small to medium-size firms, to adopt lean enterprise practices. On behalf of this customer, NESI delivered introductory workshops at the customer firm's own training facility, to which suppliers were invited in groups of about 25. The suppliers were asked to send senior managers or owners, not the sales representative. Senior supplier management from the customer was there to give the introductory remarks and make the business case to the suppliers. The workshops must have been compelling. Some suppliers were so enthused by the potential benefits to their enterprise, apart from their customer's strong encouragement to adopt lean, that they hired consultants and started to implement lean totally on their own, in many cases, initially unbeknown to their customer. Other suppliers requested help directly from the customer firm to jumpstart their lean initiatives. The customer sent lean resources to several suppliers for further training and to run some initial kaizen events and teach the suppliers how to do kaizen events themselves. In following up, this customer discovered that over half the suppliers who had been invited to the initial lean awareness training had begun to implement lean in their own companies.[4]

When measuring supplier performance, capabilities can be leading indicators that will predict success. Improved or new capabilities allow suppliers to make progress and improvements without the intervention of the customer firm. Often lack of capabilities is at the root cause of supplier problems. A good SPM system will uncover opportunities that will require improvements in supplier capabilities. Helping suppliers improve their capabilities is the best approach for ensuring, as much as possible, sustainment of progress and perpetuation of continuous improvement. The ability to do continuous improvement requires more than learning tools such as fishbone diagrams, Pareto charts, and value stream maps. Improving capabilities in a sustainable way always involves management, organization, and culture. This makes improving capabilities much more challenging than completing simple supplier improvement projects. Supplier development to improve processes and capabilities is more resource-intensive than targeted supplier development. However, the payoffs can be bigger and longer-term with less probability of backsliding than targeted projects.

CONDUCTING A SUCCESSFUL SUPPLIER DEVELOPMENT PROJECT

Here are four situations that can provide the impetus for a supplier development project:

- Supplier evaluations are indicating performance problems at a supplier that need to be solved.

---

4. *Kaizen* is a Japanese term for continual, incremental improvement. Kaizen event is a term used by lean enterprise practitioners to mean the application of kaizen techniques in an accelerated manner that focuses on a specific improvement area within a short time frame, such as several days or a week, rather than an ongoing process.

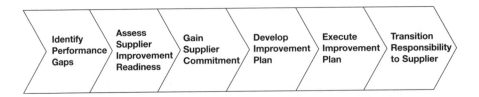

Figure 11.1 Supplier development process.

- The customer firm is implementing a specific high-performance business system such as lean enterprise, Lean Sigma, or Six Sigma internally and wants to get its suppliers on board and aligned with the initiative (thus preventing and remedying supplier performance problems).
- The customer firm has dedicated supplier development resources as part of its mode of operating and because of its belief in the payback for both its own organization and the supplier firm. It applies these resources to suppliers whose performance evaluation metrics indicate performance gaps. Or, it may use its dedicated resources to align suppliers with internal performance improvement initiatives. Examples of firms who have successfully used this approach include John Deere, Honda, Boeing, and Delphi.[5] An example of the order of magnitude of improvement achieved in dedicated supplier development team efforts is a Deere supplier that got a 57 percent reduction in cycle time (from 42 to 18 days) and a reduction in product cost of 6 percent (a $6.04 savings on a $52.35 item). The cost reduction was then shared by the customer and its supplier in subsequent purchases.[6]
- The supplier asks its customer for supplier development help.

Should the customer firm decide to pursue a supplier development initiative or project based upon one of the above situations, Figure 11.1 illustrates a suggested supplier development process.

5. Using dedicated supplier development resources is covered in detail in the book *The Purchasing Machine* by Dave Nelson, Patricia E. Moody, and Jonathan Stegner and also in *Powered by Honda: Developing Excellence in the Global Enterprise* by Dave Nelson, Patricia E. Moody, and Rick Mayo.

6. Schluter, Chris, "Framework for Manufacturing Cycle Time Reduction," an independent study done in partial fulfillment of a degree requirement at the University of Wisconsin, Madison, May 1999.

1. Identify Performance Gaps

Your supplier performance management system has identified performance gaps at the supplier. The problems are the type that requires working to improve underlying supplier capabilities such as cost issues or cycle time issues, for example, rather than fixing a few technical issues. Solving some important issues would have a measurable impact on both the customer firm and the supplier. Having identified some gaps that you want to target, you will need to do some more analysis to understand the issues in more detail. You want to better understand the scope of the effort required: root causes of the problems, how solvable the problem is in a supplier development context, the benefits of solving the problem, what resources might be required, and what it would take organizationally from both the customer and supplier side to address and improve.

2. Assess Supplier Readiness to Undertake the Development Process

Assess how ready the supplier is to address the performance gaps, make the commitment, and undertake a development process. High-impact projects require change management at the supplier. The customer company needs to assess the supplier's readiness to undergo real change. Also, there should be a reasonable degree of alignment and compatibility between the customer's expertise, attitudes, and values with those of the supplier.[7] Following are some considerations:

- What is the supplier's attitude toward change? A supplier may be paying lip service to change to please or pacify the customer, when in fact they are not truly willing and able to change. This type of attitude needs to be uncovered in advance to avoid an unsuccessful project. A supplier without the desire to truly change will try to keep the project on the periphery of its business and not address the real issues. I have seen this situation when a supplier does not really believe that the changes requested by the customer will work and chooses an area that will not have an impact on the overall business should the changes fail. The result is the impact is so insignificant that a business case for the change cannot be made for a broader implementation.
- What type of culture does the supplier have? Some supplier cultures can present challenges to supplier development. Some companies may have an authoritarian culture that does not value employee input into solving problems. The owner mentioned previously who thought his

---

7. Hartley, Janet, and Gwen Jones, "Process Oriented Supplier Development: Building the Capability for Change," *Journal of Supply Chain Management*, Summer 1997, Vol. 33, No. 3, p. 24.

operators never had and never will have an idea is an example. Many supplier firms do not have a culture of continuous improvement. In some, it reflects their level of sophistication and organizational maturity, not a lack of desire to do so. In other company cultures, suggestions for improvement are viewed as a criticism of management. It's the boss's role to do the thinking, not the associates' job. Some cultures can evolve, if management has the desire. But others are clearly not ready or have a management culture with less potential.

- What change management experience has the supplier had? There is a higher risk of failure if the supplier has little or no experience in change management. When a company is in the midst of changing the way work is done and asks its workforce to change ingrained behaviors and habits, employee feelings of confusion, worry, and frustration can result. Ability to handle the people side, not just the technical side, of the change is essential. The probability of successful change management increases in a company with a strong, competent leadership, a clear vision and strategy, effective communications, and a sense of urgency and commitment among employees. No company is perfect at managing change, but a successful track record will increase the chances of a successful supplier development project.

- What resources are available at the supplier to work on an improvement process? To have a successful development project, the supplier must be able to commit some of its own resources to the project. Customers who send teams that do all or most of the project for the supplier will find that the supplier will be unable to internalize and manage the changes. I have seen supplier development personnel come into a company and physically change an operation or develop a tool shadow board without any involvement from employees at the supplier. I have also seen a consultant set up work cells for the supplier without the supplier really learning how to do it themselves. Customer firm personnel may not know how to coach the supplier rather than do it for them. This may be a training issue for supplier development personnel. Supplier development personnel need consultancy skills rather than just the pure know-how or technical expertise to solve supplier problems. Supplier personnel need to be involved not just in providing information for the project but also to take responsibility for aspects of it. The customer firm should coach and support but not directly drive the change. Small suppliers understandably are lacking in resources and many companies feel stretched thin. If the project is significant to the supplier, the investment of supplier resources in the development project is likely to pay off in improvements that free up resources in the long run. This return on investment should be analyzed up front to help make the business case for the supplier.

- What are the current skill levels of employees? Supplier employees should have basic skills in place to work on improvement projects, such as computer basics, English as a second language, and math. Other skills such as teaming, statistics, problem solving, and root cause analysis can help support improvement projects. The customer may need to help the supplier by providing workforce training and development to its employees directly or by hooking the supplier up with workforce development resources in order to help employees reach a skill level where they can begin to undertake high-impact improvement projects.

- What are the current operational systems and to what extent may these systems need to change? The supplier may lack technology or information systems that readily support some of the changes considered to be important to the success of the project.

If it is determined that the project is not a good fit with a particular supplier, the scope can be reduced or a more targeted project could be considered as an alternative. Strategic projects should not proceed if the chances of success are limited. If several specific, more limited-scope improvements can be successfully implemented, the customer could look again at a larger scope, more strategic effort with the supplier in the future. The customer can try a proof-of-concept project at the supplier to build support and momentum for serious changes in the future. An example of this situation occurred at an electromechanical assembly supplier to a large manufacturer who was trying to spread lean enterprise processes and practices to its suppliers. Using some available government funding to deploy the resources, the customer firm selected the electromechanical assembly supplier to improve its flow and level of quality with lean. Initially, the supplier was afraid to try a pull system on its main manufacturing lines. The supplier did not commit its own resources to the project and sent the customer team to a newly acquired machine shop that was 30 miles from the main facility and that had almost no manufacturing taking place to make the changes there. It was apparent that the supplier, who was a certified supplier and historically very diligent and responsive to the customer, was paying lip service to lean. Lean was so opposite the way their manufacturing was organized that the supplier had little faith that it would work and feared that it could shut them down. So they appeared to be exiling the customer team to a place where lean couldn't hurt their business (nor could it really help it). When the person in charge of the funding (me) threatened to pull the plug, they then agreed to let the team work on a printed circuit board line at the main facility. The improvements that resulted in cycle time and quality were dramatic. Also, they gained so much additional floor space that their employees were able to stop having to have lunch breaks in multiple shifts because the cafeteria had almost disappeared for lack of space. After the initial high-impact project, the supplier committed to and then implemented a more comprehensive rollout.

3. Gain and Build Supplier Commitment and Support

If the buying firm determines that there is a good fit with the supplier for the project, then the specifics about how the project will be deployed and implemented need to be determined in conjunction with the supplier. Commitment and support from the supplier's management must be obtained. But that is just where it begins. Commitment from the parts of the organization that will be impacted must also be gained. Customer and supplier need to work together to figure out the makeup of project teams at the supplier and identify the functions and individuals who will participate. To the extent that supplier personnel are involved in designing and implementing the project, greater supplier buy-in and knowledge transfer will occur, increasing the chance that the changes will be sustainable. As demonstrated in the story about the electromechanical supplier, a project will not be successful unless the supplier's management truly commits and involves appropriate resources. Changes cannot be made on behalf of someone else.

4. Develop Improvement Plan

Improvement plan development should be a joint effort between the customer and supplier. The customer team's knowledge of how to implement the project should be combined with the supplier team's knowledge of its company, people, and processes. There should be mutual agreement about the how the project will be approached and implemented and on the composition of project teams. Supplier assessment should have helped identify important areas of opportunity for the supplier. It is likely that there are multiples areas of opportunity for improvement at the supplier. Customer and supplier should work jointly to identify the areas that have the most opportunity, have the biggest ROI, or are the most reasonable starting points for proof of concept. They should develop strategies for improvement that are in sync with the supplier's culture and resources and are practical and doable for the particular supplier. The team should then prioritize the project activities in the form of a detailed plan with actions, dates, and responsibilities. The plan should include baseline metrics and target metrics.

The plan should then be reviewed with supplier management for buy-in and approval.

5. Execute the Improvement Plan

The challenge in implementing strategic improvements in a supplier development project is making them systemic instead of just isolated pockets of excellence. This is true for bringing about high-impact change in any company. Only in this case, the changes are customer-initiated or customer-requested. So the supplier organization must clearly understand the business case for the changes and have a level of commitment to change and trust toward the customer company to be able to successfully execute the improvement plan. The customer team must have more than just technical capabilities to support the supplier. High-impact change requires team-building, coaching, and organizational skills. Ideally, the supplier will either have its own people with these capabilities or else utilize customer personnel for this purpose. If customer supplier development personnel do not have those skills and are not prepared to undertake strategic supplier development initiatives, the capabilities will need to be developed or added. Otherwise, the supplier will need the help of qualified outside consultants. Many if not most customer firms do not have dedicated supplier development teams to work with suppliers and can go only as far as identifying the development projects needed and recommending that the supplier find the consulting resources to help them. The advantage of using customer resources is the relationship-building and value-adding aspects of working together on high-impact projects to help the supplier. But depending upon the supplier's capabilities and culture and the relationship with its customer, third-party consultants may be a better choice, even though there is a cost to using them. Supplier firms may prefer to have a neutral third party work with them to solve problems and maintain the boundaries between the firms rather than exposing the details of their problems and operations to their customer.

Supplier development project implementation should consider all issues and look to remedy the root causes of problems. As we have discussed, customer firms are typically responsible for their share of problems at the supplier. Therefore, the project should also examine interfaces between the companies and the extent to which customer processes and systems may be causing some of the supplier's problems. Failing to examine and address these issues at the customer will mean that many supplier opportunities for improvement cannot be fully realized. This is why supplier development must have management support and visibility at its own (i.e., the customer firm) organization and communicate with other functional groups and management. It will need to both facilitate change at the supplier as well as communicate to its own firm its successes as well as issues that need to be resolved in order to enable suppliers to meet customer requirements and add value.

6. Transition Responsibility to the Supplier

Before the end of a customer-initiated supplier development project, the supplier needs to assume responsibility for and ongoing maintenance of the changes. Implementing significant change is challenging. Ensuring that the change is institutionalized into the company culture, then persisting with the continuous improvement process is challenging as well. In some companies, when improvement processes are successful, they can generate momentum, which needs to be nurtured and supported by management. But what you do not want to happen is that as soon as the customer leaves, the gremlins of the status quo put things back the way they were.

An extreme example of customer-initiated improvements that were short-lived is a story told to me by a former supplier manager at a photography and image products company that had an initiative to get its suppliers to adopt lean manufacturing practices. The customer team spent time at a supplier in Puerto Rico reorganizing its operation into work cells. The team returned home over the weekend. Customer firm personnel came to visit the supplier the next week, and to their surprise, the cells had been taken apart and the whole place had been put back the way it was originally, into its previous traditional departmental setup. The supplier had gone along with the customer's wishes but had not truly understood the benefits of implementing cellular manufacturing. They apparently did not have management buy-in or the organizational structure in place to support it, nor had they seen its advantages for them. This story illustrates supplier lip service in a fairly radical form. It shows the importance of the customer's role in change at suppliers as a coach, consultant, or catalyst in continuous improvement but not the responsible party.

How can the customer firm support real change and help keep the gremlins at bay? This is a challenge at both customer and supplier firms undergoing change. First, the supplier needs to assume responsibility for supplier development projects, as has been described in the previous steps. If customer personnel are directly involved in supplier development projects, they should phase their involvement out gradually and make sure the supplier is increasingly taking responsibility. This coaching approach is appropriate whether the consultants are from the customer firm or from an outside consulting firm. After new processes and practices are in place, the customer firm should support the supplier as much as possible with feedback, recognition, coaching, and training. Improvement project plans need to be mutually reviewed by both customer and supplier on a regular basis to help keep them visible and on track. By taking baseline measurements before the project begins, the supplier will be able to see the improvements in a quantitative way, as ROI and improvement will be reflected in the measurements taken after changes are implemented and also in supplier performance scores.

When the changes are really important to improving the supplier's operations, the supplier and its customers will notice the improvements in daily business, apart from what the measurements indicate. The change process at suppliers (or at any company, for that matter) can be slow and sometimes frustrating, and can require determination, patience, and perseverance. Those suppliers who have successfully undergone significant and measurable improvements should celebrate internally and recognize employees involved in the success *and* be celebrated and recognized by the customer firm. The importance of before-and-after measurements cannot be overemphasized. They help make the business case for improvement for both supplier and customer firms. At the supplier, they encourage the supplier's management to support, sustain, and continue changes and not backslide. At the customer, they demonstrate the payback for supplier performance management and supplier development and help maintain internal support and budget.

ROLLING OUT SPECIFIC INTERNAL INITIATIVES TO SUPPLIERS

As companies implement internal improvement initiatives and high-performance systems, they typically find that they need their key suppliers to be on board in order for these initiatives to work well and provide them with the promised ROI. When implementing lean enterprise, customer firms need suppliers to eliminate waste and non-value-added processes (those that do not add value to the customers). In manufacturing, lean requires orders to be made and delivered to customers as needed rather than in large quantities so that unused inventory and its associated costs do not accumulate at either the customer or the supplier. In a lean environment, suppliers who do not practice waste reduction have poorer cost structures than those who do, less competitive cycle times, and less ability to be responsive to customers. This is true for both manufacturing and nonmanufacturing environments. The metrics that are tracked in supplier performance programs are likely to reflect the above consequences of not having a high-performance business process in place (i.e., cost, waste, long cycle times, lack of responsiveness, etc.). Manufacturing suppliers who have not deployed lean are likely to hold more inventory, have wasted floor space, have lower on-time delivery rates, have significantly longer machine changeover rates, and have poorer cash flow. There is a compelling business case for suppliers' adopting lean, especially when their customer is already implementing and needs to synchronize this business system and operating philosophies with its suppliers. The customer firm will not realize all of lean's potential without engaging key suppliers, as they are all part of the same business ecosystem.

Lean turns out to have significant and proven rates of return on investment for firms. Plus, it applies well to firms of any size and type, not just big manufacturing companies. It helps get at the root causes of waste in the supply chain, rather than just attacking the symptoms. Like any major change management process, lean requires the management commitment and support just described in the supplier development process section. Many companies deploy a tools approach to lean with their suppliers. They teach them how to deploy various lean tools such as: 5S (workplace organization), work cells, setup reduction, kaizen events, and so on. Suppliers see initial big improvements. But then many of these improvements stall or lose momentum. What is happening is that they are treating lean implementation as a targeted or results-oriented improvement rather than a longer-term strategic process. Without a determination of cultural fit and the development of an overall strategy and a long-term plan for lean implementation, customer firms apply the tools at suppliers or encourage the application of lean tools, but suppliers do not get sustainable results. The initial enthusiasm may wear thin, as lean in the supply chain represents a true change management and continuous-improvement process, not a quick fix using lean tools. Admittedly, applying tools and quick fixes can be immediately gratifying and rewarding for both customer and supplier. And, it can produce dramatic and measurement results. However, lean needs the management commitment, overall planning, and strategic underpinnings to become ingrained and sustained. Another observation is that doing lean supplier development can be both exciting and threatening at the same time. Lean invariably leads to efficiencies that cause the elimination of job functions and the need to retrain or redeploy displaced employees. Many businesses can use these workers in other areas of the company, particularly when a supplier is growing or the increased responsiveness to the customer helps fuel more business from the customer or from other customers. Lean transformation positions and enables but does not guarantee growth. Therefore, management at the supplier must grapple with the realities of potential job elimination and decide how they will address it.

Another methodology that can be used for supplier development is Six Sigma. Six Sigma is a quality improvement methodology with a goal of no more than 3.4 defects per million items. It is used to reduce process variation and to identify and prevent defects in both manufacturing and service-related processes. The Six Sigma methodology is DMAIC—Define, Measure, Analyze, Improve, and Control. Six Sigma has typically been implemented in larger enterprises, since many implementation models have required a level of infrastructure, training, and expenditure that smaller companies have difficulty supporting. Six Sigma uses a suite of statistical analysis tools to uncover process variation and root causes of problems. It is particularly useful for understanding variation in highly complex processes. It can be used to discover and remedy the root causes of supplier problems identified in supplier performance reporting and is applicable to any department or process in a company.

The examples of Six Sigma projects are numerous, from helping a supplier figure out how to reduce abandoned calls in its call center to finding the causes of quality variation in a supplier's shipments. Since Six Sigma is so project-oriented, it can be used to fix various problems at suppliers. Some companies teach Six Sigma analysis to some of their suppliers by sending Black Belts to the suppliers to conduct training and coach Six Sigma projects.[8] Others will leave open slots in their own internal Six Sigma training, ask supplier representative to attend the customer firm's Six Sigma training, then coach the supplier through Six Sigma projects. Another approach is to train suppliers in Six Sigma and give them project experience by having them work on customer projects, particularly those that address customer-supplier issues or the interfaces between customer and supplier.

Six Sigma can also fall victim to the trap of the tools approach: conducting many unrelated, though important, projects, but having no overarching strategy or objective other than general continuous improvement. It can result in a lot of pockets of improvement and excellence that optimize small parts of the business but never optimize the whole. These projects can produce excellent individual and departmental results but still generate no measurable impact on the organization as a whole. Six Sigma implemented with the tools or project approach can create the sustainment problems typical of continuous improvement methodologies that are project-oriented or targeted only to specific problem areas.[9]

A current popular hybrid approach is called Lean Sigma. This method applies tools from both the lean and Six Sigma toolkits to solve problems. Some companies use lean to reduce waste and expose problems, and then use Six Sigma techniques to uncover additional waste and defects and solve more complex process variability problems that cannot be solved using lean methods alone. For example, Six Sigma tools might be used to solve complex problems attributable to process variability (i.e., what are the root causes of delays in treating patients in a hospital emergency room) in the very same organization that is using lean to improve the velocity of an administrative process. Simply put, lean focuses on increasing process velocity by improving materials and information flow, and Six

---

8. Black Belts represent the next to highest level of process improvement leaders in a Six Sigma environment. They act as coaches and leaders for green belts who are doing Six Sigma projects. Some companies have Master Black Belts, who are the highest level and who coach and support Black Belts. Black Belts typically go through extensive training and management of successful projects, starting as Green Belts.

9. For a discussion of implementing Six Sigma in smaller companies, refer to the book by Terence T. Burton and Jeff L. Sams, *Six Sigma for Small and Mid-Sized Organizations*. With suppliers under increasing pressure to implement Six Sigma, this book offers a practical and workable approach for smaller companies.

Sigma focuses on the elimination of defects through variability reduction. Together, lean and Six Sigma can support all aspects of process improvement.

SUMMARY

In summary, when flowing customer methodologies down to suppliers or synchronizing management and continuous-improvement methodologies with supplier firms, there is always the potential trade-off of short-term projects and quick hits versus longer-term change management and sustainable process improvement. Sustainable improvement of supplier performance requires change management, both in the customer and supplier firms. Implementation of sustainable change does not happen overnight, nor is it an appropriate strategy for all suppliers. The most practical approach is to get suppliers' feet wet with targeted supplier development projects that do not immediately require massive change and use them as pilots or proofs of concept to then determine which suppliers are ready for and will benefit from longer-term, more comprehensive performance improvement approaches.

This book has free material available for download from the
Web Added Value™ resource center at *www.jrosspub.com*

INDEX